STUDY GUIDE
Gwendolyn M. Parsons

ABNORMAL PSYCHOLOGY

FOURTH EDITION

Thomas F. Oltmanns

Robert E. Emery

Upper Saddle River, New Jersey 07458

© 2004 by PEARSON EDUCATION, INC.
Upper Saddle River, New Jersey 07458

All rights reserved

10 9 8 7 6 5 4 3 2 1

ISBN 0-13-049271-X

Printed in the United States of America

TABLE OF CONTENTS

Chapter 1	Examples and Definitions of Abnormal Behavior	1
Chapter 2	Causes of Abnormal Behavior: A Systems Approach	15
Chapter 3	Treatment of Psychological Disorders	34
Chapter 4	Classification and Assessment of Abnormal Behavior	50
Chapter 5	Mood Disorders and Suicide	65
Chapter 6	Anxiety Disorders	81
Chapter 7	Acute and Posttraumatic Stress Disorders, Dissociative Disorders, and Somatoform Disorders	96
Chapter 8	Stress and Physical Health	114
Chapter 9	Personality Disorders	129
Chapter 10	Eating Disorders	144
Chapter 11	Substance Use Disorders	154
Chapter 12	Sexual and Gender Identity Disorders	170
Chapter 13	Schizophrenic Disorders	186
Chapter 14	Dementia, Delirium, and Amnestic Disorders	201
Chapter 15	Mental Retardation and Pervasive Developmental Disorders	214
Chapter 16	Psychological Disorders of Childhood	230
Chapter 17	Adjustment Disorders and Life-Cycle Transitions	244
Chapter 18	Mental Health and the Law	259

CHAPTER ONE

EXAMPLES AND DEFINITIONS OF ABNORMAL BEHAVIOR

CHAPTER OUTLINE

Overview
Recognizing the Presence of Disorder
Defining Abnormal Behavior
      Harmful Dysfunction
      Cultural Considerations
Who Experiences Abnormal Behavior?
      Frequency in and Impact on Community Populations
      Cross-Cultural Comparisons
The Mental Health Professions
Psychopathology in Historical Context
      The Greek Tradition in Medicine
      The Creation of the Asylum
      Worcester Lunatic Hospital: A Model Institution
      Lessons from the History of Psychopathology
Methods for the Scientific Study of Mental Disorders
      The Uses and Limitations of Case Studies
      Clinical Research Methods
Summary

OBJECTIVES

1. Define abnormal psychology.
2. Discuss the criteria used to define abnormality.
3. Discuss the scientist-practitioner model.
4. Distinguish between epidemiology, incidence, and prevalence.
5. Describe the contributions of nature and nurture in the development of abnormal behavior.
6. Compare the individual, social, and biological systems of influence.
7. Discuss the advantages and disadvantages of reductionism.
8. Distinguish between causation and correlation or change.
9. Discuss the differences between demonological and natural scientific approaches to psychopathology.
10. Discuss the history of institutionalization for the treatment of mental disorders.
11. Discuss the relationship between cultural beliefs and the labeling of behavior as normal or abnormal.
12. Discuss the conservative approach in research, which leads to a reluctance to reject the null hypothesis.

MATCHING I

Answers are found at the end of this chapter. Match these terms and concepts with the definitions that follow:

  a. Psychology
  b. Abnormal psychology
  c. Scientist-Practitioner model
  d. Case study
  e. Comorbidity
  f. Psychopathology
  g. Psychosis
  h. Delusion
  i. Disorganized speech
  j. Bulimia nervosa
  k. Dichotomous decision
  l. Epidemiology
  m. Incidence
  n. Prevalence
  o. Lifetime prevalence
  p. Etiology

1. __e__ the presence of more than one condition within the same period of time
2. __a__ the scientific study of behavior, cognition, and emotion
3. __l__ the scientific study of the frequency and distribution of disorders within a population
4. __h__ an idiosyncratic belief, not shared by other members of the society, that is rigidly held despite its preposterous nature
5. __i__ a symptom often found in schizophrenia of speech that is odd and difficult to comprehend; a problem with the form of speech rather than content
6. __n__ the total number of active cases of a disorder present in a population during a specific period of time
7. __o__ the total proportion of people in a population who have been affected by the disorder at some point in their lives
8. __d__ a descriptive presentation of the psychological problems of one particular person
9. __c__ emphasizes the integration of science and clinical practice
10. __g__ a state of being profoundly out of touch with reality
11. __p__ the causes of a disorder
12. __k__ required in making a diagnosis; determining whether a particular person fits a diagnostic category rather than the degree to which they possess a characteristic
13. __j__ a form of eating disorder characterized by bingeing and purging
14. __f__ the manifestations of, and study of the causes of, mental disorders
15. __b__ the application of psychological science to the study of mental disorders
16. __m__ the number of new cases of a disorder that appear in a population during a specific time

MATCHING II
Answers are found at the end of this chapter. Match these terms and concepts with the definitions that follow:

1. Formal thought disorder
2. Insanity
3. Not guilty by reason of insanity
4. Nervous breakdown
5. Descriptive psychopathology
6. Syndrome
7. Schizophrenia
8. Managed Care
9. Harmful dysfunction
10. Diagnostic and Statistical Manual of Mental Disorders
11. Nature-nurture controversy
12. Biopsychosocial model
13. Psychopharmacology
14. Psychotherapy
15. Culture
16. Moral treatment movement
17. Psychiatry
18. Experimental hypothesis
19. Null hypothesis
20. Clinical psychology
21. Social work
22. Professional Counselors
23. Marriage and Family Therapy (MFT) counselors
24. Psychiatric Nursing
25. Psychosocial Rehabilitation

a. _7_ a mental disorder characterized by psychotic symptoms, disorganized speech, and emotional flatness and withdrawal
b. _18_ any new prediction made by a researcher
c. _6_ a group of symptoms that appear together and are assumed to represent a specific type of disorder
d. _17_ a specialization in medicine concerned with the study and treatment of mental disorders
e. _13_ the use of medication to treat mental disorders
f. _8_ an insurance system which places a high priority on keeping costs low
g. _3_ a legal term indicating a legal defense or finding that, although a person committed a crime, he or she is not criminally responsible for the behavior because of a mental disorder
h. _16_ a movement founded on a basic respect for human dignity and the belief that humanistic care would be effective in the treatment of mental illness, that promoted improved conditions at mental hospitals
i. _14_ the use of psychological procedures in the context of a relationship with a therapist to treat mental disorders
j. _19_ the alternative to the experimental hypothesis; predicts that the experimental hypothesis is not true
k. _2_ currently, this is a legal term referring to a person's culpability for criminal acts if he or she has a mental disorder
l. _1_ another term for disorganized speech
m. _9_ an approach to defining whether a condition is a mental disorder in terms of its harm to the person and whether the condition results from the inability of some mental mechanism to perform its natural function

n. __20__ a specialization in psychology concerned with the application of psychological science to the assessment and treatment of mental disorders
o. __15__ the values, beliefs and practices that are shared by a specific community or group of people
p. __10__ the official listing of mental disorders and their diagnostic criteria published by the American Psychiatric Association; updated regularly
q. __21__ a profession concerned with helping people achieve an effective level of psychosocial functioning; focuses less on a body of scientific knowledge than on a commitment to action
r. __11__ the debate over whether genetic or biological factors versus environmental factors cause mental disorders or abnormal behavior
s. __4__ an old-fashioned term indicating that a person became incapacitated because of an unspecified mental disorder
t. __12__ the analytic approach toward etiology combining the influences of biological, psychological, and social systems
u. __5__ psychopathology based on the signs and symptoms of a mental disorder rather than on its inferred causes
v. __24__ a degree including nursing in addition to additional training in mental health issues
w. __22__ Master's level care providers focusing on offering direct service
x. __25__ professionals who teach the severely mentally ill practical daily living skills
y. __23__ Masters' level treatment providers with a theoretical orientation focusing on couples and family issues

MATCHING III
Answers are found at the end of this chapter. Match these names with the descriptions of their contributions to the study of abnormal psychology.

    a. Jerome Wakefield   c. Dorothea Dix
    b. Hippocrates   d. Samuel Woodward

1. __C__ an early advocate for the humane treatment of the mentally ill; promoted the creation of mental institutions for treatment
2. __b__ saw mental disorders as diseases having natural causes, like other forms of physical diseases
3. __d__ argued that mental disorders could be traced to immoral behavior, stress or improper living conditions; optimistic about curing mental illnesses
4. __a__ proposed the harmful dysfunction approach to defining mental disorder

CONCEPT REVIEW

Answers are found at the end of this chapter. After you have read and reviewed the material, test your comprehension by filling in the blanks or circling the correct answer.

1. Case studies are particularly important in understanding mental disorders that are _rare_.
2. Case studies can prove that a certain factor is the cause of a disorder: true **(false)**
3. One limitation of case studies is that one person may not be _representative_ of the disorder as a whole.
4. There are several laboratory tests available to test for the presence of certain forms of mental disorders: true **(false)**
5. An unusual behavior or symptom that goes away after a few days is not clinically significant; that is, it does not indicate that a person has a disorder: **(true)** false
6. What is the problem with defining abnormal behavior based on the individual's experience of personal distress? _It is subjective, not have insight_
7. What is the problem with defining abnormal behavior based on statistical norms of rarity? _some are common & some are good_
8. The DSM-IV-TR defines mental disorder in terms of personal _distress_ or impairment of _function_ or with significantly increased risk of suffering some form of harm.
9. Why was the behavior of the Yippie Party of the 1960s, whose members threw money off the balcony at a stock exchange, not considered to be a symptom of a mental illness? _b/c protesting voluntary political gesture_
10. The DSM-IV-TR is not influenced by social or cultural forces: true **(false)**
11. Why does the DSM-IV-TR no longer consider homosexuality to be a mental disorder? _political pressure from gay activist_
12. What does the DSM-IV-TR definition of mental disorders place primary emphasis on? _consequences of certain behav. syndromes_
13. Much of our current estimates of the prevalence of mental disorder is based on the _ECA_ study.
14. Most psychopathologists view mental disorders as being culture-free: true **(false)**
15. Psychotic disorders are less influenced by culture than are nonpsychotic disorders: **(true)** false
16. Epidemiological studies indicate that the following percentage of people had at least one diagnosable condition sometime in their life: 6% **(32%)** 83%
17. People affected by severe disorders often qualify for the diagnosis of more than one disorder at the same time: **(true)** false
18. The concept of disease burden combines which two factors? _mortality & disability_
19. Mental disorders cause 1 percent of all deaths but produce 47 percent of all _disability in_ economically developed countries.
20. Almost all mental disorders occur in Western countries: true **(false)**

5

21. Scientists have come to fairly well agreed upon conclusions about the etiology of most mental disorders:
    true   **false** (circled)

22. A psychopathologist who hypothesizes that schizophrenia is caused by an infectious agent, like a virus, would be adopting which view?
    nature (circled)   nurture

23. Almost all patients who are being treated in psychotherapy are not treated with medication at the same time: true   **false** (circled)

24. Most people who have a diagnosable mental disorder receive some form of treatment for it:
    true   **false** (circled)

25. Why is it an error to conclude that when a treatment is successful in relieving a mental disorder, that treatment indicates the cause of the disorder? _b/c dont_

26. Many ancient theories of abnormal behavior see as its cause the disfavor of the gods or demonic possession: **true** (circled)   false

27. Cutting patients to make them bleed and reduce the amount of blood in the body was a form of treatment for mental illness in the 19th century: **true** (circled)   false

28. Urbanization was one of the reasons that _asylums_ were built.

29. What led to the creation of the specialization of psychiatry? _mental institution_

30. Samuel Woodward saw masturbation, among other "morally objectionable" behaviors as the cause of _disorders_.

31. Woodward claimed a success rate of _____.
    about 30 percent   about 50 percent   **about 85 five percent** (circled)

32. Fever therapy involved infecting mental patients with _malaria_ to cause a fever because symptoms sometimes disappeared in patients with a high fever.

33. What type of mental health professionals may prescribe medication? _Psychiatrist_

34. What type of mental health professionals are trained in the use of scientific research methods? _Clinical psychologist_

35. A greater number of treatment providers for mental health services are professionals other than physicians:
    true (circled)   false

CROSSWORD

Answers are found at the end of this chapter. Complete the following crossword puzzle to reinforce your understanding of this chapter's key terms and concepts:

ACROSS
1. hypothesis involving any new prediction
5. total number of active cases of a disorder
7. type of psychology which applies psychological science to study of mental disorders
9. official classification system
10. a group of symptoms which appear together to represent a specific type of disorder
11. the values, beliefs, practices shared by a group of people

DOWN
2. study of the frequency and distribution of disorders within a population
3. type of psychology concerned with assessment and treatment of mental disorders
4. in depth look at the circumstances surrounding an individual's psychological disorder
5. branch of medicine concerned with the study and treatment of mental disorders
6. number of new cases of a disorder
8. multidisciplinary field in which professionals are trained to provide psychotherapy

MULTIPLE CHOICE

Answers are found at the end of this chapter. The multiple choice questions listed will test your understanding of the material presented in the chapter. Read through each question and circle the letter representing the best answer.

1. A type of formal thought disorder characterized by significant disruptions of verbal communication:
    a. depression
    b. schizophrenia
    c. psychosis
    d. disorganized speech

2. This model combines the dimensional and categorical approaches to classification.
    a. threshold model
    b. scientist-practitioner model
    c. diathesis-stress model
    d. biopsychosocial model

3. When literally translated, the term "psychopathology" refers to
    a. "deterioration of the psyche"
    b. "pathology of the mind"
    c. "pathology of the psyche"
    d. "deterioration of the mind"

4. A mental disorder is typically defined by
    a. a person experiencing the feeling that something is wrong
    b. statistical rarity
    c. a set of characteristic features
    d. being out of contact with reality

5. Sam has been experiencing delusional thinking and hallucinations. Bob has been experiencing hallucinations and formal thought disorder. According to DSM-IV-TR
    a. they could both be classified as schizophrenic
    b. they would be given different diagnoses
    c. they probably have different etiologies
    d. they should get different treatments

6. In all but which of the following are hypotheses of the etiology of abnormal behavior?
    a. diathesis-stress model
    b. biopsychosocial model
    c. biological reductionism
    d. scientist-practitioner model

7. This approach defines psychopathology in terms of signs and symptoms rather than inferred causes.
    a. descriptive psychopathology
    b. influential psychopathology
    c. comparative psychopathology
    d. experiential psychopathology

8

8. In all but which of the following are ways case studies may be useful?
    a. they provide important insights about the nature of mental disorders
    b. they allow you to draw conclusions about a disorder from a single experience
    c. they assist a clinician in making hypotheses about a specific case
    d. they provide a rich clinical description which can be helpful in diagnosing an individual

9. These two disorders are much more common in men than they are in women.
    a. alcoholism; antisocial personality disorder
    b. anxiety disorders; depression
    c. alcoholism; depression
    d. anxiety disorders; antisocial personality disorder

10. With the exception of _____, all of the following could be considered psychotic symptoms.
    a. delusions
    b. hallucinations
    c. disorganized speech
    d. depression

11. Eating disorders may be fatal if they are not properly treated because
    a. there is a high suicide rate among people with eating disorders
    b. they affect so many vital organs of the body
    c. people with eating disorders are often unaware of the disorder and therefore are prone to developing additional disorders
    d. the majority of people with eating disorders do not view their behavior as problematic and therefore do not seek treatment

12. Cultural forces
    a. mostly affect people living in non-Western societies.
    b. do not change.
    c. only affect women.
    d. affect what we perceive as abnormal.

13. This is a general term referring to a type of severe mental disorder in which the individual is considered to be out of contact with reality.
    a. threshold
    b. syndrome
    c. psychosis
    d. schizophrenia

14. _____ is to experience as _____ is to genes.
    a. Nature; nurture
    b. Nurture; nature
    c. Quantitative; qualitative
    d. Qualitative; quantitative

15. In order for a behavior to be considered abnormal, it must include all of the following with the exception of
    a. distress or painful symptoms
    b. conflicts between the individual and society that are voluntary in nature
    c. impairment in one or more important areas of functioning
    d. increased risk of suffering death, pain, disability, or an important loss of freedom

16. Which is true about the role of value judgments in the development of diagnostic systems?
    a. values may be avoided with the use of scientific methods
    b. diagnosis is completely determined by values
    c. values have no place in the attempt to define disease
    d. values are inherent in any attempt to define disease

17. The conclusion of Murphy's study of the Inuit and Yoruba was that severe forms of mental illness
    a. are not limited to Western cultures or developed countries
    b. do appear to be limited to Western cultures or developed countries
    c. are more prevalent in Western cultures and developed countries
    d. are more prevalent in the Inuit and Yoruba populations studied

18. Nancy grew up in a society where mourners pull out their hair, go into an emotional frenzy, and begin speaking in tongues. On a visit to the U.S., she did these things in public when she heard that a relative had died. According to DSM-IV-TR, this would be considered
    a. not to be psychopathology, because it is part of her culture
    b. not to be psychopathology, because it caused no disruption in her social relationships
    c. to be psychopathology, because of her personal distress
    d. to be psychopathology, because it impaired her functioning

19. Which of the following is not considered a criterion for defining a behavior as a form of mental illness?
    a. negative effects on the person's social functioning
    b. recognition by the person that his or her behavior is problematic
    c. personal discomfort
    d. persistent, maladaptive behaviors

UNDERSTANDING RESEARCH
Answers are found at the end of this chapter.

<u>Cross-Cultural Study of Abnormal Behavior</u>: The text presents a detailed description of a study in the Research Close Up. Finding the answers to these questions will provide an understanding of this study and why it is important.

1. What did the textbook mean by the term "non-Western?" _____ Who were the two groups of people Murphy studied? _____ and _____. She lived with each of them for several _____, learned their languages, and learned how they think about problem _____.

2. Both cultures recognize certain forms of "crazy" behavior, including aberrant beliefs, feelings, and actions, hearing _____, _____ at strange times, talking in ways that don't make _____: which are like what diagnosis? _____. The specific _____ of hallucinations and delusions varies from one culture to the next, but the underlying _____ appear to be the same. Both groups saw "crazy behavior" as being different from the behaviors of the _____, who also acted

strangely at times when doing their job. "When the shaman is healing, he is out of his mind, but he is not_____."

3. Both groups believe that mental illness originates in _____. Their attitudes toward "crazy" people were neither _____ nor _____. The World _____ Organization studied schizophrenia in _____ countries and found about the same _____ of the disorder in all the countries.

SHORT ANSWER
Answer the following short answer questions. Compare your work to the material presented in the text.

1. Describe the criteria which need to be present in order for a behavior to be considered abnormal. Why is it important to have criteria to define abnormality?

2. Choose two case studies presented in this chapter and discuss how they illustrate abnormal behavior.

3. Discuss the history of institutionalization.

4. What is the importance of the null hypothesis? Provide one example.

ANSWER KEY

MATCHING I

1. e
2. a
3. l
4. h
5. i
6. n
7. o
8. d
9. c
10. g
11. p
12. k
13. j
14. f
15. b
16. m

MATCHING II

a. 7
b. 18
c. 6
d. 17
e. 13
f. 8
g. 3
h. 16
i. 14
j. 19
k. 2
l. 1
m. 9
n. 20
o. 15
p. 10
q. 21
r. 11
s. 4
t. 12
u. 5
v. 24
w. 22
x. 25
y. 23

MATCHING III

1. c
2. b
3. d
4. a

MULTIPLE CHOICE

1. d
2. a
3. b
4. c
5. a
6. d
7. a
8. b
9. a
10. d
11. b
12. d
13. c
14. b
15. b
16. d
17. a
18. b
19. b

CONCEPT REVIEW

1. rare
2. false
3. representative
4. false
5. true
6. they may not have insight
7. something rare is not necessarily bad
8. distress; functioning
9. it was voluntary and was a political gesture
10. false
11. political pressure from gay rights activists
12. consequences of certain behavioral syndromes
13. ECA
14. false
15. true
16. 32%
17. true
18. mortality and disability
19. disability
20. false
21. false
22. nature
23. false
24. false
25. it is a logical error, like thinking a lack of aspirin causes headaches
26. true
27. true
28. lunatic asylums

29. creation of institutions to treat mental patients
30. mental illness
31. about 85%
32. malaria
33. psychiatrists
34. clinical psychologists
35. true

UNDERSTANDING RESEARCH

1. People living in non-industrialized or undeveloped cultures or countries, or other than the United States, Canada, and Europe; Inuits and the Yoruba; months; behaviors
2. voices; laughing; sense; schizophrenia; content; processes; shamans; crazy
3. magic; positive; negative; Health; nine; frequency

CROSSWORD

ACROSS	DOWN
1. hypothesis involving any new prediction	2. study of the frequency and distribution of disorders within a population
5. total number of active cases of a disorder	3. type of psychology concerned with assessment and treatment of mental disorders
7. type of psychology which applies psychological science to study of mental disorders	4. in depth look at the circumstances surrounding an individual's psychological disorder
9. official classification system	5. branch of medicine concerned with the study and treatment of mental disorders
10. a group of symptoms which appear together to represent a specific type of disorder	6. number of new cases of a disorder
11. the values, beliefs, practices shared by a group of people	8. multidisciplinary field in which professionals are trained to provide psychotherapy

CHAPTER TWO

CAUSES OF ABNORMAL BEHAVIOR: A SYSTEMS APPROACH

CHAPTER OUTLINE

Overview
Brief Historical Perspective: Twentieth Century Paradigms
    General Paresis and the Biological Paradigm
    Freud and the Psychodynamic Paradigm
    Psychology, Learning, and the Cognitive Behavioral Paradigm
    Free Will and the Humanistic Paradigm
    The Problem with Paradigms
Systems Theory
    Holism
    Causality
    Developmental Psychopathology
Biological Factors
    The Neuron and Neurotransmitters
    Neurotransmitters and the Etiology of Psychopathology
    Major Brain Structures
    Cerebral Hemispheres
    Psychophysiology
    Behavior Genetics
Psychological Factors
    Basic Human Motivations and Temperament
    Emotions and Emotional Systems
    Learning and Cognition
    The Sense of Self
    Stages of Development
Social Factors
    Relationships and Psychopathology
    Gender and Gender Roles
    Prejudice and Poverty
    Societal Values
Summary

OBJECTIVES

1. Describe the biopsychosocial approach. Explain how it is a systems approach.
2. Describe several breakthroughs which led to the modern scientific study of abnormal psychology.
3. Distinguish holism from reductionism.
4. Understand how systems theory replaces several paradigms of the twentieth century.
5. Discuss issues regarding etiology. Include information pertaining to multiple pathways, correlation versus causation, equifinality, and diathesis-stress.
6. Describe the functions of the hindbrain, midbrain, and forebrain.
7. Distinguish structural from psychophysiological problems.
8. Describe the functioning of the central and peripheral nervous systems, the voluntary and autonomic nervous systems, and the sympathetic and parasympathetic divisions.
9. Understand the research design used for twin studies, adoption studies, and family incidence studies.

10. Define temperament and explain its significance in the etiology of psychopathology.
11. Describe some ways in which modeling, social cognition, and sense of self may affect abnormal behavior.

MATCHING I
Answers are found at the end of this chapter. Match these terms and concepts with the definitions that follow:

a.	Paradigm	l.	Ego
b.	Multifactional causes	m.	Reality principle
c.	Biological paradigm	n.	Superego
d.	General paresis	o.	Neurotic anxiety
e.	Syphilis	p.	Defense mechanisms
f.	Psychoanalytic theory	q.	Projection
g.	Hysteria	r.	Psychosexual development
h.	Conversion disorder	s.	Oedipal conflict
i.	Libido	t.	Electra complex
j.	Pleasure principle	u.	Unconscious
k.	Id	v.	Moral anxiety
		w.	Cognitive behavioral paradigm
		x.	Psychodynamic paradigm

1. _____ an elaborate theory of personality based on the concepts of Freud
2. _____ a set of assumptions about the substance of a theory and the scientific method used to test the theory
3. _____ unconscious processes that reduce conscious anxiety by distorting anxiety laden memories, emotions, and impulses
4. _____ the mode of operation for the ego, where the need to gratify impulses is balanced with demands of reality
5. _____ Freud's concept that a stage boys go through involves having sexual impulses toward their mothers and aggressive impulses toward their fathers; resolved by identifying with their fathers
6. _____ a psychoanalytic diagnostic category involving the conversion of psychological conflicts into physical symptoms
7. _____ Freud's theory of development
8. _____ a sexually transmitted disease caused by bacteria, the end stage of which includes psychiatric symptoms; treatable with antibiotics
9. _____ a Freudian term for the part of personality which serves as the conscience, containing societal standards of behavior
10. _____ the modern diagnostic category for hysteria
11. _____ a Freudian term for the part of personality which is the source of basic drives and motivations, including sexual and aggressive impulses
12. _____ the etiology of a disorder results from a combination of biological, psychological, and social factors
13. _____ produced by conflict between the id and the ego
14. _____ Freud's concept that a stage girls go through involves yearning for a penis, which they feel they must have lost
15. _____ focuses on biological causation
16. _____ a defense mechanism where the person perceives his or her own forbidden unconscious impulses as a characteristic of another person
17. _____ a Freudian term for sexual or life energy

18. _____ the mode of operation for the id, where impulses seek immediate gratification
19. _____ a disorder with delusions of grandeur, dementia, and progressive paralysis; progressively worsens, ending in death; caused by untreated syphilis
20. _____ a Freudian term for the part of personality which deals with the realities of the world
21. _____ mental processes or contents outside of a person's awareness, largely unavailable to the person
22. _____ produced by conflict between the ego and superego
23. _____ views abnormal behavior as caused by unconscious conflicts arising out of early childhood experiences
24. _____ assert that behavior is learned and examines the processes underlying learning

MATCHING II
Answers are found at the end of this chapter. Match these terms and concepts with the definitions that follow:

1. Introspection
2. Classical conditioning
3. Unconditioned stimulus
4. Unconditioned response
5. Conditioned stimulus
6. Conditioned response
7. Extinction
8. Operant Conditioning
9. Positive reinforcement
10. Negative reinforcement
11. Punishment
12. Response cost
13. Behaviorism
14. Humanistic psychology
15. Determinism
16. Free will
17. Systems theory
18. Holism
19. Reductionism
20. Risk factors
21. Molecular
22. Molar
23. Levels of analysis
24. Correlational study
25. Correlational coefficient

a. _____ a neutral stimulus that, when repeatedly paired with a stimulus that elicits an automatic reaction, comes to produce that reaction itself
b. _____ the idea that human behavior is not determined but a product of a person's choice
c. _____ the statistic for measuring how strongly two factors are related; it ranges between -1.0 and +1.0
d. _____ when the onset of a stimulus increases the frequency of a behavior
e. _____ the use of different perspectives, subsystems, or "lenses" to conceptualize causal factors
f. _____ when the removal of a stimulus decreases the frequency of behavior
g. _____ focus on inner experiences
h. _____ events or circumstances that are correlated with an increased likelihood of a disorder
i. _____ a paradigm that emphasizes interdependence, cybernetics, and holism
j. _____ Pavlov's form of learning through association of paired stimuli
k. _____ a research design where the relation between two factors is studied
l. _____ when the cessation of a stimulus increases the frequency of a behavior
m. _____ a stimulus that elicits an automatic reaction
n. _____ the assumption that human behavior is caused by predictable and potentially knowable internal and/or external events
o. _____ an automatic reaction to an event
p. _____ the most general
q. _____ the belief within psychology that observable behaviors are the only appropriate focus of psychological study
r. _____ a learning theory asserting that behavior is a function of its consequences; that behavior increases if it is rewarded and decreases if it is punished
s. _____ the gradual elimination of a response when learning conditions change

t. _____ the idea that the whole is more than the sum of its parts
u. _____ the most reductionistic
v. _____ the perspective that the whole is the sum of its parts, and that the task for science is to divide the world into smaller and smaller components
w. _____ when the introduction of a stimulus decreases the frequency of a behavior
x. _____ a paradigm of abnormal behavior that rejects determinism and argues that human behavior is the product of free will
y. _____ a response that is elicited by a conditioned stimulus

MATCHING III
Answers are found at the end of this chapter. Match these terms and concepts with the definitions that follow:

a. Positive correlations
b. Negative correlations
c. Third-variable
d. Diathesis-stress model
e. Equifinality
f. Reciprocal causality
g. Linear causality
h. Prognosis
i. Homeostasis
j. Developmental psychopathology
k. Developmental norms
l. Premorbid history
m. Reverse causality
n. Prognosis
o. Anatomy
p. Physiology
q. Neuroanatomy
r. Neurophysiology
s. Neurons
t. Soma
u. Dendrites
v. Axon
w. Axon Terminal
x. Synapse
y. Neurotransmitters
z. Multifinality

1. _____ a predictable course for the future
2. _____ the study of brain structures
3. _____ a pattern of behavior that precedes the onset of the disorder
4. _____ trunk of the neuron that transmits messages toward other cells
5. _____ the idea that causality is bidirectional
6. _____ cell body
7. _____ predictions about the future course of a disorder
8. _____ the same psychological disorder may have different causes
9. _____ the study of biological structures
10. _____ an approach to abnormal psychology that emphasizes the importance of age-graded averages and determining what constitutes abnormal behavior
11. _____ the study of biological functions
12. _____ the end of the axon where messages are sent out to other neurons
13. _____ as one factor goes up, the other factor goes down
14. _____ age-graded averages
15. _____ as one factor goes up, the other factor goes up
16. _____ causation operates in one direction only
17. _____ branching cell structures that receive messages from other cells
18. _____ the possibility that causation could be operating in the opposite direction; Y could be causing X instead of X causing Y
19. _____ the tendency to maintain a steady state
20. _____ the study of brain functions
21. _____ a small gap between neurons that is filled with fluid
22. _____ a correlation between two variables could be explained by their joint relation with some unmeasured factor

23. ____ nerve cells
24. ____ the same event can lead to different outcomes
25. ____ chemical substances released into the synapse that carry signals from one neuron to another
26. ____ a view of the etiology of a disorder that assumes it is produced by an interaction by a predisposition and a precipitating event

MATCHING IV
Answers are found at the end of this chapter. Match these terms and concepts with the definitions that follow:

1. Receptors
2. Reuptake
3. Neuromodulators
4. Vesicles
5. Dualism
6. Hindbrain
7. Medulla
8. Pons
9. Cerebellum
10. Midbrain
11. Reticular activating system
12. Forebrain
13. Limbic system
14. Thalamus
15. Hypothalamus
16. Cerebral hemispheres
17. Lateralized
18. Corpus callosum
19. Ventricles
20. Cerebral cortex
21. Frontal lobe
22. Parietal lobe
23. Temporal lobe
24. Occipital lobe

a. ____ a brain grouping including the medulla, pons, and cerebellum
b. ____ regulates emotion and basic learning processes
c. ____ sites on the dendrites or soma of a neuron that are sensitive to certain neurotransmitters
d. ____ the uneven surface of the brain just underneath the skull which controls and integrates sophisticated memory, sensory, and motor functions
e. ____ receives and integrates sensory information and plays a role in spatial reasoning
f. ____ controls bodily functions which sustain life, like heart rate and respiration
g. ____ the process of recapturing some neurotransmitters from the synapse before they reach the receptors of another neuron
h. ____ receives and integrates sensory information from the sense organs and from higher brain structures
i. ____ four connected chambers in the brain filled with cerebrospinal fluid
j. ____ each cerebral hemisphere serves a specialized role in brain function; the left hemisphere is involved in language and the right in spatial relations
k. ____ regulates stages of sleep
l. ____ connects the two cerebral hemispheres, and coordinates their different functions
m. ____ helps coordinate physical movement
n. ____ processes sound and smell, regulates emotions, and is involved in learning, memory, and language
o. ____ controls a number of complex functions like reasoning, planning, emotion, speech, and movement
p. ____ the view that mind and body are separable
q. ____ regulates sleep and waking
r. ____ a brain grouping which evolved last and is the location of most sensory, emotional, and cognitive processes
s. ____ the two major structures of the forebrain and the site of most sensory, emotional, and cognitive processes
t. ____ chemicals that may be released from neurons or endocrine glands which influence

u. ____ communications of many neurons by affecting the functioning of neurotransmitters
u. ____ a brain grouping which controls some motor activities, especially fighting and sex, and includes part of the reticular activating system
v. ____ receives and interprets visual information
w. ____ controls basic biological urges such as eating, drinking, and sex
x. ____ structures which contain neurotransmitters

MATCHING V

Answers are found at the end of this chapter. Match these names with the descriptions of their contributions to the study of abnormal psychology.

a. Sigmund Freud   f. John B. Watson
b. B. F. Skinner   g. Gregor Mendel
c. Rene Descartes   h. Ivan Pavlov
d. John Bowlby   i. Thomas Kuhn
e. Wilhelm Wundt   j. Abraham Maslow

1. ____ attempted to balance religious teachings with emerging scientific reasoning by proposing dualism
2. ____ founded behaviorism and applied learning theory to the study of abnormal behavior
3. ____ developed attachment theory, based in part on ethology
4. ____ developed psychoanalytic theory; focused on the importance of early childhood experiences and unconscious conflicts
5. ____ conducted a series of studies on classical conditioning
6. ____ applied the idea of paradigm to the historical study of science
7. ____ discovered genetic inheritance; made the distinction between genotypes and phenotypes
8. ____ a humanistic psychologist who explored motivation
9. ____ one of the first experimental psychologists; pioneered the scientific study of psychological phenomena
10. ____ conducted a series of studies on operant conditioning

CONCEPT REVIEW

Answers are found at the end of this chapter. After you have read and reviewed the material, test your comprehension by filling in the blanks or circling the correct answer.

1. It is likely that continuing research will answer the nature-nurture debate by demonstrating what the cause of each disorder is: **true**   **false**

2. What three major events encouraged advances in the scientific understanding of the etiology of psychopathology in the nineteenth and twentieth centuries?
_____, _____, and _____.

3. The development of a _____ for general paresis inspired a search for its cause, which took 100 years of investigation.

4. General paresis was eliminated with the advent of _____.

5. The elimination of general paresis encouraged researchers to adopt what paradigm in their research on etiology of mental disorders? _____

6. What theorist opposed the biological paradigm for mental disorders? _____
7. Freud developed his theories largely on the basis of _____ rather than scientific research.
8. What approach did Wundt use in studying psychological phenomena? _____
9. Cognitive behaviorists are primarily concerned with the _____ of mental disorders rather than understanding their causes.
10. _____ psychology was a reaction against biomedical, psychoanalytic, and behavioral theories of abnormal behavior.
11. Humanistic psychologists tend to blame dysfunctional, abnormal, or aggressive behavior on:

    the individual   society
12. What are the four paradigms the authors of your text focus on in explaining mental disorders? _____, _____, _____, and _____
13. The textbook example of the Martian scientists trying to figure out what causes automobiles to move, points out the importance of the _____ that a research approach uses.
14. A predisposition toward developing a disorder is called a: **stress   diathesis**
15. A thermostat is a good example of which systems theory concept? _____
16. The density and sensitivity of _____ on neurons has been implicated in some types of abnormal behavior.
17. All psychological experience has a representation in the biochemistry of the _____.
18. A _____ is caused by blood vessels in the brain rupturing and cutting off the supply of oxygen to parts of the brain, thereby killing surrounding brain tissue.
19. Psychophysiological **overarousal/underarousal** has been hypothesized to be responsible for excessive anxiety, while psychophysiological **overarousal/underarousal** has been linked with antisocial behavior.
20. The simple mode of dominant/recessive inheritance has been linked with forms of which of the following kinds of abnormal behavior?   **schizophrenia   mental retardation   depression**
21. The genetic contributions to most disorders are hypothesized to be caused by:

    a single gene   multiple genes
22. If a disorder is purely genetic, the concordance for MZ twins would be _____% and the concordance for DZ twins would be _____%.
23. If the concordance rates for MZ and DZ twins are the same, then what type of factors are responsible for the disorder?   **genetic   environmental**
24. Family incidence studies ask whether diseases _____.
25. If a disorder is shown to be genetic, then nothing can change it: **true   false**
26. According to attachment theorists, displays of distress by human infants serve to keep caregivers in _____, making infants more likely to survive.

27. Emotions are often experienced grouped in a constellation or system rather than alone:
    true   **false**

28. The most effective parents are those who provide both high levels of _____ and _____ .

29. Two prominent stage theories are those proposed by which theorists? _____ and _____

30. There is a correlation between marital status of parents and emotional _____ of children.

31. A close relationship with an adult outside the family can protect children from the effects of troubled family circumstances: **true**   **false**

32. Some theorists have suggested that _____ are responsible for the much higher rates of depression among women.

33. One study found that 12 percent of school-aged children had seen a _____ in the streets outside their homes in a Washington neighborhood.

CROSSWORD

Answers are found at the end of this chapter. Complete the following crossword puzzle to reinforce your understanding of this chapter's key terms and concepts:

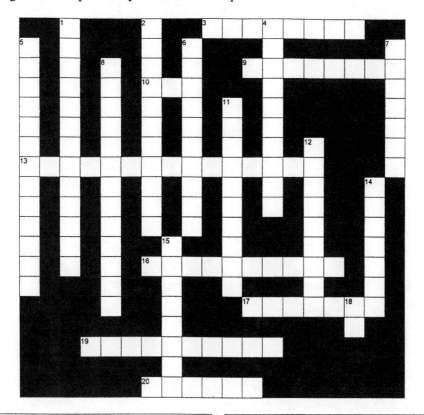

ACROSS	DOWN
3. observational learning	1. type of study which focuses on the relation between two factors
9. cause	2. tendency to maintain a steady state
10. part of personality operating of the reality principle	4. occurs when CS is no longer paired with US
13. intellectually justifying a feeling or event; a defense mechanism	5. increases likelihood of a behavior repeating
16. paradigm which focuses on notion of free will	6. paradigm which looks for biological abnormalities
17. paralysis	7. space between nerve cells
19. attributing one's own feelings to other people; a defense mechanism	8. paradigm which focuses on unconscious conflict
20. central principle of systems theory	11. selective bond with caregiver
	12. system of glands
	14. theory which integrates biological, psychological, and social variables
	15. equivalent to the conscience in psychodynamic model
	18. source of basic drives

MULTIPLE CHOICE

Answers are found at the end of this chapter. The multiple choice questions listed will test your understanding of the material presented in the chapter. Read through each question and circle the letter representing the best answer.

1. Which of the following views psychopathology as resulting from physical factors that form a predisposition, combined with a threatening or challenging experience?
    a. medical model
    b. diathesis-stress model
    c. threshold model
    d. biopsychosocial model

2. The assumption that biological explanations are more useful than psychological explanations because they deal with smaller units is called:
    a. biological perspective
    b. genetic predisposition
    c. biological reductionism
    d. medical model

3. Which regulates the function of various organs, such as the heart and stomach?
    a. somatic nervous system
    b. autonomic nervous system
    c. sympathetic nervous system
    d. parasympathetic nervous system

4. According to Freud, this is the part of the personality that attempts to fulfill id impulses while at the same time dealing with the realities of the world.
    a. ego
    b. id
    c. superego
    d. libido

5. In all but which of the following are methods of learning?
    a. classical conditioning
    b. operant conditioning
    c. introjection
    d. modeling

6. Developmental theory suggests that children whose parents are _____ and _____ are better adjusted than those whose parents are inadequate on one or both of these dimensions.
    a. loving; firm in their discipline
    b. authoritative; hold high expectations of their child
    c. demanding; promote individuality
    d. congenial; encourage separation and independence

7. Freud was trained by this neurologist who successfully used hypnosis to treat what used to be called hysteria.
    a. Skinner
    b. Bertalanffy
    c. Perls
    d. Charcot

8. While watching her daughter play kickball in the street of their neighborhood, Mrs. Jones sees her daughter being hit by a car. Soon thereafter, Mrs. Jones loses her vision. After visits to numerous doctors, there is no known organic impairment to cause the blindness. What might her diagnosis be?
    a. depression
    b. conversion disorder
    c. hysteria
    d. hypochondriasis

9. Which of the following could be considered an uncertain or ambivalent parent-child relationship that is a consequence of inconsistent and unresponsive parenting, particularly during the first year of life?
    a. anxious attachment
    b. neurotic attachment
    c. oppositional attachment
    d. apathetic attachment

10. All of the following are associated with the humanistic approach, with the exception of
    a. Rogers
    b. Skinner
    c. Perls
    d. Maslow

11. In the famous experiments on which classical conditioning was based, the bell served as the _____ and the meat powder was the _____.
    a. conditioned response; unconditioned response
    b. unconditioned response; conditioned response
    c. conditioned stimulus; unconditioned stimulus
    d. unconditioned stimulus; conditioned stimulus

12. The enigma written by Lord Byron and presented in this chapter illustrates that
    a. paradigms are unscientific and should not be used in evaluating situations
    b. the hidden meanings in life are sometimes difficult to comprehend, however the use of a paradigm can aid in this process
    c. we should use our paradigm to reveal the meaning from certain situations
    d. assumptions made by a paradigm can at times act as blinders and lead an investigator to overlook what otherwise might be obvious

13. Brad's mother took away his privilege to use the computer for two days because he hit his sister. This is an example of:
    a. punishment
    b. response cost
    c. extinction
    d. negative reinforcement

14. Systems theory has roots in all of the following fields, with the exception of
    a. biology
    b. engineering
    c. philosophy
    d. all of the above

15. _____ are chainlike structures found in the nucleus of cells.
    a. Neurotransmitters
    b. Genes
    c. Chromosomes
    d. Lobes

16. Which is a pattern of behavior that precedes the onset of the disorder?
    a. prognosis
    b. premorbid history
    c. determinism
    d. self-fulfilling prophecy

17. Advances in the scientific understanding of the etiology of psychopathology did not appear until the nineteenth and early twentieth centuries when all of the following major events occurred, except
    a. the number of people diagnosed with some form of psychopathology rapidly increased
    b. the cause of general paresis was discovered
    c. the emergence of Sigmund Freud
    d. the creation of a new academic discipline called psychology

18. According to Freud's theory of psychosexual development, a son's forbidden sexual desire for his mother is called (a/an):
    a. defense mechanism
    b. neurotic anxiety
    c. Electra complex
    d. Oedipal conflict

19. As described by the bipolar dimensions of personality, this domain is characterized by trusting and kind versus hostile and selfish.
    a. conscientiousness
    b. agreeable
    c. neuroticism
    d. extraversion

20. According to the psychodynamic paradigm, the cause of abnormality is
    a. early childhood experiences
    b. social learning
    c. frustrations of society
    d. genes, infection, or other physical damage

21. The cornerstone of humanistic psychology is _____. It is the assumption that human behavior is not determined but is a product of how people choose to act.
    a. holism
    b. self-fulfilling prophecy
    c. individuation
    d. free will

22. Which of the following is a communication and control process that uses feedback loops to adjust progress toward a goal?
    a. homeostasis
    b. neuromodulators
    c. cybernetics
    d. neurotransmitters

23. This nervous system is responsible for controlling activities associated with increased arousal and energy expenditure.
    a. sympathetic nervous system
    b. parasympathetic nervous system
    c. autonomic nervous system
    d. somatic nervous system

24. Freud can be credited with all of the following, with the exception of
    a. offering specific, empirically-derived hypotheses about his theory
    b. calling attention to unconscious processes
    c. formulating a stage theory of child development
    d. identifying numerous intra-psychic defenses

25. Which of the following are characteristic ways of behaving according to the expectations of the social situation?
    a. prescribed roles
    b. social roles
    c. gender roles
    d. transitional roles

26. All of the following statements are true from a systems perspective regarding the etiology of psychopathology, except
    a. there may be biopsychosocial contributions to psychopathology, but clear hypotheses must still be supported by empirical evidence
    b. social domains of behavior are the most significant contribution to the causes of abnormal behavior
    c. different types of abnormal behavior have very different causes
    d. causes of almost all forms of abnormal behavior are unknown at present

27. According to the behavioral paradigm, the inborn human nature is
    a. aggressive
    b. basically good
    c. basically selfish, but having some altruism
    d. neutral, like a blank slate

28. Which of the following is a defense mechanism that includes the insistence that an experience, memory, or internal need did not occur or does not exist?
    a. sublimation
    b. reaction formation
    c. denial
    d. repression

29. This occurs when a conditioned stimulus is no longer presented together with an unconditioned stimulus.
    a. extinction
    b. punishment
    c. negative reinforcement
    d. response cost

30. A _____ is an individual's actual genetic structure.
    a. locus
    b. phenotype
    c. negative reinforcement
    d. response cost

31. This theory suggests that depression is caused by wrongly attributing bad events to internal, global, and stable causes.
    a. labeling theory
    b. learned helplessness theory
    c. modeling theory
    d. social cognition theory

32. The concept that one particular event can lead to different outcomes is known as:
    a. reciprocal causality
    b. equifinality
    c. linear causality
    d. multifinality

UNDERSTANDING RESEARCH
Answers are found at the end of this chapter.

Marriage and Mental Health: The text presents a detailed description of a study in the Research Close-Up. Finding the answers to these questions will provide an understanding of this study and why it is important.

1. A factor commonly found to be correlated with psychological well-being is _____. This study, the _____ study, involved interviewing _____ of people. There were consistent correlations between marriage and _____ health. Of people still in their first marriage, _____% were diagnosed with depression in the past year; of people who were never married, the rate was _____%; among those divorced once the rate was _____%; among those divorced more than once the rate was _____%.

2. What other diagnostic category was found to be correlated with marital status? _____ What percentage of people in their first marriage had ever had this diagnosis? _____%. What percentage of people never married? _____% What percentage of people divorced once? _____% What percentage of people divorced more than once? _____% Another disorder that was correlated was _____. Marital status was correlated with virtually _____ psychological disorder that was diagnosed in this study.

3. One explanation for these findings is that not being married _____ mental disorders, because having a spouse may provide emotional support, and divorce and _____ and loss of support may increase

susceptibility to disorders. However, emotional problems may _____ marital status. Psychologically disturbed people may have more trouble _____ and forming relationships, and may have shakier marriages. This explanation is called _____. Another explanation is the _____ interpretation, which states that another factor may cause a _____ correlation between marital status and abnormal behavior. One possible factor to consider is _____.

4. These different explanations result in very different implications for _____ of mental disorders and social _____. What should be done if the third variable hypothesis is correct? _____ What do most researchers conclude about the correlation between marriage and mental health? It remains after controlling for _____ variables; for disorders like schizophrenia, marital status is a reaction to, not a cause of, the _____ problem; and marital status does have causal impact on disorders like _____.

SHORT ANSWER

Answer the following short answer questions. Compare your work to the material presented in the text.

1. Compare and contrast the following behavior genetics investigations: twin studies, adoption, and family incidence studies. In what ways are these findings helpful? In what ways could these findings possibly be misinterpreted?

2. Discuss Bowlby's attachment theory. Does this theory have empirical support? Explain.

3. Compare and contrast Freud and Erikson's theories of development. Which theory makes the most sense to you and your personal experience? Why?

4. Discuss why it is not enough to focus on one subsystem or level of analysis when viewing psychopathology. What do you gain by focusing on multifactorial causes?

5. Why is it important not to infer causation from correlation?

ANSWER KEY

MATCHING I

1. f
2. a
3. p
4. m
5. s
6. g
7. r
8. e
9. n
10. h
11. k
12. b
13. o
14. t
15. c
16. q
17. i
18. j
19. d
20. l
21. u
22. v
23. x
24. w

MATCHING II

a. 5
b. 16
c. 25
d. 9
e. 23
f. 12
g. 1
h. 20
i. 17
j. 2
k. 24
l. 10
m. 3

n. 15
o. 4
p. 22
q. 13
r. 8
s. 7
t. 18
u. 21
v. 19
w. 11
x. 14
y. 6

MATCHING III

1. h
2. q
3. l
4. v
5. f
6. t
7. n
8. e
9. o
10. j
11. p
12. w
13. b

14. k
15. a
16. g
17. u
18. m
19. i
20. r
21. x
22. c
23. s
24. z
25. y
26. d

MATCHING IV

a. 6
b. 13
c. 1
d. 20
e. 22
f. 7
g. 2
h. 14
i. 19
j. 17
k. 8
l. 18

m. 9
n. 23
o. 21
p. 5
q. 11
r. 12
s. 16
t. 3
u. 10
v. 24
w. 15
x. 4

MATCHING V

1. c
2. f
3. d
4. a
5. h

6. i
7. g
8. j
9. e
10. b

CONCEPT REVIEW

1. false
2. discovery of the cause of general paresis; Freud; birth of psychology
3. diagnostic category
4. Penicillin
5. Biological
6. Freud
7. introspection
8. the scientific method
9. treatment
10. Humanistic
11. society
12. systems theory; biological factors; psychological factors; social factors
13. level of analysis
14. diathesis
15. cybernetics
16. receptors
17. brain
18. stroke
19. overarousal; underarousal
20. mental retardation
21. multiple genes
22. 100; 50
23. environmental
24. run in families
25. false
26. proximity
27. true
28. love, discipline
29. Freud; Erikson
30. problems
31. true
32. gender roles
33. dead body

MULTIPLE CHOICE

1. b
2. c
3. b
4. a
5. c
6. a
7. d
8. b
9. a
10. b
11. c
12. d
13. b
14. d
15. c
16. b

17. a
18. d
19. b
20. a
21. d
22. c
23. a
24. a
25. b
26. b
27. d
28. c
29. a
30. a
31. b
32. d

UNDERSTANDING RESEARCH

1. marital status; ECA; thousands; mental; 1.5; 2.4; 4.1; 5.8
2. alcoholism; 8.9; 15; 16.2; 24.2; schizophrenia; every
3. causes; conflict; cause; dating; reverse causality; third variable; spurious; poverty
4. treatment policy; intervention should focus on changing the third variable; third; emotional; depression

CROSSWORD

ACROSS		DOWN	
3.	observational learning	1.	type of study which focuses on the relation between two factors
9.	cause	2.	tendency to maintain a steady state
10.	part of personality operating of the reality principle	4.	occurs when CS is no longer paired with US
13.	intellectually justifying a feeling or event; a defense mechanism	5.	increases likelihood of a behavior repeating
16.	paradigm which focuses on notion of free will	6.	paradigm which looks for biological abnormalities
17.	paralysis	7.	space between nerve cells
19.	attributing one's own feelings to other people; a defense mechanism	8.	paradigm which focuses on unconscious conflict
20.	central principle of systems theory	11.	selective bond with caregiver
		12.	system of glands
		14.	theory which integrates biological, psychological, and social variables
		15.	equivalent to the conscience in psychodynamic model
		18.	source of basic drives

CHAPTER THREE

TREATMENT OF PSYCHOLOGICAL DISORDERS

CHAPTER OUTLINE

Overview
- Frances and the Four Paradigms
- Brief Historical Perspective

Biological Treatments
- Electroconvulsive Therapy
- Psychosurgery
- Psychopharmacology

Psychodynamic Psychotherapies
- Freudian Psychoanalysis
- Ego Analysis
- Psychodynamic Psychotherapy

Cognitive Behavior Therapy
- Systematic Desensitization
- Other Exposure Therapies
- Aversion Therapy
- Contingency Management
- Social Skills Training
- Cognitive Techniques
- Beck's Cognitive Therapy
- Rational-Emotive Therapy
- Integration: Empiricism Reigns

Humanistic Therapy
- Client-Centered Therapy
- Gestalt Therapy
- A Means, Not an End?

Research on Psychotherapy
- Does Psychotherapy Work?
- Psychotherapy Process Research

Changing Social Systems: Couples, Family, and Group Therapy
- Couples Therapy
- Family Therapy
- Group Therapy
- Prevention

Specific Treatments for Specific Disorders

Summary

OBJECTIVES

1. Discuss the systems approach to psychotherapy.
2. Distinguish between the biological, psychodynamic, cognitive, behavioral, and humanistic approaches to treatment.
3. Describe electroconvulsive therapy and psychosurgery and their current applications.
4. Discuss the effectiveness of psychopharmacology in the treatment of mental illness.
5. Describe the basic goals and primary techniques involved in psychoanalysis.
6. Discuss the theory underlying ego analysis and distinguish between psychoanalysis and psychodynamic psychotherapy.
7. Discuss the ways in which classical conditioning principles are utilized in treatment.
8. Describe contingency management and social skills training programs.
9. Discuss the principles of attribution therapy, self-instruction training, cognitive therapy, and rational therapy.
10. Discuss how client-centered therapy reflects the underlying principles of humanistic psychology.
11. Describe the findings of psychotherapy outcome studies.
12. Define psychotherapy process research and describe some of its basic findings.
13. Discuss the goals, techniques, and outcomes of couples therapy, family therapy, and group therapy.
14. Discuss several recommendations which may improve the effectiveness of psychotherapy.

MATCHING I

Answers are found at the end of this chapter. Match these terms and concepts with the definitions that follow:

a.	Psychotherapy	l.	Genuineness
b.	Psychotherapy outcome research	m.	Trephining
c.	Psychotherapy process research	n.	Symptom alleviation
d.	Eclectic	o.	Electroconvulsive therapy (ECT)
e.	Biological therapies	p.	Bilateral ECT
f.	Psychodynamic therapies	q.	Unilateral ECT
g.	Psychotropic drugs	r.	Psychosurgery
h.	Cognitive therapies	s.	Prefrontal lobotomy
i.	Humanistic therapies	t.	Cingulotomy
j.	Defensive style	u.	Psychopharmacology
k.	Homework		

1. ____ investigates similarities in practice by studying aspects of the client-therapist relationship
2. ____ an ancient form of surgery to treat mental disorders consisting of chipping a hole in the patient's skull
3. ____ treatments based on Freud's writings and later related theorists; focus on exploring the patient's past and unconscious to promote insight
4. ____ electroconvulsive therapy through both brain hemispheres
5. ____ treatments based on the perspective that mental illness is like physical illness
6. ____ a procedure in which the frontal lobes of the brain are surgically destroyed
7. ____ ability to be oneself
8. ____ treatments focusing on present feelings which encourage the client to take responsibility for their actions
9. ____ a type of therapy focused on changing the client's cognition and behavior
10. ____ surgical destruction of specific regions of the brain

11. ____ treatment for mental illness involving the induction of a seizure by passing electricity through the brain
12. ____ electroconvulsive therapy through one brain hemisphere
13. ____ protecting oneself from being aware of inner feelings
14. ____ compares the effectiveness of alternative forms of treatment
15. ____ a form of limited psychosurgery that may be effective for very severe cases of obsessive-compulsive disorder
16. ____ the study of the use of medications to treat psychological disturbances
17. ____ the use of psychological techniques to try to produce change in the context of a special, helping relationship
18. ____ activities assigned to the client designed to continue treatment outside the therapy session
19. ____ an approach of picking different treatments according to the needs of individual disorders and individual clients
20. ____ chemical substances that affect psychological state
21. ____ reducing the dysfunctional symptoms of a disorder but not eliminating its root cause

MATCHING II

Answers are found at the end of this chapter. Match these terms and concepts with the definitions that follow:

1. Catharsis
2. Free association
3. Psychoanalysis
4. Insight
5. Interpretation
6. Therapeutic neutrality
7. Transference
8. Countertransference
9. Psychodynamic
10. Ego analysis
11. Short term psychodynamic psychotherapy
12. Behaviorism
13. Experiment
14. Hypothesis
15. Independent variable
16. Experimental group
17. Control group
18. Random assignment
19. Dependent variable
20. Statistically significant
21. Confounded
22. Internal validity
23. External validity

a. ____ bringing formerly unconscious material into conscious awareness
b. ____ a form of treatment involving active focus on a particular emotional issue rather than free association, usually completed in about twenty five sessions
c. ____ subjects who receive an active treatment
d. ____ an analyst's suggestion to the patient of what is the hidden meaning of his or her symptoms, dreams, or verbalizations
e. ____ the outcome that is hypothesized to vary according to the manipulations of the independent variable
f. ____ the sudden release of pent-up emotions in therapy which reduces psychic strain
g. ____ the belief that observable behaviors rather than cognitive or emotional states are the appropriate focus of psychological study
h. ____ subjects who receive no treatment or a placebo
i. ____ a purposeful stance the therapist takes of being distant and uninvolved to minimize his or her influence on free association
j. ____ changes in the dependent variable can be accurately attributed to changes in the independent variable
k. ____ a therapeutic technique where patients report without censorship whatever thoughts cross their mind, no matter how trivial
l. ____ a type of scientific investigation which can establish cause and effect

m. ____ the factor that is controlled and manipulated by the experimenter
n. ____ revisions of psychoanalysis where the therapist is more engaged and directive and treatment is often briefer
o. ____ where the independent variable is unknowingly related to some other unmeasured factor which is not evenly distributed among the treatment groups
p. ____ the form of psychological therapy developed by Freud
q. ____ the experimenter's specific prediction about cause and effect
r. ____ the probability that the observed difference between the groups occurred by chance alone rather than the effect of the independent variable is less than five percent
s. ____ the process whereby patients transfer their feelings about key people in their lives onto their therapist
t. ____ ensuring that each subject has a statistically equal chance of receiving different levels of the independent variable
u. ____ the process whereby therapists' feelings and reactions toward their patients affects their responses to them
v. ____ findings of an experiment can be validly generalized to other circumstances
w. ____ innovations on psychoanalytic theory giving more importance to the ego and the role of society and culture

MATCHING III
Answers are found at the end of this chapter. Match these terms and concepts with the definitions that follow:

a. Counterconditioning
b. Systematic desensitization
c. Progressive muscle relaxation
d. Hierarchy of fears
e. In vivo desensitization
f. Flooding
g. Aversion therapy
h. Contingency management
i. Token economy
j. Social skills training
k. Assertiveness training
l. Role playing
m. Social problem solving
n. Cognitive behavior therapy
o. Attribution retraining
p. Self-instruction training
q. Beck's cognitive therapy
r. Rational-emotive therapy (RET)
s. Emotional awareness
t. Client-centered therapy
u. Empathy
v. Self-disclosure
w. Unconditional positive regard
x. Gestalt therapy
y. Empty chair technique
z. Psychotherapy integration

1. ____ the therapist's description of his or her own feelings and reactions
2. ____ a technique for challenging negative distortions in thinking where the therapist gently confronts the client's fallacies
3. ____ teaching clients new, desirable ways of behaving that are likely to be rewarded in the everyday world
4. ____ ordering fears ranging from very mild to very frightening
5. ____ a treatment for impulsive children where an adult first models an appropriate behavior while saying the self-instruction aloud, then the child does so, and gradually shifts from saying the self-instruction aloud to saying it silently to themselves
6. ____ non-judgmentally valuing clients for whom they are regardless of their behavior
7. ____ gradually being exposed to the feared stimulus in real life while simultaneously maintaining a state of relaxation
8. ____ the client has a dialogue with another part of himself or herself that is imagined sitting in an empty chair

9. ____ a humanistic therapy that follows the client's lead where the therapist offers warmth, empathy, and genuineness but the client solves his or her own problems
10. ____ an improvisational acting technique that allows clients to rehearse new social skills
11. ____ emotional understanding of others' unique feelings and perspectives
12. ____ exposure at full intensity to the feared stimulus with prevention of avoidance of the stimuli until the fear response is eliminated through extinction
13. ____ a technique of problem solving where the problem is first assessed in detail, alternative solutions are brainstormed, the different options are evaluated, one alternative is implemented, and its success is evaluated objectively
14. ____ a formalized contingency management system adopted in an institutional setting
15. ____ teaching clients to be direct about their feelings and wishes
16. ____ a cognitive behavior therapy technique designed to directly challenge irrational beliefs about oneself and the world
17. ____ a method of inducing a calm state through the contraction and subsequent relaxation of all the major muscle groups
18. ____ trying to change how a person ascribes causes to various events in his or her life by abandoning intuitive strategies for more scientific methods
19. ____ a form of humanistic therapy that underscores affective awareness and expression, genuineness, and experiencing the moment
20. ____ a treatment for overcoming fears involving systematic exposure to imagined, feared events while simultaneously maintaining relaxation
21. ____ altering existing responses by pairing new responses with old stimuli
22. ____ pairing an unpleasant response with the stimuli that was previously sought; used for helping people stop smoking and drinking alcohol
23. ____ recognizing and experiencing true feelings
24. ____ the application of behavior therapy into the cognitive realm
25. ____ focuses on directly changing the rewards and punishments for various behaviors: rewarding the desired behavior and punishing the undesirable behavior
26. ____ combining the best elements of different treatments into a unified theory of psychotherapy

MATCHING IV

Answers are found at the end of this chapter. Match these names with the descriptions of their contributions to the study of abnormal psychology:

a. Egas Moniz
b. Joseph Breuer
c. Sigmund Freud
d. Harry Stack Sullivan
e. Erik Erikson
f. Karen Horney
g. John Bowlby
h. John B. Watson
i. Joseph Wolpe
j. Aaron Beck
k. Albert Ellis
l. Carl Rogers
m. Fritz Perls
n. Jerome Frank

1. ____ proposed a theory that people have conflicting ego needs to move toward, against, and away from others
2. ____ developed attachment theory
3. ____ developed client-centered therapy
4. ____ abandoned the cathartic method for free association
5. ____ an ego analyst who focused on interpersonal relationships rather than intrapsychic dynamics
6. ____ developed rational-emotive therapy
7. ____ pioneered the cathartic method
8. ____ investigated the common factors of different psychotherapies
9. ____ developed behaviorism
10. ____ won a Nobel Prize for discovering prefrontal lobotomy
11. ____ developed a cognitive behavior therapy for depression
12. ____ developed Gestalt therapy
13. ____ developed systematic desensitization
14. ____ developed a psychosocial stage theory of development

CONCEPT REVIEW

Answers are found at the end of this chapter. After you have read and reviewed the material, test your comprehension by filling in the blanks or circling the correct answer.

1. There are hundreds of different types of psychotherapy: **true**   **false**

2. The surgical removal of sexual organs was one biological treatment used for emotional problems in the past: **true**   **false**

3. The development of ECT originated in attempts to treat schizophrenia that were based on the incorrect conclusion that schizophrenia was rare among people who had _____.

4. Which type of ECT produces less memory loss: **unilateral**   **bilateral**

5. Which type of ECT is more effective: **unilateral**   **bilateral**

6. Research has shown electroconvulsive therapy to be quite effective in treating what type of mental illness?_____

7. Psychosurgery is a reversible treatment: **true**   **false**

8. What percentage of people treated with prefrontal lobotomy died?
    1-2%   **11%**   **25%**

9. What was the number one selling prescription medicine for any type of ailment in the 1990s?_____

10. What was the number one selling prescription medicine for any type of ailment in the 1970s?_____

11. According to psychoanalysis, uncovering unconscious material and sharing the _____ view of their intra-psychic life, is necessary for treatment.

12. Why is timing so important in interpreting the patient's dynamics to him or her in psychoanalysis?_____

13. Psychoanalysis is thought to be more effective for what types of disorders? _____

14. Sullivan hypothesized that there are two basic dimensions of interpersonal relationships: _____and_____

15. Horney stressed the need for a person to have _____ among the three styles in which they relate to others.
16. Research shows that systematic desensitization is an effective form of treatment for fears and phobias:
    true   false
17. Research shows that aversion therapy is effective in the long-term alleviation of substance use:
    true   false
18. What is the shortcoming of the use of token economies? _____
19. Attribution retraining is effective for what type of mental disorder? _____
20. One of the main strengths of the behavior therapy approach is its focus on demonstrating its effectiveness through _____.
21. Humanistic psychotherapists are very active in directing therapy: **true   false**
22. When a client in Gestalt therapy is phony, the therapist is _____
23. There is no research evidence that psychotherapy works: **true   false**
24. Research has documented that psychotherapy is more effective in treating mental disorders than chemotherapy is in treating breast cancer: **true   false**
25. What proportion of people improve without any treatment:
    one quarter   one third   two thirds
26. The quickest improvements in therapy occur in the first several months of therapy:
    true   false
27. What does YAVIS stand for? _____
28. Cognitive behavior therapy may be more effective in the treatment of _____
29. In the classic study by Sloane and colleagues comparing behavior therapy and psychodynamic psychotherapy, both forms of therapy were more effective than no treatment, but were not significantly different from each other: **true   false**
30. In that same study, the single most important aspect of both types of therapy for the client was his or her _____.
31. The "file drawer problem" refers to the scientist hesitating before _____ findings that contradict their expectation.
32. Potent placebo effects have been demonstrated in cancer treatment and in surgery: **true   false**
33. All forms of therapy emphasize the importance of _____ in the therapist-client relationship.
34. According to family systems therapists, a well-functioning family is one where the primary alliance is between _____.
35. One shortcoming of self-help groups is the lack of _____.

CROSSWORD

Answers are found at the end of this chapter. Complete the following crossword puzzle to reinforce your understanding of this chapter's key terms and concepts.

ACROSS	DOWN	
3. prevention which focuses on developoment of new cases	1. statistical technique	10. type of therapy designed to challenge cognitive distortions
5. a prediction	2. example of contingency management	12. inert substance or treatment
9. humanistic approach used by Rogers	3. medications which affect psychological state	13. group consisting of those who receive no treatment or merely a placebo
11. bringing unconscious material into conscious awareness	4. perceived causes	
	6. deliberate induction of a seizure	
14. an exposure technique	7. involves surgical destruction of specific regions of the brain	
	8. belief that observable behaviors are the appropriate focus of psychology	

MULTIPLE CHOICE
Answers are found at the end of this chapter. The multiple choice questions listed will test your understanding of the material presented in the chapter. Read through each question and circle the letter representing the best answer.

1. According to attribution theory, depressed people often attribute _____ to themselves and _____ to others.
    a. success; failure
    b. failure; success
    c. irrational beliefs; rational beliefs
    d. rational beliefs; irrational beliefs

2. Treatment outcome researchers widely accept the finding that approximately _____ of clients improve as a result of psychotherapy.
    a. one-third
    b. two-thirds
    c. one-quarter
    d. one-half

3. Empathy involves
    a. trying to put yourself in someone else's shoes in order to understand their feelings and perspectives
    b. trying to understand the etiology of someone else's behavior
    c. feeling sorry for someone because of their life situation
    d. all of the above

4. The "placebo effect" is treatment
    a. in which the client has a dialogue with an imagined part of himself or herself
    b. in which the client is taught relaxation skills for the condition being evaluated
    c. that contains no "special ingredient" for treating the condition being evaluated
    d. which involves full intensity exposure to feared stimuli

5. Every day that Sally completes all of her chores at home her mother gives her a star. After Sally has accumulated fifteen stars, her mother will take her out for ice cream. Her mother is most likely using which of the following to get Sally to do her chores?
    a. token economy
    b. counterconditioning
    c. in vivo desensitization
    d. classical conditioning

6. Which of the following would most likely ask a patient to do homework?
    a. a biological therapist
    b. a psychodynamic psychotherapist
    c. a humanistic therapist
    d. a cognitive behavior therapist

7. The following is a/are possible side effect(s) of electroconvulsive therapy.
    a. fractures
    b. death
    c. long-term memory loss
    d. all of the above

8. All of the following are examples of cognitive behavior therapy with the exception of
    a. flooding
    b. social skills training
    c. aversion therapy
    d. empty chair technique

9. An experiment has internal validity if
    a. the findings can be generalized to other circumstances
    b. changes in the dependent variable can be accurately attributed to changes in the independent variable
    c. the researcher can control all aspects of the experimental environment
    d. the researcher is able to control and manipulate the dependent variable

10. This type of therapy is primarily used to treat substance abuse disorders such as alcoholism and cigarette smoking.
    a. cognitive therapy
    b. psychodynamic therapy
    c. aversion therapy
    d. contingency therapy

11. Sam is a first-year college student who is extremely afraid of heights. He entered therapy after failing his first semester chemistry course because it was located on the fifth floor of a building, and Sam was too afraid to go the fifth floor to attend class. Sam's therapist gradually exposes Sam to increasing heights while having Sam simultaneously maintain a state of relaxation. Sam's therapist is using which technique to help Sam alleviate his fear of heights?
    a. in vivo desensitization
    b. systematic desensitization
    c. flooding
    d. counterconditioning

12. Albert Ellis is to _____ as Aaron Beck is to _____.
    a. client-centered therapy; ego analysis
    b. ego analysis; client-centered therapy
    c. rational-emotive therapy; cognitive therapy
    d. cognitive therapy; rational-emotive therapy

13. According to Freud, all of the following are ways to reveal aspects of the unconscious mind except for
    a. slips of the tongue
    b. countertransference
    c. dreams
    d. free association

14. One major difference in technique between humanistic and cognitive behavior therapists is
    a. humanistic psychotherapists view the nature of the therapist-client relationship differently than behavior therapists
    b. humanistic psychotherapists focus on the patients' past and present interpersonal relationships
    c. humanistic psychotherapists focus on treatment irrespective of its causes
    d. none of the above

15. All of the following have caused a decline in the practice of classical psychoanalysis except
    a. the substantial amount of time required
    b. the accessibility of treatment only by those who are relatively financially secure
    c. research has proven classical Freudian psychoanalysis to be ineffective
    d. the limited data available on the outcome of treatment

16. In the 1990s this medication has outsold every prescription medication, including all medications used to treat physical ailments.
    a. Valium
    b. Prozac
    c. Ritalin
    d. Lithium

17. All of the following can be viewed as goals of psychoanalysis except
    a. to rid the patient of his or her defenses
    b. to increase self-understanding
    c. to bring unconscious material into conscious awareness
    d. to release pent-up emotions and unexpressed feelings

18. Pavlov is to _____ as Skinner is to _____.
    a. in vivo desensitization; systematic desensitization
    b. systematic desensitization; in vivo desensitization
    c. operant conditioning; classical conditioning
    d. classical conditioning; operant conditioning

19. Psychotherapy outcome research indicates that:
    a. clients who are young, attractive, verbal, intelligent, and successful tend to improve more in psychotherapy
    b. if psychotherapy is going to be effective, it will be effective rather quickly
    c. psychotherapy is generally effective when compared with no treatment at all
    d. all of the above

20. Aversion therapy is a _____ technique.
    a. classical conditioning
    b. operant conditioning
    c. cognitive-behavior
    d. social skills training

21. Collaborative empiricism involves:
    a. relieving a client's symptoms through the use of medication
    b. revealing aspects of a client's unconscious drives and conflicts
    c. role-playing and assertiveness training
    d. challenging a client's negative distortions

22. _____ is one of the earliest examples of a spiritual or religious tradition of healing.
    a. Taboo death
    b. Exorcism
    c. Trephining
    d. Stoning

23. Research indicates that _____ is the most effective approach to treating psychological disorders.
    a. humanistic psychotherapy
    b. psychodynamic psychotherapy
    c. cognitive behavior therapy
    d. research generally reveals few differences among approaches

24. The term "unconditional positive regard" refers to
    a. valuing a client for who they are and refraining from judging them
    b. making positive comments to a client and never devaluing them as a person
    c. the relationship between the client and therapist
    d. none of the above

25. _____ has been the most promising avenue of biological treatment.
    a. Psychosurgery
    b. Classical conditioning
    c. Operant conditioning
    d. Psychopharmacology

26. In order for a finding to be statistically significant, it would need to occur by chance alone in less than
    a. 1 out of every 5 experiments
    b. 1 out of every 10 experiments
    c. 1 out of every 15 experiments
    d. 1 out of every 20 experiments

27. _____ is used in training clients to use relaxation techniques to cope with thoughts, feelings, or situations that provoke anxiety.
    a. Progressive relaxation
    b. Specific muscle relaxation
    c. Applied relaxation
    d. Primary relaxation

28. This method became the cornerstone of Freud's psychoanalysis.
    a. free association
    b. hypnosis
    c. catharsis
    d. interpretation

UNDERSTANDING RESEARCH
Answers are found at the end of this chapter.

<u>Identifying Common Factors and Specific Active Ingredients:</u> The text presents a detailed description of a study in the Research Close-Up. Finding the answers to these questions will provide an understanding of this study and why it is important.

1. This is an example of psychotherapy _____ research. The researchers were looking at the effectiveness of types of _____ therapy in treating generalized _____ disorder. What were the two types of behavior therapy used? _____ and _____. What was the third type used? _____

Why did they include ND?_____. How many sessions were involved?_____

2. How many clients were in the study?_____ How were the clients assigned to treatment group? _____Who supervised the ND cases? _____How were the sessions monitored? _____What were the four times that clients were measured?_____ When were no differences among the groups found? _____What two groups were doing much better right after treatment?_____ A year after treatment, _____% of the CBT group was functioning in the normal range of _____, while _____% of the AR and _____% of the ND clients were.

3. This study showed that both _____ and _____ were important to treatment outcome. The best predictor of successful outcome in all three groups was the client's expectation for _____.

SHORT ANSWER

Answer the following short answer questions. Compare your work to the material presented in the text.

1. Compare and contrast the biological, psychodynamic, cognitive behavioral, and humanistic approaches to treating psychological disorders. In what ways might they be similar in working with a patient with depression? In what ways might they be different?

2. Discuss how the ideas of ego analysts differ from the original ideas of Freud. In what ways are they still similar?

3. Discuss some of the issues addressed by psychotherapy researchers.

4. Outline the design of the experimental method. Provide one example.

ANSWER KEY

MATCHING I

1. c
2. m
3. f
4. p
5. e
6. s
7. l
8. i
9. h
10. r
11. o

12. q
13. j
14. b
15. t
16. u
17. a
18. k
19. d
20. g
21. n

MATCHING II

- a. 4
- b. 11
- c. 16
- d. 5
- e. 19
- f. 1
- g. 12
- h. 17
- i. 6
- j. 22
- k. 2
- l. 13
- m. 15
- n. 9
- o. 21
- p. 3
- q. 14
- r. 20
- s. 7
- t. 18
- u. 8
- v. 23
- w. 10

MATCHING III

1. v
2. q
3. j
4. d
5. p
6. w
7. e
8. y
9. t
10. l
11. u
12. f
13. m
14. i
15. k
16. r
17. c
18. o
19. x
20. b
21. a
22. g
23. s
24. n
25. h
26. z

MATCHING IV

1. f
2. g
3. l
4. c
5. d
6. k
7. b
8. n
9. h
10. a
11. j
12. m
13. i
14. e

MULTIPLE CHOICE

1.	b	5.	a	9.	b	13.	b	17.	a	21.	d	25.	d
2.	b	6.	d	10.	c	14.	a	18.	d	22.	c	26.	d
3.	a	7.	d	11.	a	15.	c	19.	d	23.	d	27.	c
4.	c	8.	d	12.	c	16.	b	20.	a	24.	a	28.	a

47

CONCEPT REVIEW

1. true
2. true
3. epilepsy
4. unilateral
5. bilateral
6. severe depression
7. false
8. 25%
9. Prozac
10. Valium
11. analyst's
12. premature interpretations will be rejected and may be considered too threatening
13. milder forms of depression and anxiety
14. power and closeness
15. balance
16. true
17. false
18. they do not generalize to uncontrolled environments
19. depression
20. research
21. false
22. confrontational
23. false
24. true
25. one third
26. true
27. young, attractive, verbal, intelligent, and successful
28. anxiety
29. true
30. relationship with the therapist
31. publishing
32. true
33. warmth
34. the parents
35. research on process and outcome

UNDERSTANDING RESEARCH

1. outcome; behavior; anxiety; Applied relaxation and Cognitive behavior therapy; Nondirective therapy; to control for common factors; 12

2. 55; randomly; an expert nondirective therapist; audiotape; immediately before and after therapy, 6 months and 1 year after therapy; before therapy; AR and CBT; 58; anxiety; 37; 28

3. specific treatment factors; common factors; success

CROSSWORD

ACROSS		DOWN	
3.	prevention which focuses on developoment of new cases	1.	statistical technique
5.	a prediction	2.	example of contingency management
9.	humanistic approach used by Rogers	3.	medications which affect psychological state
11.	bringing unconscious material into conscious awareness	4.	perceived causes
14.	an exposure technique	6.	deliberate induction of a seizure
		7.	involves surgical destruction of specific regions of the brain
		8.	belief that observable behaviors are the appropriate focus of psychology
		10.	type of therapy designed to challenge cognitive distortions
		12.	inert substance or treatment
		13.	group consisting of those who receive no treatment or merely a placebo

CHAPTER FOUR

CLASSIFICATION AND ASSESSMENT OF ABNORMAL BEHAVIOR

CHAPTER OUTLINE

Overview
Basic Issues in Classification
    Categories versus Dimensions
    From Description to Theory
Classifying of Abnormal Behavior
    Brief Historical Perspective
    The DSM-IV-TR System
Evaluating Classification Systems
    Reliability
    Validity
    Unresolved Questions
    Problems and Limitations of the DSM-IV-TR System
Basic Issues in Assessment
    Purposes of Clinical Assessment
    Assumptions about Consistency of Behavior
    Evaluating the Usefulness of Assessment Procedures
    Types of Assessment Procedures
Assessing Psychological Systems
    Interviews
    Observational Procedures
    Personality Tests and Self-Report Inventories
    Projective Personality Tests
Assessing Social Systems
Assessing Biological Systems
    Psychophysiological Assessment
    Brain Imaging Techniques
Summary

OBJECTIVES

1. Define classification system, assessment, and diagnosis.
2. Distinguish between categorical and dimensional approaches to classification.
3. Explain why the DSM-III represented a turning point in the diagnosis of psychiatric disorders.
4. Describe the axes utilized in the DSM-IV-TR.
5. Discuss the meaning and implications of reliability and validity in diagnosis and classification.
6. Discuss the advantages and limitations of interview data for assessment.
7. Discuss several observational procedures used in assessment.
8. Describe the strengths and weaknesses of the MMPI-2.
9. List several advantages and limitations of utilizing projective tests for assessment and diagnosis.
10. Describe the applications of psychophysiological assessment procedures and discuss the limitations of this approach.
11. Distinguish between static and dynamic brain imaging techniques.

MATCHING I

Answers are found at the end of this chapter. Match the following terms and concepts with the definitions that follow:

a. Assessment
b. Diagnosis
c. Classification system
d. Categorical approach
e. Dimensional approach
f. Stigma
g. Phenylketonuria (PKU)
h. Dementia praecox
i. Manic-depressive psychosis
j. Diagnostic and Statistical Manual of Mental Disorders (DSM)
k. International Classification of Diseases (ICD)
l. Labeling theory
m. Multiaxial classification
n. Inclusion criteria
o. Exclusion criteria
p. Reliability
q. Inter-rater reliability
r. Validity
s. Kappa
t. Etiological validity
u. Concurrent validity
v. Predictive validity
w. Comorbidity
x. Test-retest reliability
y. Split-half reliability

1. ____ an old term for what we now call schizophrenia
2. ____ a system for grouping together objects or organisms that share certain properties
3. ____ a system in which the person is rated with regard to several separate aspects of behavior or adjustment
4. ____ the process of gathering and organizing information about a person's behavior
5. ____ looks at the social context in which abnormal behavior occurs; sees mental disorders as maladaptive social roles
6. ____ assumes that distinctions between members of different categories are qualitative
7. ____ concerned with factors that contribute to the onset of the disorder
8. ____ the diagnostic system for mental disorders published by the World Health Organization
9. ____ describes the objects of classification in terms of continuous dimensions
10. ____ concerned with the present time and with correlations between the disorder and other symptoms, circumstances, and test procedures
11. ____ the simultaneous appearance of two or more disorders in the same person
12. ____ an old term for what we now call bipolar mood disorder
13. ____ the diagnostic system for mental disorders published by the American Psychiatric Association
14. ____ symptoms or characteristic features that must be present in order for a person to meet the diagnostic criteria for a particular disorder
15. ____ the identification or recognition of a disorder on the basis of its characteristic symptoms
16. ____ an inherited metabolic disorder that, uncontrolled, produces mental retardation
17. ____ symptoms or conditions that are used to rule out the presence of a particular disorder
18. ____ a statistic of reliability that reflects the proportion of agreement that occurred above and beyond what would have occurred by chance alone
19. ____ the meaning or systematic importance of a construct or measurement
20. ____ the consistency of measurements over time
21. ____ a label that sets the person apart from others in a negative way
22. ____ concerned with the future and with the stability of the problem over time
23. ____ agreement among clinicians
24. ____ the internal consistency of items within a test
25. ____ the consistency of measurements

MATCHING II
Answers are found at the end of this chapter. Match these terms and concepts with the definitions that follow:

1. Structured interviews
2. Informal observations
3. Rating Scales
4. Behavioral coding systems
5. Self-monitoring
6. Reactivity
7. Personality tests
8. Personality inventories
9. Minnesota Multiphasic Personality Inventory
10. Validity scales
11. Actuarial interpretation
12. Beck Depression Inventory
13. Self-report inventories
14. Projective tests
15. Rorschach test
16. Thematic Apperception Test
17. Exner system
18. Family Environment Scale
19. Family Interaction Coding System
20. Computerized topographic scanning
21. Magnetic resonance imaging
22. Positron emission tomography
23. Single photon emission computed tomography
24. Basal ganglia
25. Yale-Brown Obsessive Compulsive Scale

a. ____ a procedure where clients record their own behavior
b. ____ analysis of test results based on an explicit set of rules derived from empirical research
c. ____ objective tests consisting of a series of straightforward statements that the person indicates how true or false they are in relation to himself or herself
d. ____ a projective test also known as the inkblot test
e. ____ a static brain imaging technique which passes X-rays through brain tissue to measure the density of the tissue
f. ____ a dynamic brain imaging technique using special radioactive elements to produce relatively detailed images of the brain, which can reflect changes in brain activity as a person performs various tasks
g. ____ personality tests in which the person is asked to interpret a series of ambiguous stimuli
h. ____ focus on the frequency of specific behavioral events, requiring fewer inferences on the part of the observer
i. ____ a self-report inventory designed to measure social characteristics of families
j. ____ a brain imaging technique which passes electromagnetic phenomena through brain tissue to provide a static image of brain structures
k. ____ an objective personality inventory aimed at a focal topic or at one aspect of a person's adjustment
l. ____ people altering their behavior, either intentionally or unintentionally, when they know they are being observed
m. ____ a self-report inventory used as an index of severity of depression
n. ____ standardized situations where a person's behavior can be sampled, and reflects on underlying abilities or personality traits
o. ____ a coding system for observations of interactions between parents and children in their homes
p. ____ an assessment interview that follows a specific question-and-answer format
q. ____ a projective test consisting of a series of drawings that depict human figures in various ambiguous situations
r. ____ reflect the person's attitude toward the test and the openness and consistency with which the questions were answered
s. ____ an assessment device where the observer makes judgments that place the person along a dimension
t. ____ a dynamic brain imaging technique using single-photon-emitting compounds
u. ____ objective scoring procedure for Rorschach

v. ____ a part of the thalamus implicated in obsessions and compulsions
w. ____ a very widely used personality inventory with a true-false format that produces scores on ten clinical scales and four validity scales
x. ____ qualitative observations of a person's behavior and/or environment with no attempt to quantify the observed characteristics
y. ____ an interview-based rating scale used extensively to assess obsessions and compulsions

MATCHING III

Answers are found at the end of this chapter. Match these names with the descriptions of their contributions to the study of abnormal psychology:

    a. Emil Kraepelin   b. Thomas Scheff   c. Hermann Rorschach

1. ____ a proponent of labeling theory
2. ____ pioneered the type of categorical classification system currently used
3. ____ developed the best-known projective test, the inkblot test

CONCEPT REVIEW

Answers are found at the end of this chapter. After you have read and reviewed the material, test your comprehension by filling in the blanks or circling the correct answer.

1. In the field of psychopathology, assigning a diagnosis implies the etiology of the person's problem:

   true   **false**

2. Classification systems can be based on descriptive or _____ similarities.

3. Which type of emphasis typically comes first in the development of scientific classification systems?

   etiological factors   **description**

4. What were three criticisms of psychiatric classification systems during the 1950s and 1960s? _____, _____, and _____.

5. The major change that occurred in the third edition of the DSM was a focus on clinical description rather than on _____.

6. Labeling theory views symptoms of mental disorders as violations of residual _____.

7. Labeling theory predicts that people from lower status groups, like the impoverished are **more/less** likely to receive a diagnosis.

8. The authors of your text conclude that labeling theory provides a good account for abnormal behavior:

   true   **false**

9. How many diagnostic axes are there in the DSM-IV-TR? _____

10. The presence of general medical conditions are coded on one of the axes of a DSM-IV-TR diagnosis:

    true   **false**

11. One example of a culture-bound syndrome, amok, is found among mostly men in Malaysia and consists of a period of brooding and paranoid thinking followed by an angry, aggressive outburst in response to a perceived _____.

12. Clinicians have been more willing to drop old categories in revisions of the DSM than to include new categories: **true**   **false**

13. Comorbidity rates among mental disorders as defined in the DSM system are very low: **true**   **false**

14. What are the three primary goals which guide most assessment procedures? _____

15. The meaning or importance of an assessment procedure is known as its: **reliability**   **validity**

16. There are only a few select assessment procedures available to clinicians today: **true**   **false**

17. Clinical interviews provide clinicians with the opportunity to assess a person's appearance and nonverbal behavior: **true**   **false**

18. Clinical interviews are either structured or_____.

19. One advantage of structured interviews is that anybody can conduct them, saving the expense of a clinician's time: **true**   **false**

20. Clinical interviews are of limited use with young children: **true**   **false**

21. Observations provide a more realistic view of behavior than do people's recollections of their actions and feelings: **true**   **false**

22. One problem with observational procedures is that they can be time-consuming and expensive: **true**   **false**

23. Why do some clinicians prefer to use the original version of the MMPI? _____

24. One advantage of the MMPI is that it allows the clinician to use his or her intuition in coming up with scores on the clinical scales: **true**   **false**

25. A unique feature of the MMPI are the **clinical/validity** scales.

26. Which is a more complex assessment tool?   **the MMPI**   **the BDI**

27. If a person scores as being significantly depressed on the Beck Depression Inventory, he or she definitely will meet diagnostic criteria for depression: **true**   **false**

28. The Exner system, a new scoring system for the Rorschach test, is based more on which of the following?   **content**   **form**

29. One strength of the original Rorschach scoring system was its high reliability: **true**   **false**

30. Projective tests are more likely to be used by a therapist with which type of theoretical orientation?

    psychodynamic   **behavioral**

31. List three types of physiological measures that provide information about a person's psychological state:_____

32. Men who exhibit physiological responses that indicate intense arousal during discussions with their wives about marital conflicts but who do not express their arousal _____ are more likely to divorce.

33. Brain imaging techniques are used to rule out _____ as a cause of behavioral or cognitive deficits.

CROSSWORD

Answers are found at the end of this chapter. Complete the following crossword puzzle to reinforce your understanding of this chapter's key terms and concepts:

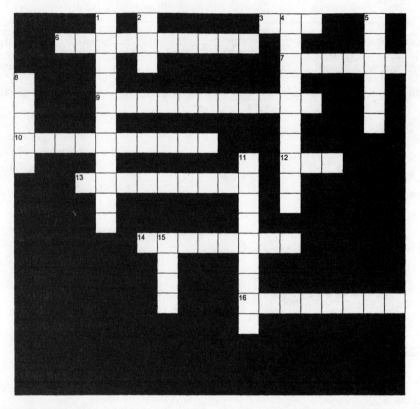

ACROSS	DOWN
3. uses strong magnetic field to generate images	1. simultaneous appearance of two or more disorders in a person
6. tests characterized by series of ambiguous stimuli	2. measures glucose utilization within the brain
7. axis which calls for information about life events	4. characterized by changes in behavior as the result of being observed
9. consistency of measurements	5. refers to a label that sets a person apart from others
10. validity concerned with the stability of the problem over time	8. indicates the proportion of agreement that occurs above and beyond that of chance
12. diagnostic system published by the World Health Organization	11. current edition of Diagnostic and Statistical Manual
13. identification of a disorder based on characteristic symptoms	15. culture bound syndrome triggered by perceived insult
14. refers to the meaning or importance of a measurement	
16. science of arranging living organisms into groups	

MULTIPLE CHOICE

Answers are found at the end of this chapter. The multiple choice questions listed will test your understanding of the material presented in the chapter. Read through each question and circle the letter representing the best answer.

1. A characteristic of all projective tests is
    a. a true-false response format
    b. the use of a list of open-ended sentences that the individual must answer
    c. the use of items describing various thoughts, feelings, and behaviors that the individual must rate
    d. the use of ambiguous stimuli

2. Which approach to classification is based on an ordered sequence or on quantitative measurements rather than qualitative judgments?
    a. dimensional approach
    b. categorical approach
    c. diagnostic approach
    d. interview approach

3. Which of the following is not an axis of DSM-IV-TR?
    a. global rating of adaptive functioning
    b. psychosocial and environmental problems
    c. general medical conditions that may be relevant to the patient's current behaviors or that may affect treatment
    d. familial communication style

4. Which would not be considered a limitation of a clinical interview?
    a. the information gathered is subjective and may be influenced or distorted by errors in memory or perception
    b. the person may be reluctant to directly share with the interviewer experiences that are embarrassing or socially undesirable
    c. interviews are expensive and time-consuming
    d. people may not be able to give a rational account of their problems due to the presence of limited verbal skills, a psychotic process, etc.

5. Analyzing a test on the basis of an explicit set of rules based on empirical research is referred to as what type of procedure?
    a. actuarial
    b. self-report
    c. diagnostic
    d. cookbook

6. A criticism of psychiatric diagnosis in the 1950s and 1960s was that
    a. the system in use was too detailed and included too many categories
    b. the system was too descriptive and did not make assumptions about etiology
    c. once labeled with a diagnosis, individuals did not receive the appropriate treatment
    d. once labeled with a diagnosis, an individual might be motivated to continue to act in a manner expected from someone who is mentally ill

7. Research of psychiatric diagnosis in the 1950s and 1960s was that
    a. wives who do not express their negative emotions often display sleep difficulties
    b. husbands who do not express their negative emotions often display changes in heart rate and skin conductance that indicate intense arousal
    c. wives who verbally report negative emotion do not display any physiological changes
    d. husbands who verbally express their negative emotions also show changes in their sleep patterns

8. Which of the following does not reflect a rationale for classifying abnormal behavior?
    a. a diagnostic system can be used to help clinicians more effectively communicate with one another
    b. a diagnostic system can be used to organize information that may be helpful for research purposes
    c. a diagnostic system can be used to label people who are socially deviant
    d. a diagnostic system can be used in making management and treatment decisions

9. When an observer is asked to make judgments about some aspect of an individual's behavior along a dimension, the observer would be using
    a. a projective instrument
    b. a rating scale
    c. a self-report inventory
    d. a structured interview

10. Interpretation of a person's responses to the MMPI-2 is based upon
    a. reviewing the clinical scale for which the person received the highest score
    b. reading through all of the inventory items and noting how the person answered each one
    c. reviewing the clinical scale for which the person received the lowest score
    d. examining the pattern of scale scores, paying particular attention to those scales that have elevated scores

11. An example of a type of observational procedure would be
    a. the Rorschach test
    b. the MMPI-2
    c. a behavioral coding system
    d. dynamic brain imaging

12. Which would not be considered a primary goal of assessment?
    a. making predictions
    b. reconstructing people's developmental history
    c. planning interventions
    d. evaluating interventions

13. An advantage of the MMPI-2 is that
    a. it provides information about the individual's test-taking attitude
    b. it assesses a wide range of problem areas that would take a clinician several hours to review in an interview
    c. it is scored objectively and is not influenced by the clinician's personal opinion about the individual taking the test
    d. all of the above

14. How many axes are included in the DSM-IV-TR?
    a. 3
    b. 4
    c. 5
    d. 6

15. What would be considered an advantage of a structured clinical interview compared to a regular clinical interview?
    a. it provides the interviewer with a series of systematic questions that allow for the collection of important diagnostic information
    b. it allows for the establishment of a better therapeutic rapport with the client
    c. it allows the interviewer flexibility in gathering information
    d. all of the above

16. Projective techniques place considerable emphasis upon which of the following?
    a. the importance of unconscious motivations such as conflicts and impulses
    b. the importance of familial values that may influence the person's behavior
    c. the presence of symptoms, which suggest that the person has lost contact with reality and is presently psychotic
    d. the importance of the person's cultural background in understanding his or her personality

17. An example of a measure that assesses a social system is
    a. Positron Emission Tomography
    b. the Family Interaction Coding System
    c. the Beck Depression Inventory
    d. the Yale-Brown Obsessive-Compulsive Scale

18. Which type of study could be used to validate a clinical syndrome?
    a. a follow-up study that demonstrated a distinctive course or outcome
    b. a family study supporting that the syndrome "breeds true"
    c. a study demonstrating an association between the clinical syndrome and an underlying biochemical abnormality
    d. all of the above

19. An advantage of psychophysiological assessment is that
    a. these types of procedures do not depend on self-report and may be less likely to be under the person's control
    b. physiological reactivity and stability is very consistent across people
    c. physiological assessment is less expensive and less time consuming than the use of personality inventories
    d. physiological procedures are frequently used in clinical settings

20. The most commonly used procedure in psychological assessment is
    a. self-report inventories
    b. projective testing
    c. clinical interview
    d. behavioral observation

21. A limitation of brain-imaging procedures is that
    a. brain-imaging procedures can only be used with certain populations
    b. although useful for research, brain-imaging procedures cannot be used for diagnostic purposes because norms have not yet been established
    c. brain-imaging procedures tend to give imprecise information
    d. the results of brain-imaging procedures tend to be overly responsive to outside factors such as whether the person is presently medicated

22. Which of the following problems could not be assessed through the use of an observational measure?
    a. hand-washing
    b. crying
    c. low self-esteem
    d. hitting, punching, or spitting in school

23. A limitation of the use of projective tests is
    a. information obtained from projective tests tends to duplicate what can already be obtained from a clinical interview
    b. projective tests cannot be used with children
    c. projective tests cannot be used with psychotic individuals
    d. the reliability of scoring and interpretation appears to be low

24. Which type of study could be used to demonstrate the reliability of a set of diagnostic criteria?
    a. a study demonstrating that clinicians using the same set of criteria arrived at the same diagnosis for the same set of individuals
    b. a study supporting that individuals with the same diagnosis responded to the same kind of treatment
    c. a study supporting that the set of diagnostic criteria could be meaningful to other cultures when properly translated
    d. all of the above

25. The L Scale of the MMPI-2 is an example of which type of scale?
    a. reactivity
    b. clinical
    c. projective
    d. validity

26. The first two axes of the DSM-IV-TR primarily focus on
    a. symptomatic behaviors
    b. family functioning
    c. medical history
    d. intrapsychic functioning

27. Which would not be considered a drawback of using a physiological assessment measure?
    a. the equipment used may be intimidating to certain people
    b. physiological responses can be influenced by many outside factors such as age and medication
    c. physiological response measures have not demonstrated adequate validity
    d. the stability of physiological response systems vary from person to person

UNDERSTANDING RESEARCH
Answers are found at the end of this chapter.

<u>Ataques de Nervios and the Anthropology of Emotion:</u> The text presents a detailed description of a study in the Research Close-Up. Finding the answers to these questions will provide an understanding of this study and why it is important.

1. The glossary of culture-bound syndromes lists unique ways a certain culture expresses negative _____. Ataques de nervios are unique to _____. Researchers interviewed _____ people and found that _____% had experienced this during their life.

2. These ataques involved loss of _____ relating to four dimensions: outbursts of screaming and crying with overwhelming anxiety, depression, and anger constituted the _____ dimension; the bodily sensations dimension included trembling, weakness, fatigue, heart palpitations, and _____; suicidal gestures and trouble eating and sleeping were under _____, and there were alterations in _____.

3. Many ataques occurred after _____ problems. They may serve to rally _____. Many who had experienced them were _____. They were most likely to carry a psychiatric diagnosis of _____.

SHORT ANSWER
Answer the following short answer questions. Compare your work to the material presented in the text.

1. Discuss the major assumptions of labeling theory. Do you agree with its major points?

2. Review examples of both scientific and nonscientific factors that affect the development of diagnostic systems. When do you believe nonscientific factors play an important role in this process?

3. Describe the major purposes of clinical assessment. What are the major assumptions regarding the nature of human behavior upon which the assessment process is based?

4. Assume the role of a clinician who has just received a call from a potential client. The problem for which the client is seeking treatment is depression. What assessment procedures reviewed in your chapter could you use to determine whether or not the client is depressed? What type of information would you expect to obtain from each method?

ANSWER KEY

MATCHING I

1. h
2. c
3. m
4. a
5. l
6. d
7. t
8. k
9. e
10. u
11. w
12. i
13. j
14. n
15. b
16. g
17. o
18. s
19. r
20. x
21. f
22. v
23. q
24. y
25. p

MATCHING II

a. 5
b. 11
c. 8
d. 15
e. 20
f. 22
g. 14
h. 4
i. 18
j. 21
k. 13
l. 6
m. 12
n. 7
o. 19
p. 1
q. 16
r. 10
s. 3
t. 23
u. 17
v. 24
w. 9
x. 2
y. 25

MATCHING III

1. b
2. a
3. c

MULTIPLE CHOICE

1. d	6. d	11. c	16. a	21. b	26. a
2. a	7. b	12. b	17. b	22. c	27. c
3. d	8. c	13. d	18. d	23. d	
4. c	9. b	14. c	19. a	24. a	
5. a	10. d	15. a	20. c	25. d	

CONCEPT REVIEW

1. false
2. structural
3. description
4. lack of consistency in diagnoses among clinicians; diagnoses are problems in living, not medical disorders; labels might increase maladaptive behavior
5. theories of psychopathology
6. rules
7. more
8. false
9. 5
10. true
11. insult
12. false
13. false
14. making predictions, planning interventions, and evaluating interventions
15. validity
16. false
17. true
18. nondirective
19. false
20. true
21. true
22. true
23. because of all the research done with it
24. false
25. validity
26. MMPI
27. false
28. form
29. false
30. psychodynamic
31. heart rate, respiration rate, and skin conductance
32. verbally
33. brain tumors

UNDERSTANDING RESEARCH

1. emotion; Puerto Rico and the Caribbean; 912; 16

2. central; Emotional Expressions; false seizures; Actions and Behaviors; consciousness

3. family; support; women; panic disorder

CROSSWORD

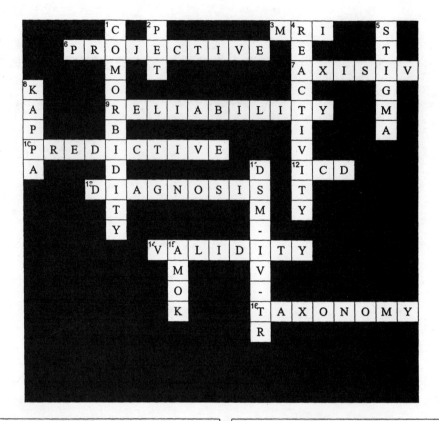

ACROSS

3. uses strong magnetic field to generate images
6. tests characterized by series of ambiguous stimuli
7. axis which calls for information about life events
9. consistency of measurements
10. validity concerned with the stability of the problem over time
12. diagnostic system published by the World Health Organization
13. identification of a disorder based on characteristic symptoms
14. refers to the meaning or importance of a measurement
16. science of arranging living organisms into groups

DOWN

1. simultaneous appearance of two or more disorders in a person
2. measures glucose utilization within the brain
4. characterized by changes in behavior as the result of being observed
5. refers to a label that sets a person apart from others
8. indicates the proportion of agreement that occurs above and beyond that of chance
11. current edition of Diagnostic and Statistical Manual
15. culture bound syndrome triggered by perceived insult

CHAPTER FIVE

MOOD DISORDERS AND SUICIDE

CHAPTER OUTLINE

Overview
Typical Symptoms and Associated Features
    Emotional Symptoms
    Cognitive Symptoms
    Somatic Symptoms
    Behavioral Symptoms
    Other Problems Commonly Associated with Depression
Classification
    Brief Historical Perspective
    Contemporary Diagnostic Systems
    Course and Outcome
Epidemiology
    Incidence and Prevalence
    Gender Differences
    Cross-Cultural Differences
    Risk for Mood Disorders Across the Life Span
    Comparisons Across Generations
Etiological Considerations and Research
    Social Factors
    Psychological Factors
    Biological Factors
    The Interaction of Social, Psychological, and Biological Factors
Treatment
    Unipolar Disorders
    Bipolar Disorders
    Electroconvulsive Therapy
    Seasonal Mood Disorders
Suicide
    Classification of Suicide
    Epidemiology of Suicide
    Etiology of Suicide
    Treatment of Suicidal People
Summary

OBJECTIVES

1. Distinguish between major depressive disorder and dysthymic disorder.
2. Define emotion, affect, mood, depression, and mania.
3. Identify the major emotional, cognitive, and somatic symptoms involved in depression.
4. Describe the features of bipolar disorder and cyclothymic disorder and distinguish between them.
5. Discuss the etiology of depression.
6. Discuss several perspectives related to the etiology and treatment of mood disorders.
7. Discuss the interaction between social, psychological, and biological factors in the development and maintenance of mood disorders.

8. Discuss the effectiveness of several treatment approaches for depression and bipolar disorders.
9. Discuss Durkheim's theory of suicide.
10. Discuss the incidence of suicide and theoretical perspectives on its causes.
11. Discuss suicide prevention efforts.

MATCHING I
Answers are found at the end of this chapter. Match these terms and concepts with the definitions that follow:

a.	Emotion		l.	Dysphoria
b.	Affect		m.	Euphoria
c.	Mood		n.	Somatic symptoms
d.	Depression		o.	Psychomotor retardation
e.	Depressed mood		p.	Comorbidity
f.	Clinical depression		q.	Dysthymia
g.	Mania		r.	Hypomania
h.	Mood disorders		s.	Cyclothymia
i.	Unipolar mood disorder		t.	Melancholia
j.	Bipolar mood disorder		u.	Seasonal affective disorder
k.	Manic-depressive disorder		v.	Double depression

1. u   a mood disorder with onset of episodes associated with changes in the seasons
2. m   a state of incredible well-being and elation
3. d   a term for a mood or a clinical syndrome that involves sadness, despair, and disappointment
4. v   a combination of major depression and dysthymia
5. q   chronic, mild depression lasting for at least two years
6. b   observable behaviors associated with a person's feelings
7. p   having more than one mental disorder at the same time
8. g   a disturbance in mood which can include elation, decreased need for sleep, pressured speech, inflated self-esteem
9. n   symptoms related to bodily functions, like sleep and appetite disturbance
10. t an especially severe form of depression
11. a subjective states of feeling, often accompanied by physiological changes
12. h a category of mental disorders involving episodes of disturbance of mood, characterized either by clinical depression or mania
13. s chronic, mild form of bipolar disorder with episodes of hypomania and depression lasting at least two years
14. c a pervasive, long-standing emotional response that affects a person's perception of their world
15. i a classification of mood disorder involving periods of depression only
16. j a classification of mood disorder involving periods of depression and mania, or sometimes mania alone
17. e a mood state involving sadness and despair that is not a psychiatric syndrome
18. k the former term for bipolar disorder
19. f a psychiatric syndrome involving sadness and despair as well as fatigue, sleep disturbance, loss of energy, or changes in appetite
20. l a state of depression, despondency, sadness
21. r an episode of increased energy that is not as extreme as mania
22. o significant slowing of movements or speech

66

MATCHING II
Answers are found at the end of this chapter. Match these terms and concepts with the definitions that follow:

1. Remission
2. Relapse
3. Neurasthenia
4. Schema
5. Learned helplessness theory
6. Hopelessness
7. Catecholamine
8. PFC
9. Hypothalamic-pituitary-adrenal axis
10. Dexamethasone suppression test
11. Analogue studies
12. Tricyclics
13. Monoamine oxidase inhibitors
14. Selective serotonin reuptake inhibitors
15. Lithium carbonate
16. ECT

a. _11_ studies that focus on behaviors that are similar to mental disorders, or features of mental disorders; often animal models of psychopathology
b. _7_ norepinephrine is an example
c. _~~7~~ 13_ a category of antidepressant medication which must not be taken with certain foods, especially cheese and chocolate
d. _~~?~~ 6_ a theory that depression may be related to a person's expectation that good things will not happen and bad things will, regardless of his or her actions
e. _4_ a lasting and highly organized cognitive structure that influences how people perceive and interpret events in their environment
f. _1_ a period of recovery from a mental disorder
g. _3_ a diagnostic term referring to multiple complaints involving physical symptoms, such as headaches and weakness
h. _15_ a medication often used to treat bipolar disorder
i. _8_ abnormal patterns of activation are seen in this area in association with depression
j. _9_ a pathway in the endocrine system that regulates hormone secretions by the adrenal glands; may be involved in the etiology of depression
k. _16_ a series of treatments in which electric current is run through the patient's brain; effective in the treatment of severe depression
l. _2_ the return of active symptoms in a person who had recovered from a previous episode
m. _10_ used to study endocrine dysfunction in people with mood disorders; half of depressed patients show an abnormal response to this test
n. _14_ a new class of antidepressants which have fewer side effects than older medications
o. _12_ an older class of antidepressants which benefit many depressed people
p. _5_ a theory that depression is like the passive behavior of animals exposed to uncontrollable electric shock, that depressed people do not see a relation between their behavior and events that occur in their lives

MATCHING III
Answers are found at the end of this chapter. Match these names with the descriptions of their contributions to the study of abnormal psychology.

      a. Aaron Beck   d. Emil Kraeplin
      b. James Coyne   e. Peter Lewinsohn
      c. Emile Durkheim   f. Martin Seligman

1. ____ conceptualized depression as cognitive in origin, arising from distortions, errors, and biases common in the thinking of depressed people
2. ____ identified four types of suicide based on the type of society in which the person lives
3. ____ proposed the first classification system for mental disorders, dividing disorders into dementia praecox and manic-depressive psychosis
4. ____ proposed the interpersonal perspective of depression, where depressed people's behavior drives away important people in their lives
5. ____ proposed a behavioral model of depression where adaptive behavior is not positively reinforced by the environment and therefore decreases
6. ____ proposed the learned helplessness model of depression

CONCEPT REVIEW
Answers are found at the end of this chapter. After you have read and reviewed the material, test your comprehension by filling in the blanks or circling the correct answer.

1. Major depression is the leading cause of disability worldwide: **true**   false
2. Many depressed and manic patients are irritable: **true**   false
3. People who are depressed often have trouble with their thinking. They have trouble _____, and can't make _____.
4. The depressive triad is typical of depressed patients. They focus on the negative aspects of enviro, _____, and _____.
5. People with _____ can be easily distracted, incoherent, and grandiose.
6. People with _____ may be preoccupied with thoughts of suicide.
7. Sometimes depressed people have difficulty falling asleep and wake up throughout the night or very early in the morning. However, it is more common for a depressed person to sleep much more than usual: **true**   **false**
8. Depressed people typically eat more than usual: **true**   **false**
9. People with _____ are less likely to initiate sexual activity and people with _____ are more likely to do so.
10. List three types of disorders that have high comorbidity with mood disorders (and are also found in higher rates than expected among relatives of people with mood disorders): _____, _____, and _____.

11. Some people with mood disorders experience psychotic symptoms during their episodes of depression or mania: **true**   **false**
12. Most people with unipolar disorder experience only a single, isolated episode during their lifetimes:
    true   **false**
13. People with Bipolar I Disorder have clear cut _____ episodes, while people with Bipolar II Disorder do not.
14. Rapid cycling bipolar patients typically do not respond as well to treatment as other bipolar patients:
    true   **false**
15. People with seasonal depression are more likely to gain weight and sleep more than people with non-seasonal depression patterns: **true**   **false**
16. The average age of onset of a first episode of unipolar disorder is at which age:
    adolescence (15-25)   **young adulthood (25-35)**   **middle age (40-50)**
17. The average number of lifetime depressive episodes of people with unipolar disorder is _____.
18. A person's risk of _____ of depression goes down the longer they are in remission.
19. The average age of onset of a first episode of bipolar disorder is at which age:
    adolescence (15-25)   **young adulthood (25-35)**   **middle age (40-50)**
20. People with bipolar disorder tend to have more episodes than those with unipolar disorder:
    true   **false**
21. Lifetime risk for major depressive disorder is _____%; for dysthymia is _____%; and for bipolar disorder is _____%.
22. Many, even most, people with mood disorders do not seek treatment: **true**   **false**
23. What sex is more likely to experience major depression and dysthymia? _____
24. There are no significant gender differences in rates of _____.
25. Some studies indicate similar frequencies of mood disorders in different countries and cultures, but differences in specific symptoms. For example, depressed people in Europe and North America are more likely to exhibit _____ while depressed people in non-Western countries, like China, are more likely to exhibit _____.
26. Mood disorders are less common among the elderly than among young and middle-aged adults:
    true   **false**
27. The frequency of depression has decreased in recent years: **true**   **false**
28. Prospective research design has demonstrated that which one comes first, depression or stressful events? _____
29. Research has shown that the _____ of an important person or role precipitates depression.
30. Once a person is depressed, their behavior leads to an increase in their levels of stress: **true**   **false**

31. Bipolar patients who leave the hospital to live with hostile, critical family members are more likely to experience _____.

32. Research indicates that communities with the highest rates of severe events have the highest prevalence of _____.

33. Beck described several types of cognitive distortions he thought were related to depression. Research has shown that these distortions are present during an episode of depression but not before or after an episode:

    true   false

34. A depressogenic attributional style is characterized by a tendency to explain negative events, like failing an exam, in which of the following terms:

    external/internal   stable/unstable   specific/global

35. College students who had negative cognitive styles at the beginning of freshman year were much more likely to develop _____.

36. Lewinsohn hypothesized that some depressed behaviors may initially be reinforced by friends and family and the strength and frequency of these behaviors are:

    increased   decreased

37. Coyne hypothesized that depressed people actually do have smaller and less supportive social networks, and that it is not just their perceptions but the actual situation that is negative. Does the research evidence support this? _____

38. People with a ruminative style have **more/less** depression that people with a distracting style. Men are **more/less** likely to have a ruminative style than women.

39. Among relatives of people with unipolar disorder, there **is/is not** an increased risk for unipolar disorder, and there **is/is not** an increased risk for bipolar disorder.

40. Which disorder, major depressive disorder, bipolar disorder, or dysthymia, shows the highest rate of twin concordance (genetic heritability)? _____ Which shows the lowest? _____

41. Researchers think that the genetic influence on mood disorders is due to:

    a single gene   multiple genes

42. Current research on the role of neurotransmitters in the etiology of depression suggests that the early theories were too complex: **true   false**

43. There are approximately **3/50/100** different neurotransmitters in the central nervous system.

44. Brain imaging studies have failed to find any differences in brain function related to mood: **true   false**

45. Rats exposed to stressful events in the laboratory develop symptoms similar to those of depressed people. Antidepressant drugs given to these animals can reverse or prevent these symptoms: **true   false**

46. In treating depressed people, _____ therapy focuses on changing the client's negative schemas and irrational beliefs, and _____ therapy focuses on changing current relationships.

47. Antidepressants typically are effective within 24 hours if they are going to be helpful at all:
    true   false

48. Antidepressant medication is far more effective in treating depression than either cognitive or interpersonal therapy: **true   false**

49. Among patients with seasonal affective disorder, exposure to broad-spectrum light is actually <u>not</u> effective in reducing depression: **true   false**

50. ECT almost always interferes with memory: **true   false**

51. What percentage of people with mood disorders will eventually commit suicide?
    1-3%   15-20%   50-55%

52. Suicide is increasing among adolescents in recent decades: **true   false**

53. There are gender differences in rates of suicide: more **males/females** make suicide attempts, and more **males/females** actually complete a suicide.

54. Which group has the highest rate of suicide:
    young black men,   middle aged white women,   older white men?

55. Does suicide run in families? _____

56. Media coverage of a suicide increases the rate of suicides committed: **true   false**

57. Suicide hotlines decrease suicide rates: **true   false**

CROSSWORD

Answers are found at the end of this chapter. Complete the following crossword puzzle to reinforce your understanding of this chapter's key terms and concepts.

ACROSS
1. depressed mood
5. elated mood
9. pervasive emotional response
11. negative views of self, the world, and the future
13. observable behaviors associated with subjective feelings
14. Celexa is an example
15. return to active symptoms
18. axis within endocrine system important to the understanding of mood disorders
19. disorders such as major depression and dysthymia

DOWN
2. negative expectations about future events; symptom of depression
3. when symptoms are diminished or improved
4. pertaining to two directions
6. episodes of increased energy experienced by some individuals with bipolar disorder
7. near tip of hippocampus; important part of neural circuit involved in emotion
8. type of unipolar disorder characterized by chronic mild depressive condition
10. neurotransmitter enhanced by medications such as Prozac
12. abnormal patterns of activation in this region of the brain are often associated with depression
16. state of arousal defined by subjective states of feeling
17. bodily symptoms

MULTIPLE CHOICE

Answers are found at the end of this chapter. The multiple choice questions listed will test your understanding of the material presented in the chapter. Read through each question and circle the letter representing the best answer.

1. Which of the following is not a general area describing the signs and symptoms representative of mood disorders?
    a. emotional symptoms
    b. psychological symptoms
    c. somatic symptoms
    d. cognitive symptoms

2. A promising form of treatment for seasonal affective disorder is
    a. light therapy
    b. lithium
    c. nutritional therapy
    d. meditation

3. What is the percent of completed suicides that occur as a result of a primary mood disorder?
    a. under 15%
    b. under 30%
    c. over 50%
    d. over 78%

4. Which is an example of a somatic symptom?
    a. suicidal ideation
    b. loss of interest
    c. sleep disturbance
    d. low self-esteem

5. An advantage of an analogue study is that
    a. experimental procedures may be employed
    b. it is easy to generalize the results beyond the laboratory
    c. human subjects are not used
    d. it is easy to reproduce a clinical disorder in the laboratory

6. Which symptom would not be considered diagnostic for clinical depression?
    a. racing thoughts
    b. loss of energy
    c. feelings of worthlessness
    d. difficulty concentrating

7. Why might it be more difficult to diagnose depression in the elderly?
    a. cognitive impairment or other problems common in the elderly may mask the symptoms of depression
    b. the elderly are more reluctant to seek treatment for depression
    c. the symptoms and features of depression change as age increases
    d. the elderly are less likely to report somatic symptoms associated with depression

8. Results from the Treatment of Depression Collaborative Research Program indicate that
    a. both types of psychological treatment (interpersonal and cognitive) were as effective as antidepressant medication
    b. patients who received interpersonal therapy did not show gains with cognitive problems
    c. placebo was equally effective to antidepressant medication
    d. cognitive therapy was superior to interpersonal therapy in its effectiveness

9. Which age group has experienced increased rates of suicide since the 1960s?
    a. adolescents
    b. people who are in their 30s
    c. people between the ages of 45 and 55 years
    d. people over 65

10. When two loci occupy positions close together on the same chromosome they are
    a. polygenic
    b. matched
    c. homogenous
    d. linked

11. Which is a social factor which may contribute to the onset of depression?
    a. the belief that one cannot control events in one's life
    b. cognitive distortions
    c. stressful life events
    d. neuroendocrine disturbances

12. Which disorder is often comorbid with a mood disorder?
    a. schizophrenia
    b. dissociative disorder
    c. paranoid personality disorder
    d. alcoholism

13. What age would a person most likely have a first episode of bipolar disorder?
    a. 18 - 23 years
    b. 28 – 33 years
    c. 38 - 43 years
    d. 48 - 53 years

14. Which of the following is a common element of suicide?
    a. the common goal of suicide is cessation of consciousness
    b. the common emotion in suicide is anger
    c. the common purpose of suicide is to get revenge
    d. the common stressor in suicide is financial difficulties

15. Decreased need for sleep, pressure to keep talking, grandiosity, and distractibility are common symptoms of which disorder?
    a. mania
    b. dysthymia
    c. major depression
    d. cyclothymia

16. Advantages of selective serotonin reuptake inhibitors include all except
    a. fewer side effects
    b. less likely to have multiple episodes of depression
    c. less dangerous in the case of an overdose
    d. ease of ingestion

17. Which is an example of a depressogenic premise?
    a. "I find time in my day to relax"
    b. "I should be at the top of my performance at all times"
    c. "I congratulate myself when I finish a hard day at work"
    d. "I try to forgive myself when I screw things up"

18. Research on electroconvulsive therapy supports that
    a. memory impairment may be permanent
    b. only bipolar depressed patients respond to ECT
    c. ECT is as effective as placebo
    d. some depressed patients may respond to ECT more than to antidepressants

19. Which statement is not true about unipolar depression?
    a. episodes of unipolar depression tend to be longer in duration, compared to episodes of depression in bipolar disorder
    b. at least half of unipolar patients will experience more than one episode
    c. female patients tend to relapse more quickly than male patients
    d. unipolar patients have their first episode at a much younger age than do bipolar patients

20. Some depressed people exhibit a depressogenic attributional style that is characterized by the tendency to explain negative events in terms of:
    a. internal, stable, global factors
    b. internal, unstable, specific factors
    c. external, unstable, specific factors
    d. external, stable, specific factors

21. A standard part of cognitive treatment for depression would be
    a. gaining insight into suppressed anger in close relationships
    b. developing a better understanding of family relationships
    c. substituting more flexible self-statements for rigid and absolute ones
    d. nondirect discussions of unexpressed emotions

22. An important assumption of the hopelessness theory of depression is
    a. loss of a parent early in life increases risk for depression
    b. desirable events will not occur regardless of what the person does
    c. depressed people are more likely to feel in control of the events of their lives
    d. depressed people have a positive impact on other people's moods

23. Which type of coping behavior is associated with longer and more severely depressed moods?
    a. processing style
    b. ruminative style
    c. intellectual style
    d. distracting style

24. Studies investigating genetic transmission of mood disorders indicate that
    a. genetic factors are more influential in bipolar disorders than major depressive disorder
    b. the concordance rate for mood disorders is higher for DZ than MZ twins
    c. there is no increased risk of bipolar disorder for relatives of bipolar patients
    d. genetic factors account for about 90% of the variance for dysthymia

25. How do depressed people often respond to a test dose of dexamethasone?
    a. they show a suppression of cortisol secretion
    b. they show a failure of suppression of cortisol secretion
    c. they show a dramatic increase of cortisol secretion
    d. they show an abnormal fluctuation of cortisol secretion

26. An example of a DSM-IV-TR subtype of depression is
    a. retarded
    b. dysphoric
    c. narcissistic
    d. melancholic

27. Which of the following areas of the brain have not been found to show changes in activity when mood is disturbed?
    a. cerebellum
    b. amygdala
    c. hypothalamus
    d. limbic system

UNDERSTANDING RESEARCH
Answers are found at the end of this chapter.

<u>Social Origins of Depression in Women:</u> The text presents in detailed description of a study in the Research Close-Up. Finding the answers to these questions will provide an understanding of this study and why it is important.

1. Did men or women participate? _____ Ages of subjects were from _____ to _____.
   Why did all subjects selected have children living at home? _____

2. What information did they gather for each subject? Psychological adjustment (such as symptoms of _____ and self-_____) Living circumstances (such as _____ relationships and social _____)

3. At follow-up one year later, they asked about _____ events and difficulties of the previous year, and they asked again about _____ of mental disorders. Judges rating each description of life events could use all information for making ratings but _____ and _____.

4. How many women were not depressed at Time I? _____ What percentage of women who did not experience a severe event during the follow up year became depressed? _____% What percentage of women who became depressed had experienced a severe event prior to becoming depressed? _____% What does this show as associated? _____

5. Only 3 percent of women experiencing a severe event involving _____ became depressed, but almost ____% of those did when the event was considered _____. Also, feeling of _____ made a woman three times more likely to become depressed.

6. Why is the use of a prospective design important here? _____
_____. What is the direction of effect indicated by these findings? _____ cause(s) _____

SHORT ANSWER
Answer the following short answer questions. Compare your work to the material presented in the text.

1. Discuss the controversy regarding the definition of mood disorders. What issues are involved? Would you advocate the use of sub-typing? Why?

2. Discuss the methodological problems in studying mood disorder across cultures. How have cross-cultural investigations assisted our understanding of mood disorders?

3. Describe the model of depression that emphasizes the interplay between cognitive and interpersonal factors.

4. Discuss the key differences between correlational and experimental studies. What are analogue studies? Provide an example of each.

ANSWER KEY

MATCHING I

1. u
2. m
3. d
4. v
5. q
6. b
7. p
8. g
9. n
10. t
11. a

12. h
13. s
14. c
15. i
16. j
17. e
18. k
19. f
20. l
21. r
22. o

MATCHING II

a. 11
b. 7
c. 13
d. 6
e. 4
f. 1
g. 3
h. 15

i. 8
j. 9
k. 16
l. 2
m. 10
n. 14
o. 12
p. 5

MATCHING III

1. a
2. c
3. d
4. b
5. e
6. f

CONCEPT REVIEW

1. true
2. true
3. concentrating, decisions
4. themselves, their environment, the future
5. mania
6. depression
7. false
8. false
9. depression; mania
10. alcoholism, eating disorders, anxiety disorders
11. true
12. false
13. manic
14. true
15. true
16. middle age (40-50)
17. 5 or 6
18. relapse
19. young adulthood (25-35)
20. true
21. 5; 3; 1
22. true
23. females
24. bipolar disorder
25. guilt and suicidal feelings; somatic feelings
26. true
27. false
28. stressful event
29. loss
30. true
31. relapse
32. depression
33. true
34. internal, stable, global
35. major depressive disorder
36. increased
37. yes
38. more; less
39. is; is not
40. bipolar disorder, dysthymia
41. multiple genes
42. false
43. 100
44. false
45. true
46. cognitive, interpersonal
47. false
48. false
49. false
50. false
51. 15-20%
52. true
53. females, males
54. older white men
55. yes
56. true
57. false

MULTIPLE CHOICE

1. b
2. a
3. c
4. c
5. a
6. a
7. a
8. a
9. a
10. d
11. c
12. d
13. b
14. a
15. a
16. b
17. b
18. d
19. d
20. a
21. c
22. b
23. b
24. a
25. a
26. d
27. a

UNDERSTANDING RESEARCH

1. women; 18; 50; because they found that women with children at home are more likely to become depressed

2. mental disorders; esteem; personal; support

3. life; symptoms; the woman's mental status; how she responded to the stressful event

4. 303; 2; 90; stressful life events and depression

5. danger; 40; humiliating; entrapment

6. It shows that the depression follows the stressful life event; stressful life events; depression

CROSSWORD

ACROSS
1. depressed mood
5. elated mood
9. pervasive emotional response
11. negative views of self, the world, and the future
13. observable behaviors associated with subjective feelings
14. Celexa is an example
15. return to active symptoms
18. axis within endocrine system important to the understanding of mood disorders
19. disorders such as major depression and dysthymia

DOWN
2. negative expectations about future events; symptom of depression
3. when symptoms are diminished or improved
4. pertaining to two directions
6. episodes of increased energy experienced by some individuals with bipolar disorder
7. near tip of hippocampus; important part of neural circuit involved in emotion
8. type of unipolar disorder characterized by chronic mild depressive condition
10. neurotransmitter enhanced by medications such as Prozac
12. abnormal patterns of activation in this region of the brain are often associated with depression
16. state of arousal defined by subjective states of feeling
17. bodily symptoms

CHAPTER SIX

ANXIETY DISORDERS

CHAPTER OUTLINE

Overview
Typical Symptoms and Associated Features
    Anxiety
    Excessive Worry
    Panic Attacks
    Phobias
    Obsessions and Compulsions
Classification
    Brief Historical Perspective
    Contemporary Diagnostic Systems (DSM-IV-TR)
    "Lumpers" and "Splitters"
    Course and Outcome
Epidemiology
    Prevalence
    Comorbidity
    Gender Differences
    Anxiety Across the Life Span
    Cross-Cultural Comparisons
Etiological Considerations and Research
    Adaptive and Maladaptive Fear
    Social Factors
    Psychological Factors
    Biological Factors
Treatment
    Psychological Interventions
    Biological Interventions
Summary

OBJECTIVES

1. Define anxiety and describe its symptoms and associated features.
2. Define and describe panic disorder. Distinguish panic attacks from other types of anxiety.
3. Compare specific phobias with generalized anxiety disorder.
4. Define obsessions and compulsions
5. Describe the historical connection between anxiety and neurosis.
6. Discuss the manner in which DSM-IV-TR classifies panic disorder, specific phobia, social phobia, generalized anxiety disorder, obsessive-compulsive disorder, and agoraphobia.
7. Discuss the prevalence of anxiety disorders.
8. Understand the role of preparedness in anxiety and anxiety disorders.
9. Recognize the role of social factors in the development of anxiety disorders.
10. Describe several theoretical perspectives regarding anxiety disorders.
11. Recognize the role of neurochemistry in anxiety disorders.
12. Describe the various treatment approaches for anxiety disorders.

MATCHING I
Answers are found at the end of this chapter. Match these terms and concepts with the definitions that follow:

   a. Fear
   b. Anxiety
   c. Worry
   d. Panic Attack
   e. Phobia
   f. Agoraphobia
   g. Social Phobia
   h. Specific Phobia
   i. Preparedness
   j. Observational Learning
   k. Neurosis

1. _____ induced in laboratory animals under stressful performance requirements; characterized by anxiety and agitation, increased startle responses, and disruption of feeding
2. _____ a sudden, overwhelming experience of focused terror
3. _____ an emotion experienced in the face of real, immediate danger
4. _____ phobia of public spaces, or being in situations where escape might be difficult
5. _____ phobia cued by doing something, such as speaking or eating, in front of other people who might scrutinize the performance
6. _____ an emotional reaction out of proportion to threats from the environment
7. _____ a phobia cued by the presence of a specific object or situation
8. _____ persistent, irrational fears associated with a specific object or situation that lead the person to avoid the feared stimulus
9. _____ organisms are biologically predisposed, on the basis of neural pathways, to learn certain types of associations more quickly
10. _____ a more or less uncontrollable sequence of negative, emotional thoughts and images concerned with possible future danger
11. _____ learning behaviors through imitation of a model

MATCHING II
Answers are found at the end of this chapter. Match these terms and concepts with the definitions that follow:

1. Obsessions
2. Compulsions
3. Neurosis
4. Signal anxiety
5. Generalized anxiety disorder
6. Catastrophic misinterpretation
7. Situational exposure
8. Introceptive exposure
9. Thought suppression
10. Pharmacological challenge procedures
11. False suffocation alarm
12. Flooding
13. Benzodiazepines
14. Azapirones
15. Breathing retraining

a. ____ indicates that an instinctual impulse previously associated with punishment and disapproval is about to be acted upon
b. ____ exposure beginning with the most frightening stimuli
c. ____ repetitive, unwanted, intrusive thoughts, images, or impulses
d. ____ tranquilizers frequently used in the treatment of anxiety disorders
e. ____ an active attempt to stop thinking about something that often leads to the paradoxical effect of an increase in strong emotions associated with unpleasant thoughts
f. ____ repetitive, ritualistic behavior aimed at reducing anxiety; the person perceives it as irrational and tries to resist performing it but cannot
g. ____ a disorder characterized by excessive and uncontrollable worry about a number of events or activities and associated symptoms of arousal
h. ____ a misfire of the system that detects carbon dioxide, which can also be set off by lactate infusion; may cause panic attacks
i. ____ a psychoanalytic term describing persistent emotional disturbances, such as anxiety or depression, in which anxiety is the key characteristic
j. ____ perceiving bodily sensations as a signal of an impending disastrous event, such as a heart attack
k. ____ a research procedure where a particular brain mechanism is stressed by the artificial administration of chemicals, which if it leads to a panic attack may implicate that brain mechanism in the etiology of panic attack
l. ____ a treatment for agoraphobia which involves repeatedly confronting the situation that has previously been avoided
m. ____ learning to take slow deep breaths
n. ____ a treatment for panic disorder which involves standardized exercises that produce sensations often felt during a panic attack
o. ____ antianxiety medications which act on serotonin transmission

MATCHING III

Answers are found at the end of this chapter. Match these names with the descriptions of their contributions to the study of abnormal psychology:

a. Susan Mineka
b. David Clark
c. Sigmund Freud
d. Thomas Borkovec
e. John Bowlby
f. Kenneth Kendler
g. Martin Seligman

1. ____ studied the influence of genes and environment on anxiety disorders; found that their influences are fairly disorder-specific
2. ____ conducted a series of studies with rhesus monkeys that combined observational learning with preparedness theory
3. ____ proposed preparedness theory, that people are prepared to develop intense, persistent fears to certain stimuli
4. ____ developed a theory of anxiety based on work with many patients; sees anxiety as warning the person they are about to do or think something that is unacceptable and triggering ego defenses to prevent the thought or action
5. ____ saw anxiety as an innate response to separation or threat of separation from caregiver
6. ____ conducted research on catastrophic misinterpretation
7. ____ researched uncontrollable worry; conceptualized it as a verbal rather than visual event

CONCEPT REVIEW
Answers are found at the end of this chapter. After you have read and reviewed the material, test your comprehension by filling in the blanks or circling the correct answer.

1. There is considerable overlap between anxiety disorders and depression: **true   false**

2. Maladaptive anxiety, or anxious apprehension, consists of:
    1) _____, 2) _____, and 3) _____.

3. Panic attacks have what type of onset: **gradual   sudden**

4. Panic attacks can happen when the person is in bed: **true   false**

5. Agoraphobia is different from other phobias in that agoraphobics are often afraid they will lose _____ in public.

6. List two ways that obsessions are different from worry. Obsessions
    1) _____, and 2) _____.

7. Normal people seldom experience obsessions: **true   false**

8. Which is a common compulsion?   **scratching   coughing   cleaning**

9. People with anxiety disorders typically require hospitalization: **true   false**

10. The Freudian perspective of obsessive-compulsive disorder focuses on which emotion? _____

11. Experts who classify mental disorders may be described as "lumpers" or "splitters." Earlier classification systems used the **lumping/splitting** approach and contemporary systems use the **lumping/splitting** approach.

12. Intrusive thoughts about real problems are one form of obsession: **true   false**

13. Panic disorder usually goes away without treatment: **true   false**

14. Many patients with obsessive-compulsive disorder show improved levels of functioning over time, although they may continue to have some symptoms: **true   false**

15. Anxiety disorders are the most common form of mental disorder: **true   false**

16. What percent of people who meet the criteria for one anxiety disorder also meet the criteria for another anxiety disorder?   **5%   20%   50%**

17. Anxiety and depression are closely related concepts, but Clark and Watson have proposed a model using positive and negative affect to help distinguish between them. Anxiety and depression both share high negative affect, but anxiety alone is characterized by _____ and depression alone is characterized by _____.

18. Depressive disorders and anxiety disorders show high comorbidity; another disorder with high comorbidity with anxiety disorders is _____.

19. People with an anxiety disorder have a greater risk of developing alcohol dependence: **true   false**

20. Which are more likely to experience specific phobias?   **men**   **women**
21. Which anxiety disorder occurs equally among men and women? _____
22. Men are more likely to relapse from an anxiety disorder than women: **true   false**
23. What age group has the lowest prevalence of anxiety disorders? _____
24. Anxiety disorders are almost entirely specific to people in Western societies: very few people in nonindustrialized countries experience them: **true   false**
25. Stressful life events have been linked to both depressive disorders and anxiety disorders. In one study, women who experienced an event involving _____ were more likely to experience depression and those who experienced an event involving _____ were more likely to experience anxiety.
26. What type of anxiety disorder is often preceded by interpersonal conflict? _____
27. Two types of childhood adversity are linked to adult anxiety disorders, especially panic disorder; they include _____ and _____ .
28. People who have agoraphobia were more likely to have had an _____ attachment to their parents as toddlers.
29. Seligman identified several shortcomings with the classical conditioning model of phobias. These include: 1) Conditioned fear responses learned in a laboratory are easy to _____, while phobic responses are extremely persistent; 2) Phobias developed after traumatic experiences, in contrast to those learned in the laboratory, are developed after _____ trial, and 3) The theory states that any stimulus can be conditioned to provoke fear, but phobias of guns, cars, and electrical outlets, and other potentially dangerous objects, are _____.
30. Monitoring one's heart rate when aroused minimizes the fear response: **true   false**
31. Rhesus monkeys raised in the wild **are/are not** afraid of snakes, while those raised in a laboratory **are/are not** afraid of snakes.
32. Monkeys can learn to fear snakes by watching videotapes of other monkeys exhibiting fear reactions toward snakes: **true   false**
33. People who believe they are able to control their environment are **more/less** likely to show symptoms of anxiety than people who believe they are helpless.
34. One example of the limitation of the catastrophic misinterpretation model of panic attacks is that they can occur while a person is _____.
35. In contrast to a depressed person, who is convinced that failure will occur, an anxious person is _____ that failure will occur.
36. Thought suppression has been found to be quite effective in reducing worrying and intrusive thoughts: **true   false**

37. Relatives of people with panic disorder are more likely to have panic disorder but not more likely to have generalized anxiety disorder: true   false
38. Relatives of people with generalized anxiety disorder are more likely to have GAD but not more likely to have panic disorder: true   false
39. Relatives of people with OCD are more likely to have OCD but not more likely to have other anxiety disorders: true   false
40. There is no evidence that the findings that anxiety disorders run in families can be explained in part by genetic influences: true   false
41. In one study, patients with anxiety disorders who were injected with lactate almost always experienced a panic attack, while only a few control subjects experienced one: true   false
42. Which of the following substances may trigger panic attacks in patients with anxiety?
    alcohol   caffeine   aspirin
43. Exposure to the feared object, situation, or behavior is an effective treatment for anxiety disorders: true   false
44. The best form of behavior therapy for OCD is _____.
45. Cognitive therapy for anxiety disorders often involves analyzing errors in the patient's _____ as well as the process of _____.
46. Antianxiety medications are particularly effective in reducing a person's worry and problems with rumination: true   false
47. Benzodiazepines are more effective in the treatment of _____ and _____ and less effective in the treatment of _____ and _____.
48. Benzodiazepines are addictive: true   false
49. Antidepressants are effective in treating some anxiety disorders: true   false

CROSSWORD

Answers are found at the end of this chapter. Complete the following crossword puzzle to reinforce your understanding of this chapter's key terms and concepts:

ACROSS	DOWN
1. repetitive behaviors	2. learning which involves imitation
7. model which suggests evolutionary component to fear	3. experienced in the face of real, immediate danger
10. feelings of unreality	4. sudden, overwhelming experience of fright
11. repetitive, intrusive thoughts	5. affect common in anxiety and depression
12. neurotransmitter regulating nervous activity	6. type of antidepressant which has become preferred medication to treat anxiety disorders
13. brain structure which processed threatening stimuli	8. characterized by free-floating anxiety
15. irrational, narrowly defined fear of specific object	9. key in the treatment of OCD
16. important relationship exists between perception of this and anxiety	14. refers to a mood or a syndrome

MULTIPLE CHOICE

Answers are found at the end of this chapter. The multiple choice questions listed will test your understanding of the material presented in the chapter. Read through each question and circle the letter representing the best answer.

1. The most frequently used types of minor tranquilizers for the treatment of anxiety disorders are
    a. tricyclics
    b. benzodiazepines
    c. serotonin
    d. GABA inhibitors

2. Which of the following is least likely to be present in an anxiety disorder?
    a. lack of insight
    b. social impairment
    c. significant personal distress
    d. negative emotional response

3. Which of the following is an example of a potential unconditioned stimulus which could contribute to the development of a phobia?
    a. loss of a relationship
    b. chronic occupational difficulties
    c. a painfully loud and unexpected noise
    d. a sad song

4. _____ is experienced in the face of real, immediate danger, _____ is a diffuse reaction that is out of proportion to threats from the environment.
    a. anxiety, fear
    b. worry, anxiety
    c. fear, anxiety
    d. worry, fear

5. Results of family studies investigating transmission of anxiety disorders suggest
    a. there appears to be no genetic component to OCD
    b. social phobia is the most inheritable form of anxiety disorder
    c. panic disorder and GAD are etiologically separate disorders
    d. the most inheritable anxiety disorder is specific phobia

6. The two most common types of compulsions are
    a. counting and repeating
    b. cleaning and checking
    c. sorting and counting
    d. checking and writing

7. A junior in college, Jimmy is acutely distressed at the thought of having to write in front of others. He is afraid that he will drop his pen, lose control of his writing, or somehow embarrass himself while other people are watching. This fear has impaired his ability to take notes in class. His diagnosis may be
    a. specific phobia
    b. agoraphobia
    c. generalized anxiety disorder
    d. social phobia

8. The discovery of laboratory procedures that reliably induce panic attacks is important because
    a. they offer investigators the opportunity to research the antecedents and consequences of panic attacks
    b. brain activities that occur during a panic attack may be monitored
    c. such procedures may be fruitful in developing a map of the specific areas of the brain that mediate anxiety symptoms
    d. all of the above

9. Which of the following is the most common type of abnormal behavior?
    a. anxiety disorders
    b. major depression
    c. generalized anxiety disorder
    d. dysthymia

10. Specific phobias may be best understood in terms of learning experiences. The association between the object and intense fear can develop through all but which of the following?
    a. direct experience
    b. observational learning
    c. exposure to fear-irrelevant stimuli
    d. exposure to warnings about dangerous situations

11. Which is true regarding the relationship between anxiety and other disorders?
    a. substance dependence is rarely associated with anxiety disorders
    b. anxiety disorders overlap considerably with other anxiety disorders
    c. anxiety disorders usually overlap with psychotic disorders
    d. anxiety disorders do not appear to be associated with depressive disorders

12. "Free-floating" anxiety would be most characteristic of which anxiety disorder?
    a. social phobia
    b. panic disorder
    c. obsessive-compulsive disorder
    d. generalized anxiety disorder

13. Which of the following is not consistent with Freud's model of anxiety?
    a. repression is the product of anxiety
    b. anxiety is the result of a harsh superego in conflict with the defense mechanisms that are employed by the ego
    c. the specific form of overt symptoms is determined by the defense mechanisms that are employed by the ego
    d. different types of anxiety disorders can be distinguished by many factors within the analytic framework, for example, the developmental stage at which the person experiences problems

14. Anxiety disorder categories did not emerge in psychiatric classifications during the last century primarily because
    a. the prevalence of anxiety disorders was much lower during the last century
    b. they were considered to be neurological disorders
    c. very few cases of anxiety disorders required institutionalization
    d. physicians were not trained to recognize the symptoms of anxiety disorders

15. Which of the following is not a symptom of a panic attack?
    a. feeling of choking
    b. trembling
    c. nausea
    d. headache

16. Research on the relationship between stressful life events and anxiety disorders suggests that
    a. the onset of agoraphobia may be associated with interpersonal conflict
    b. marital distress is associated with the onset of simple phobia
    c. the onset of agoraphobia may be associated with the experience of a conditioning event, such as a sudden painful injury
    d. severe loss is associated with the onset of an anxiety disorder

17. Which cognitive factor shares an important relationship with panic attacks?
    a. perception of control over events in one's environment
    b. thought suppression
    c. cognitive minimization of traumatic events
    d. all-or-none thinking about future events

18. Which is not included in the DSM-IV-TR's classification of anxiety disorders?
    a. panic disorder
    b. agoraphobia
    c. cyclothymia
    d. obsessive-compulsive disorder

19. If a panic attack only occurs in the presence of a particular stimulus, it is said to be
    a. a situationally cued attack
    b. an anticipated attack
    c. a below threshold attack
    d. a cognitively processed attack

20. Karen has consistent worries that she is going to lose her job, that something is going to happen to her husband, and that her health may take a turn for the worse. She knows that her worries are causing friction in her marriage, but she feels that she cannot control them. Although she has always been a "worrier," the intensity and frequency of her worries has worsened in the past year. Her diagnosis may be
    a. agoraphobia
    b. panic disorder
    c. generalized anxiety disorder
    d. simple phobia

21. The most serious adverse side effects of benzodiazepines is
    a. heart palpitations
    b. significant weight gain
    c. necessary dietary restrictions
    d. their potential for addiction

22. The types of symptoms most characteristic of a panic attack are
    a. interpersonal difficulties
    b. physical symptoms
    c. emotional reactions
    d. cognitive reactions

23. Cross-cultural research on anxiety disorders suggests that
    a. anxiety disorders are not experienced in certain cultures
    b. phobic avoidance is the most commonly reported symptom across cultures
    c. the focus of typical anxiety complaints can vary dramatically across cultures
    d. anxiety disorders are more common in preliterate cultures

24. An important consideration in diagnosing panic disorder is that the person must
    a. experience recurrent, situationally cued panic attacks
    b. experience recurrent panic attacks in anticipation of a feared event
    c. report the experience of feeling out of control
    d. experience recurrent unexpected panic attacks

25. Which of the following is not included in the DSM-IV-TR as criteria to establish the boundary between normal behavior and compulsive rituals?
    a. the rituals cause marked distress
    b. the rituals can be observed by other people
    c. the rituals interfere with normal occupational and social functioning
    d. the rituals take more than one hour per day to perform

26. Which of the following would be a typical situation that would cause problems for an agoraphobic?
    a. traveling on the subway
    b. speaking to a friend on the phone
    c. cleaning the house
    d. encountering a snake

27. According to recent research, what percent of the people who qualify for an anxiety disorder diagnosis actually seek treatment for their disorder?
    a. fifteen percent
    b. twenty-five percent
    c. forty percent
    d. fifty percent

28. What is an important difference between compulsions and some addictive behaviors such as gambling?
    a. addictive behaviors reduce anxiety more effectively than compulsions
    b. compulsions are more resistant to treatment
    c. addictive behaviors are not repetitive in nature
    d. compulsions reduce anxiety but they do not produce pleasure

29. Women are about twice as likely as men to experience all but which of the following anxiety disorders?
    a. social phobia
    b. agoraphobia
    c. GAD
    d. panic disorder

UNDERSTANDING RESEARCH
Answers are found at the end of this chapter.

Panic and Perception of Control: The text presents a detailed description of a study in the Research Close-Up. Finding the answers to these questions will provide an understanding of this study and why it is important.

1. All of the procedures researchers have used to induce a panic attack in a laboratory situation produce a range of peripheral _____ sensations, such as _____, chest _____, and _____ headedness.

2. In this study they used air enriched with _____ but manipulated the subjects' impressions of whether they were in _____ of the air mixture. All subjects met diagnostic criteria for _____ disorder.

3. Each person sat _____ in a quiet room, breathing through a gas _____, and rated his or her _____ level. They were told when the box was _____ they could adjust the mixture of carbon dioxide by using the dial on their _____. In reality the dial had _____ effect. All patients received _____ minutes of compressed air, then _____ minutes of carbon-dioxide enriched air. For _____ of the _____ patients the light went on, and for the rest it never went on.

4. Following the procedure, subjects were all interviewed to see if they experienced a _____. Eight of the 10 subjects in the _____ group had a panic attack. Two of the 10 subjects in the _____ group had a panic attack. Those in the no illusion group reported more than _____ as many symptoms than those in the illusion of control group. Both groups had symptoms of breathlessness and _____ sensations, dizziness, _____ headedness, and a pounding _____.

5. This study is important because it shows how biological and psychological factors _____ to produce the experience of panic. Biological factors were important but alone were not _____ to produce an attack. Feelings of _____ were particularly important.

SHORT ANSWER
Answer the following short answer questions. Compare your work to the material presented in the text.

1. Learning processes have been associated with the etiology of phobias, while cognitive factors have been used to explain the development of panic attacks. Review several learning and cognitive theories which account for each type of disorder. Do differences in etiological processes imply that these disorders are unrelated? Why or why not?

2. Discuss the relationship between anxiety and depression. Do you believe anxiety and depression are separate types of disorders, or do you think that they represent different manifestations of the same problem? What evidence supports your position?

3. Consider the following psychological interventions used for the treatment of anxiety disorders: desensitization, flooding, prolonged exposure and response prevention, and cognitive therapy. Select an anxiety disorder and discuss how you would approach the treatment of this disorder. Which intervention technique(s) would you choose? Why?

ANSWER KEY

MATCHING I

1. k
2. d
3. a
4. f
5. g
6. b
7. h
8. e
9. i
10. c
11. j

MATCHING II

a. 4
b. 12
c. 1
d. 13
e. 9
f. 2
g. 5
h. 11
i. 7
j. 6
k. 10
l. 7
m. 15
n. 8
o. 14

MATCHING III

1. f
2. a
3. g
4. c
5. e
6. b
7. d

MULTIPLE CHOICE

1. b
2. a
3. c
4. c
5. c
6. b
7. d
8. d
9. a
10. c
11. b
12. d
13. b
14. c
15. d
16. a
17. a
18. c
19. a
20. c
21. d
22. b
23. c
24. d
25. b
26. a
27. b
28. d
29. a

CONCEPT REVIEW

1. true
2. high levels of negative emotion, a sense of lack of control, and self preoccupation
3. sudden
4. true
5. control
6. are out of the blue, and involve socially unacceptable and horrific themes
7. false
8. cleaning
9. false
10. anger or aggression
11. lumping; splitting
12. false
13. false
14. true
15. true
16. 50 percent
17. physiological hyperarousal; absence of positive affect
18. alcoholism
19. true
20. women
21. OCD
22. false
23. the elderly
24. false
25. loss; danger
26. agoraphobia
27. parental indifference; physical abuse
28. insecure-anxious
29. extinguish; one; rare
30. false
31. are; are not
32. true
33. less
34. asleep
35. not sure
36. false
37. true
38. true
39. false
40. false
41. true
42. caffeine
43. true
44. prolonged exposure with response prevention
45. thinking; decatastrophizing
46. false
47. GAD; social phobia; specific phobia; OCD
48. true
49. true

UNDERSTANDING RESEARCH

1. somatic; palpitations; tightness; light
2. carbon dioxide; control; panic
3. alone; mask; anxiety; lit; lap; no; 5; 15; 10; 20
4. panic attack; no illusion; illusion of control; twice; smothering; light; heart
5. interact; sufficient; control

CROSSWORD

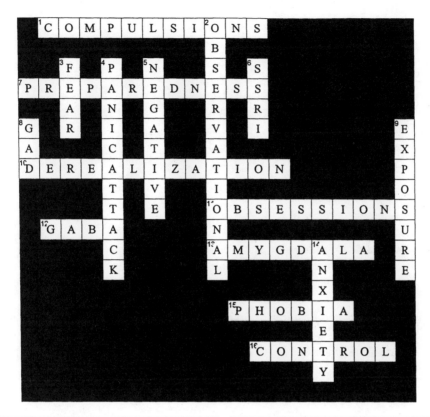

ACROSS	DOWN
1. repetitive behaviors	2. learning which involves imitation
7. model which suggests evolutionary component to fear	3. experienced in the face of real, immediate danger
10. feelings of unreality	4. sudden, overwhelming experience of fright
11. repetitive, intrusive thoughts	5. affect common in anxiety and depression
12. neurotransmitter regulating nervous activity	6. type of antidepressant which has become preferred medication to treat anxiety disorders
13. brain structure which processed threatening stimuli	8. characterized by free-floating anxiety
15. irrational, narrowly defined fear of specific object	9. key in the treatment of OCD
16. important relationship exists between perception of this and anxiety	14. refers to a mood or a syndrome

CHAPTER SEVEN

ACUTE AND POSTTRAUMATIC STRESS DISORDERS, DISSOCIATIVE DISORDERS, AND SOMATOFORM DISORDERS

CHAPTER OUTLINE

Overview
Acute and Posttraumatic Stress Disorders
    Typical Symptoms and Associated Features of ASD and PTSD
    Classification of Acute and Posttraumatic Stress Disorders
    Epidemiology of Trauma, PTSD, and ASD
    Etiological Considerations and Research on PTSD and ASD
    Prevention and Treatment of ASD and PTSD
Dissociative Disorders
    Hysteria and Unconscious Mental Processes
    Typical Symptoms of Dissociative Disorders
    Classification of Dissociative Disorders
    Epidemiology of Dissociative Disorders
    Etiological Considerations and Research on Dissociative Disorders
    Treatment of Dissociative Disorders
Somatoform Disorders
    Typical Symptoms and Associated Features of Somatoform Disorders
    Classification of Somatoform Disorders
    Epidemiology of Somatoform Disorders
    Etiological Considerations and Research on Somatoform Disorders
    Treatment of Somatoform Disorders
Summary

OBJECTIVES

1. Describe the features of posttraumatic stress disorder.
2. Distinguish between posttraumatic stress disorder and acute stress disorder.
3. Describe several treatment approaches for posttraumatic stress disorder.
4. Distinguish between dissociative and somatoform disorders.
5. Describe several perspectives of hysteria. Compare these perspectives with current views.
6. Define dissociation and psychogenic amnesia.
7. Discuss the connection between psychological trauma and fugue, amnesia, and multiple personality disorder.
8. Define retrograde, posttraumatic, anterograde, and selective amnesia.
9. Identify the DSM-IV-TR criteria for depersonalization disorder and dissociative identity disorder.
10. Define prosopagnosia and explain the significance of this disorder from the biological perspective.
11. Discuss the psychological view of dissociative disorders.
12. Describe the ways in which hypnosis and abreaction may aid in the integration of dissociated memories.
13. Discuss the DSM-IV-TR criteria for body dysmorphic disorder, hypochondriasis, somatization disorder, pain disorder, and conversion disorder.
14. Discuss the danger in misdiagnosing somatoform disorders.

15. Discuss Freud's theory of primary and secondary gain as these relate to somatoform symptoms.
16. Describe the behavioral approach in treating chronic pain.
17. Outline the manner in which physicians should treat patients who present multiple physical concerns that are not physiologically based.

MATCHING I

Answers are found at the end of this chapter. Match these terms and concepts with the definitions that follow:

a. Traumatic stress
b. Acute Stress Disorder (ASD)
c. Posttraumatic stress disorder (PTSD)
d. Dissociative Disorders
e. Somatoform Disorders
f. Malingering
g. Factitious Disorder
h. Flashbacks
i. Depersonalization
j. Derealization
k. Dissociative amnesia
l. Selective amnesia
m. Depersonalization disorder
n. Dissociative identity disorder
o. Multiple personality disorder
p. Hypnosis
q. Prosopagnosia
r. Retrospective reports
s. State-dependent learning
t. Iatrogenesis
u. Abreaction
v. Secondary victimization
w. Interpersonality amnesia
x. Priming

1. ____ a disorder characterized by the sudden inability to recall extensive and important personal information
2. ____ a sense of feeling cut off from oneself or one's environment
3. ____ impairment of face recognition sometimes resulting from brain damage
4. ____ characterized by persistent, maladaptive disruptions in the integration of memory, consciousness, or identity
5. ____ a marked sense of unreality about oneself or one's environment
6. ____ recollections about the past that have questionable reliability and validity
7. ____ an altered state of consciousness during which people are especially susceptible to suggestion
8. ____ occurs within four weeks of exposure to a trauma; characterized by dissociative symptoms, re-experiencing of the event, avoidance of reminders of the event, and anxiety or arousal
9. ____ lasts over a month after exposure to a trauma, or has a delayed onset (6 or more months after trauma); characterized by dissociative symptoms, reexperiencing of the event, avoidance of reminders of the event, and anxiety or arousal
10. ____ when professionals increase a rape victim's emotional burden
11. ____ exposure to some event that involves actual or threatened death or serious injury to self or others
12. ____ the emotional reliving of a past traumatic experience
13. ____ a dissociative disorder characterized by the existence of two or more distinct personalities in a single individual, which repeatedly take over the person's behavior outside of their awareness
14. ____ the previous term for dissociative identity disorder
15. ____ sudden, intrusive, vivid memories during which a trauma is replayed in images or thoughts
16. ____ pretending to have a psychological disorder in order to achieve some external gain
17. ____ pretending to have a psychological disorder in order to assume the sick role
18. ____ a dissociative disorder characterized by severe and persistent feelings of being detached from oneself
19. ____ learning that occurs in one state of affect or consciousness is recalled most accurately while in that same state
20. ____ a form of amnesia in which people do not lose their memory completely but are unable to remember only certain personal events and information

21. ____ characterized by unusual physical symptoms that occur in the absence of a known physical illness
22. ____ creation of a disorder by attempts at treatment
23. ____ showing a set of stimuli and later testing subjects with a degraded form of the stimuli
24. ____ lack of awareness of the experiences of one personality by an alter

MATCHING II

Answers are found at the end of this chapter. Match these terms and concepts with the definitions that follow:

1. Victimization
2. Two-factor theory
3. Trauma desensitization
4. EMDR
5. Recovered memories
6. False memories
7. Dissociative fugue
8. Hysteria
9. Amnesia
10. Psychogenic amnesia
11. Conversion disorder
12. Somatization disorder
13. La belle indifference
14. Briquet's syndrome
15. Hypochondriasis
16. Pain disorder
17. Body dysmorphic disorder
18. Diagnosis by exclusion
19. Primary gain
20. Secondary gain
21. Prosopagnosia
22. Thought suppression
23. Explicit memory
24. Implicit memory

a. ____ a pattern of response among victims of violent crime that includes fear, guilt, self-blame, powerlessness, and lowered self-esteem
b. ____ a somatoform disorder characterized by preoccupying fear or belief that one is suffering from a physical illness, even in the face of a clean bill of health by a physician
c. ____ a somatoform disorder characterized by physical symptoms that mimic those found in neurological diseases, but which often do not make sense anatomically
d. ____ amnesia that is psychologically caused, resulting from trauma or emotional distress
e. ____ a process of identifying somatoform disorders by ruling out physical causes that could account for the symptoms
f. ____ avoidance of memories or thoughts of a trauma
g. ____ a controversial treatment using rapid back-and-forth eye movements to induce relaxation while reliving a traumatic event
h. ____ a somatoform disorder characterized by constant preoccupation with some imagined or grossly exaggerated defect in physical appearance
i. ____ dramatic recollections of a long-forgotten traumatic experience
j. ____ partial or complete loss of recall for a particular event or time period
k. ____ an unintentionally invented memory of an event that did not actually occur
l. ____ a psychoanalytic term that a symptom protects the ego from an unacceptable thought by serving as a symbolic, disguised expression of that thought
m. ____ a somatoform disorder characterized by multiple, somatic complaints in the absence of organic impairment
n. ____ a rare disorder characterized by sudden, unplanned travel, the inability to remember details about the past, and identity confusion or assumption of a new identity
o. ____ a psychoanalytic term that a symptom is rewarding because it allows a patient to avoid responsibility or elicit sympathy or attention from others
p. ____ a flippant lack of concern about the physical symptoms of a somatoform disorder
q. ____ a historic diagnostic category that included both dissociative and somatoform disorders; based on the ancient Greek idea that these symptoms were caused by a "dislodged, wandering uterus."

r. ____ a somatoform disorder characterized by preoccupation with pain in which psychological factors are involved
s. ____ explains the development of symptoms following trauma using a combination of classical and operant conditioning, whereby classical conditioning creates fears and operant conditioning maintains them
t. ____ treatment method where the client is first taught to relax, and while relaxed, gradually relives the traumatic event through discussion or fantasy
u. ____ impairment of face recognition
v. ____ a name sometimes used to refer to somatization disorder
w. ____ changes in memory but with no conscious recollection
x. ____ conscious recollection of a past event

MATCHING III

Answers are found at the end of this chapter. Match these names with the descriptions of their contributions to the study of abnormal psychology:

a. Pierre Janet
b. Edna Foa
c. Nicholas Spanos
d. Jean Charcot
e. Sigmund Freud

1. ____ argued that multiple personalities are caused by role playing
2. ____ viewed dissociation as a normal process, similar to repression, whereby the ego defends itself against unacceptable thoughts
3. ____ used hypnosis to treat hysteria
4. ____ viewed dissociation as an abnormal process indicative of psychopathology
5. ____ explains PTSD symptoms using the two-factor theory

CONCEPT REVIEW

Answers are found at the end of this chapter. After you have read and reviewed the material, test your comprehension by filling in the blanks or circling the correct answer.

1. PTSD is characterized by these three symptoms: _____, _____, and _____.

2. ASD is characterized by the above three symptoms and_____.

3. Sometimes the re-experiencing of PTSD and ASD occurs as a(n) _____ state, which is usually brief.

4. In PTSD, avoidance may manifest as _____, where feelings seem dampened or nonexistent.

5. Many people with PTSD and ASD are jumpy and nervous, showing an "exaggerated _____response."

6. The development of ASD as a diagnostic category was, in part, an attempt to _____ the development of PTSD by providing early treatment.

7. What was wrong with earlier definitions of trauma? _____.

8. What are five types of experience that often lead to the development of PTSD? _____, _____, _____, _____, and _____.

9. A woman cannot become pregnant as the result of a sexual assault: **true** **false**

10. What three disorders commonly co-occur with PTSD? _____, _____, and _____.

11. It is thought that about _____% of women and _____% of men will develop PTSD at some point in their lives.
12. People who experience what type of trauma develop PTSD in the highest proportions? _____
13. People with a history of emotional problems are **more/less** likely to experience trauma and are **more/less** likely to develop PTSD.
14. There is evidence to suggest that some patients with PTSD dissociate, because they report low anxiety but tests show they have _____ arousal.
15. What are the three models that attempt to explain why not everybody that experiences a traumatic event develops PTSD? _____, _____, and _____.
16. Monozygotic (MZ) twins had a **higher/lower** concordance rate than dizygotic (DZ) twins for experiencing trauma in the form of exposure to combat, and for developing PTSD symptoms in a study of Vietnam veterans.
17. Research suggests that high levels of thought _____ are associated with severe symptoms of PTSD.
18. Research has suggested that an increase in the production of the neurotransmitter _____ in response to trauma causes the increased arousal and anxiety seen in PTSD, and that the increase in production of endogenous _____ in response to trauma causes the numbing.
19. One study showed that Vietnam veterans with PTSD showed **more/less** pain sensitivity following exposure to a film of combat.
20. People cope **better/worse** with trauma when they anticipate its onset.
21. What three characteristics of an attack increase the chance that victims of sexual assault will develop PTSD? _____, _____, and _____.
22. What three types of experiences among Vietnam veterans increase the risk of PTSD? _____, _____, and _____.
23. Social support **increases/decreases** the risk for PTSD.
24. Research **supports/does not support** the idea that immediate, emergency psychological treatment is effective in preventing PTSD.
25. What was the conclusion of the study in the Netherlands comparing the effectiveness of trauma desensitization, hypnotherapy, and psychodynamic therapy in improving PTSD? _____.
26. Although painful and difficult, _____ is the essential component of effective treatment for PTSD.
27. EMDR is a highly effective treatment method: **true   false**
28. There is no evidence that repression of memories of traumatic events occurs: **true   false**
29. It is very difficult to establish whether a recovered memory is accurate: **true   false**
30. Freud viewed the unconscious mind as being **dumb/smart** while contemporary scientists view it as **dumb/smart**.

31. One study found that 80 percent of patients with dissociative identity disorder also met criteria for what disorder? _____.
32. What traumatic experience is hypothesized to play a role in the etiology of many dissociative disorders? _____
33. Only two hundred case histories of _____ disorder appeared in the entire world literature before 1980; a 1986 report suggested that about 6,000 cases of it had been diagnosed in North America alone, yet the diagnosis remains extremely rare in Europe and Japan.
34. Some professionals question the existence of dissociative identity disorder, arguing that it is created by the power of _____.
35. What is one important way that the multiple identity enactment created in laboratory studies differs from the multiple identities found in dissociative identity disorder? _____
36. Patients with prosopagnosia demonstrate the normal preference for viewing faces that are familiar. This finding implies a dissociation between _____ and _____ cognitive processes.
37. An adequate test of the hypothesized relation between child abuse and dissociative disorders requires _____ research following trauma victims from childhood into adult life with assessments of dissociation at different times.
38. A twin study found _____ genetic contribution to dissociative symptoms.
39. Some psychologists argue that dissociative identity disorder is produced by iatrogenesis; in other words, who causes the disorder? _____
40. The goal of treatment for dissociative identity disorder is _____.
41. What kind of professional do people with somatoform disorders typically see? _____.
42. Multisomatoform disorder has been proposed and requires _____ physical symptoms.
43. In one study, twenty seven percent of women undergoing what type of surgery actually suffered from somatization disorder? _____
44. Somatization disorder must have its onset in: **young adulthood**   **middle age**
45. Conversion disorders are **more/less** common now than in the past.
46. Somatization disorder is more common in which of the following:
    women/men   **blacks/whites**   **less educated/more educated**
47. Somatoform disorders show high comorbidity with _____.
48. People with somatization disorder are more likely to have male relatives with _____ disorder.
49. In one study, what percentage of patients diagnosed with conversion disorders were eventually found to have a neurological disease? _____
50. Somatoform disorders are not more frequent in non-industrialized countries: **true**   **false**

CROSSWORD

Answers are found at the end of this chapter. Complete the following crossword puzzle to reinforce your understanding of this chapter's key terms and concepts:

ACROSS		DOWN	
1. shares symptoms of ASD but is longer lasting or has a delayed onset	19. personal sense of commitment, control, and challenge in facing stress	2. theory which combines principles of classical and operant conditioning	15. type of support which plays crucial role in alleviating long term effects of trauma
7. disruption of normally integrated mental processes		3. occurs within four weeks after exposure to traumatic stress	16. sudden memory during which trauma is replayed in images or thoughts
9. characterized by sense of unreality about oneself		4. general term referring to normal responses to trauma	
12. critical incident stress debriefing		5. axis in area of brain known to be stimulated by normal stress	
13. disorders characterized by unusual physical problems occuring in the absence of physical illness		6. impairment of face recognition	
14. characterized by two or more personalities coexisting within single individual		8. use of rapid back and forth eye movements to reduce anxiety	
17. type of processing which involves facing fear		10. symptom of ASD and PTSD which is oftentimes marked or persistent	
18. characterized by inability to recall past, confusion about identity		11. manufacture of dissociative disorders by their treatment	

MULTIPLE CHOICE

Answers are found at the end of this chapter. The multiple choice questions listed will test your understanding of the material presented in the chapter. Read through each question and circle the letter representing the best answer.

1. Many people who suffer from PTSD also meet the diagnostic criteria for another mental disorder, particularly _____ and _____.
    a. depression; substance abuse
    b. hypomanic; antisocial personality disorder
    c. depression; adjustment disorder
    d. hypomanic; paranoid personality disorder

2. All of the following are cultural myths of sexual assault with the exception of
    a. women who are raped provoke it
    b. women who are raped seldom sustain physical injuries
    c. women who are raped often enjoy it
    d. many women who are raped are raped by an acquaintance

3. Jack, a Vietnam Veteran, runs for cover every time he hears an airplane pass by overhead. Jack's reaction can best be described as a:
    a. flashback
    b. dissociative state
    c. brief psychotic reaction
    d. hallucination

4. According to one study conducted in the St. Louis area, the most common cause of PTSD among men was
    a. observing domestic violence in the home as a child
    b. being a victim of physical abuse as a child
    c. participation in the Vietnam War
    d. witnessing a friend or relative die from a traumatic event

5. Surveys have found that approximately _____ of U.S. women have been raped.
    a. 2%
    b. 10%
    c. 30%
    d. 40%

6. All of the following are factors that increase the risk for PTSD, with the exception of
    a. having a history of emotional problems
    b. being a minority group member
    c. being female
    d. being wealthy

7. As many as _____ of all stranger rapes are not reported to authorities.
    a. one-third
    b. two-thirds
    c. one-quarter
    d. one-half

8. Some research indicates that it is helpful to recount stressful experiences because
    a. it can reduce the various psychophysiological indicators of the stress response
    b. it helps dissipate negative feelings associated with the stressful experiences
    c. it helps the person "let go" of the experience and continue with his or her life
    d. there is no research that supports the effectiveness of recounting stressful experiences

9. Studies show that _____ is the most effective treatment for PTSD.
    a. hypnotherapy
    b. psychodynamic therapy
    c. trauma desensitization
    d. no significant differences were detected among any of the above therapies

10. _____ is the help and understanding received from friends and family as well as from professionals.
    a. A personal network
    b. Social support
    c. Psychotherapy
    d. None of the above

11. Which of the following is not typically a symptom of PTSD?
    a. difficulty falling or staying asleep
    b. irritability or outbursts of anger
    c. paranoid thoughts or ideas
    d. difficulty concentrating

12. A horrifying experience that leads to general increases in anxiety and arousal, avoidance of emotionally charged situations, and the frequent reliving of the traumatic event is called
    a. posttraumatic stress disorder
    b. victimization
    c. acute stress disorder
    d. generalized anxiety disorder

13. Sudden, unplanned travel, the inability to remember certain past details, and confusion about one's identity are primary features of
    a. general amnesia
    b. Briquet's syndrome
    c. body dysmorphic disorder
    d. dissociative fugue

14. Abnormal fears of having a serious medical disorder, even after a thorough medical evaluation reveals nothing wrong, is characteristic of
    a. hypochondriasis
    b. depersonalization disorder
    c. somatization disorder
    d. conversion disorder

15. This term is used to describe people who habitually and deliberately pretend to have a physical illness.
    a. hypochondriasis
    b. psychosis
    c. factitious disorder
    d. adjustment disorder

16. An unfortunate consequence of having a somatoform disorder is
    a. the patient does not attend to the medical aspects of the disorder, resulting in underutilization of health care
    b. the psychological nature of the patient's problems go unnoticed, and unnecessary medical procedures are performed
    c. the seriousness of the physical complaints are overlooked, and necessary medical treatments are refused
    d. mental health professionals are consulted instead of physicians, resulting in poor physical health care

17. Which disorder does not appear to overlap with somatoform disorders?
    a. anxiety disorders
    b. depression
    c. antisocial personality disorder
    d. multiple personality disorder

18. Freud believed that both dissociative and somatoform disorders were
    a. expressions of unresolved anger
    b. reactions of the superego toward repressed impulses
    c. expressions of unconscious conflict
    d. conscious reactions to traumatic situations

19. "La belle indifference" is occasionally exhibited by patients with
    a. multiple personality disorder
    b. pain disorder
    c. psychogenic amnesia
    d. somatization disorder

20. Whenever Tom looks into the mirror, the first thing he notices is his large and somewhat pointed ears. Although friends have reassured him otherwise, he is convinced that his ears are the first thing others notice about him, too. In fact, he wonders whether some people may call him Mr. Spock behind his back. He has consulted with several plastic surgeons and his first surgery has just been scheduled. Tom displays symptoms of
    a. somatization disorder
    b. Briquet's syndrome
    c. conversion disorder
    d. body dysmorphic disorder

21. Sally is depressed about her relationship with her boyfriend as she studies for her spring chemistry final. The next fall, she takes another chemistry course and easily remembers the material from her spring course while studying for her first quiz. She is also depressed now due to a fight with her girlfriend. This is
    a. state-dependent learning
    b. abreaction
    c. hypnotic recall
    d. recovered memory

22. How might antianxiety, antipsychotic, or antidepressant medications be helpful in the treatment of dissociative disorders?
    a. they facilitate reintegration of the dissociated states
    b. they reduce the level of the patient's emotional distress
    c. they increase the likelihood of having one personality become dominant over other personalities
    d. they are not recommended treatment for dissociative disorders

23. A critical consideration in the diagnosis of a somatoform disorder is that the person
    a. may be aware of the psychological factors producing the disorder
    b. may minimize their physical complaints, resulting in not detecting the disorder
    c. may also have coexisting multiple personalities
    d. may actually have a real but as yet undetected physical illness

24. Which disorder is not a type of somatoform disorder?
    a. depersonalization disorder
    b. body dysmorphic disorder
    c. conversion disorder
    d. pain disorder

25. A distinguishing feature of somatization disorder is
    a. the physical complaints involve multiple somatic systems
    b. the physical complaints are limited to only one somatic system
    c. the patient appears very serious, obsessive, and emotionally withdrawn
    d. the onset of the disorder rarely occurs before age 30

26. The separation of mental processes such as memory or consciousness that are usually integrated is referred to as
    a. abreaction
    b. dissociation
    c. repression
    d. deja vu

27. Which of the following is the best definition of a conversion symptom?
    a. a physical symptom in one part of the body that is actually referred pain or trauma from another part of the body
    b. a symptom produced by psychological conflict that mimics a symptom found in a neurological disease
    c. a symptom produced by injury which is exacerbated by psychological conflict
    d. an emotional symptom such as depressed mood produced by physical trauma

28. When is the diagnosis of a dissociative disorder not appropriate?
    a. when the patient has a history of child sexual abuse
    b. when the dissociative process is abrupt in onset
    c. when the patient additionally reports feeling depressed
    d. when the dissociation occurs in the presence of substance abuse or organic pathology

29. Joe, a house painter, reports to his family doctor that he has not been able to work for six months because of pain in his legs. He can barely walk to the kitchen from his bedroom because of the pain. No injury occurred that would explain the situation. His wife has been taking care of him but is very concerned about the financial strain this is causing. His doctor orders a thorough examination. If nothing is found, what diagnosis should his doctor consider?
    a. conversion disorder
    b. hypochondriasis
    c. pain disorder
    d. somatoform disorder

30. The onset of a dissociative episode
    a. is typically abrupt and precipitated by a traumatic event
    b. is slow and insidious in nature
    c. can be traced to certain metabolic deficiencies
    d. typically happens following a severe head injury

31. A conversion symptom that serves the function of protecting the conscious mind by expressing the conflict unconsciously is referred to as
    a. la belle indifference
    b. primary gain
    c. diagnosis by exclusion
    d. abreaction

32. While both disorders involve memory loss, a major difference between dissociative amnesia and dissociative fugue is that
    a. dissociative fugue is characterized by sudden and unexpected travel away from home
    b. the memory loss in dissociative amnesia has a physical basis
    c. dissociative amnesia is characterized by the emergence of at least one additional personality
    d. dissociative fugue additionally includes persistent feelings of being detached from oneself

33. Research on the prevalence of somatoform disorders suggests that they
    a. appear to be more common than depression in the general population
    b. appear to be less common during war time
    c. appear to be rare in the general population
    d. have increased in prevalence since Freud's time

34. The sociocultural view of the etiology of somatoform disorders suggests that
    a. people with education and financial security have greater access to physicians who will listen to their somatic complaints
    b. people in nonindustrialized societies have a greater sense of community and are more likely to describe their inner distress to others in their social network
    c. people in industrialized societies have more opportunity to develop a more sophisticated vocabulary for their physical symptoms
    d. people with less education or financial security have less opportunity to learn how to describe their inner turmoil in psychological terms

35. A person with which of the following would be at risk for developing a dissociative disorder?
    a. a family history of depression
    b. a history of child sexual abuse
    c. a history of violent behavior
    d. all of the above

36. Why are people with somatoform disorders likely to reject a referral to a mental health professional from their physicians?
    a. people may have difficulty accepting the possibility of the psychological basis to their physical symptoms
    b. people may feel that their physician is belittling their problems
    c. people may feel that their physician is not being empathetic
    d. all of the above

37. Which statement is not correct about somatization disorder?
    a. it is more common among higher socioeconomic groups
    b. it is more common among women
    c. it is more common among African Americans than whites
    d. somatic symptoms are more frequent among people who have lost a spouse

38. Every Friday, Sarah's fifth grade class has a spelling test. Every Friday morning, she complains of a stomach ache to her mother. This may be an example of
    a. expressing an emotional concern that has a genuine emotional basis
    b. expressing an emotional concern in terms of a physical complaint
    c. expressing a physical complaint that has been reinforced by the environment
    d. expressing a psychological symptom that has an organic basis

39. Somatoform disorders are characterized by
    a. physical complaints that can be traced to organic impairment
    b. patients who deliberately lie about the presence of physical symptoms
    c. physical symptoms that cannot be explained on the basis of underlying physical illness
    d. physical symptoms which are consciously linked to psychological difficulties

40. Although their presenting symptoms differ greatly in appearance, a common link between dissociative and somatoform disorders is
    a. both involve memory loss
    b. both require extensive medical treatment
    c. both apparently involve unconscious processes
    d. all of the above

41. In contrast to Freud, contemporary cognitive scientists
    a. do not recognize the existence of unconscious processes
    b. believe that unconscious processes are much less influential in shaping both normal and abnormal behavior
    c. believe that unconscious processes are more influential than conscious processes in shaping both normal and abnormal behavior
    d. have a much less restricted view of unconscious processes and their role in shaping behavior

42. The analogue experiments conducted by Spanos and his colleagues on the symptoms of dissociative identity disorder suggest that
    a. hypnosis had no relationship to the presence of symptoms of this disorder
    b. they disappeared under hypnosis
    c. they can be induced through role-playing and hypnosis
    d. experimental hypnosis increases risk for dissociative identity disorder

43. An example of a sociological theory of the cause of dissociative identity disorder is
    a. it is caused by disturbances in the temporal lobe of the brain
    b. it is caused by a perceptual disturbance that impairs the ability to recognize faces
    c. it is produced by iatrogenesis, specifically, through the leading questions of therapists
    d. it is produced by recovered memories of the loss of a parent

44. Which of the following is not a characteristic of hypnosis?
    a. people vary in how easy they are to hypnotize
    b. some researchers feel that it is simply a social role
    c. it is usually intentionally faked
    d. hypnosis can have powerful effects

UNDERSTANDING RESEARCH
Answers are found at the end of this chapter.

<u>Implicit Memory in Dissociative Identity Disorder:</u> The text presents a detailed description of a study in the Research Close-Up. Finding the answers to these questions will provide you with an understanding of this study and why it is important.

1. There is debate about whether dissociative identity disorder is _____ or real.

   Implicit memory tasks assess subtle mental processes that are _____ to feign.

2. The study used two tasks: reading and rating a set of words and reviewing a series of

   partial but increasingly complete _____ until they were identified. Participants

   later were presented with word _____ corresponding with the earlier words and repeated the partial

   _____.

3. One _____ was primed and the _____ was tested for _____ memory effects.

4. Priming effects in the word test were stronger when they were conducted within the same _____.

   However, there were no differences on the _____ completion task. _____ between personalities

   does occur but is not _____.

SHORT ANSWER
Answer the following short answer questions. Compare your work to the material presented in the text.

1. Briefly describe Posttraumatic Stress Disorder (PTSD). Provide an example of an experience that may result in PTSD and identify the various symptoms that may accompany this disorder.

2. While some professionals believe that multiple personalities are real and more common than previously thought, others believe that the condition is no more than role-playing. Discuss this controversy, citing the research and clinical evidence that supports both points of view.

3. Are recovered memories examples of dissociation or are they produced through the power of suggestion? Defend your position.

4. Review the methodological concerns surrounding the use of retrospective reports. What questions have been raised regarding their reliability and validity? What are the implications of these concerns?

5. If you are a primary care physician with a patient who has a number of vague and inconsistent physical complaints, but an extensive medical evaluation reveals no organic pathology, what types of questions would you consider? How would you approach the treatment of this patient if a diagnosis of somatization disorder was assigned?

ANSWER KEY

MATCHING I

1. k
2. i
3. q
4. d
5. j
6. r
7. p
8. b
9. c
10. v
11. a
12. u
13. n
14. o
15. h
16. f
17. g
18. m
19. s
20. l
21. e
22. t
23. x
24. w

MATCHING II

a. 1
b. 15
c. 11
d. 10
e. 18
f. 22
g. 4
h. 17
i. 5
j. 9
k. 6
l. 19
m. 12
n. 7
o. 20
p. 13
q. 8
r. 16
s. 2
t. 3
u. 21
v. 14
w. 24
x. 23

MATCHING III

1. c
2. e
3. d
4. a
5. b

MULTIPLE CHOICE

1. a	8. a	15. c	22. b	29. c	36. d	43. c
2. d	9. d	16. b	23. d	30. a	37. a	44. c
3. b	10. b	17. d	24. a	31. b	38. b	
4. c	11. c	18. c	25. a	32. a	39. c	
5. b	12. a	19. d	26. b	33. c	40. c	
6. d	13. d	20. d	27. b	34. d	41. b	
7. b	14. a	21. a	28. d	35. b	42. c	

CONCEPT REVIEW

1. re-experiencing, avoidance, and arousal or anxiety
2. dissociative symptoms
3. dissociative
4. numbing of responsiveness
5. startle
6. prevent
7. they defined trauma as outside usual experience but trauma is not that rare
8. war, rape, child sexual abuse, spouse abuse, witnessing disasters
9. false
10. depression, anxiety disorders, substance abuse
11. 10; 5
12. rape
13. more; more
14. high
15. threshold; diathesis-stress; illness
16. higher
17. suppression
18. norepinephrine; opioids
19. less
20. better
21. rape is completed; if they were physically injured; if their life was threatened
22. being wounded; being involved in death of civilians; witnessing atrocities
23. decreases
24. supports
25. all were equally effective
26. reexposure
27. false
28. false
29. true
30. smart; dumb
31. PTSD
32. child sexual abuse
33. dissociative identity
34. suggestion
35. amnesia is absent in the enactment but typical in the disorder
36. conscious; unconscious
37. prospective
38. no
39. a therapist

40. to reintegrate the personalities into one
41. physician
42. fewer
43. hysterectomy
44. young adulthood
45. less
46. women; blacks; less educated
47. depression
48. antisocial personality
49. 25%
50. true

UNDERSTANDING RESEARCH

1. fake; difficult
2. drawings; stems; drawings
3. personality; alter; implicit
4. personality; picture; Amnesia; complete

CROSSWORD

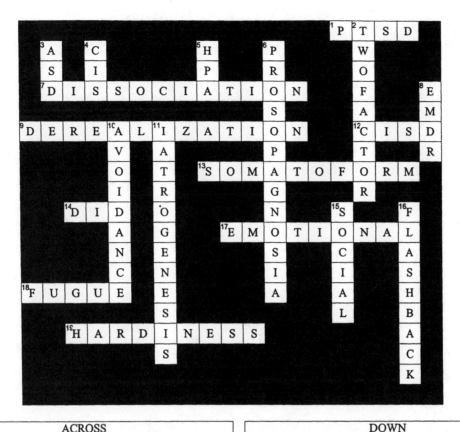

ACROSS		DOWN	
1.	shares symptoms of ASD but is longer lasting or has a delayed onset	2.	theory which combines principles of classical and operant conditioning
7.	disruption of normally integrated mental processes	3.	occurs within four weeks after exposure to traumatic stress
9.	characterized by sense of unreality about oneself	4.	general term referring to normal responses to trauma
12.	critical incident stress debriefing	5.	axis in area of brain known to be stimulated by normal stress
13.	disorders characterized by unusual physical problems occuring in the absence of physical illness	6.	impairment of face recognition
14.	characterized by two or more personalities coexisting within single individual	8.	use of rapid back and forth eye movements to reduce anxiety
17.	type of processing which involves facing fear	10.	symptom of ASD and PTSD which is oftentimes marked or persistent
18.	characterized by inability to recall past, confusion about identity	11.	manufacture of dissociative disorders by their treatment
19.	personal sense of commitment, control, and challenge in facing stress	15.	type of support which plays crucial role in alleviating long term effects of trauma
		16.	sudden memory during which trauma is replayed in images or thoughts

CHAPTER EIGHT

STRESS AND PHYSICAL HEALTH

CHAPTER OUTLINE

Overview
Defining Stress
      Stress as a Life Event
      Stress as an Appraisal of Life Events
Typical Symptoms: Responding to Stress
      Psychophysiological Responses to Stress
      Immune System Responses
      Illness and Chronic Stress
      Coping
      Health Behavior
Classification of Stress and Physical Illness
      Brief Historical Perspective
      Contemporary Approaches
      Illness as a Cause of Stress
The Role of Psychological Factors in Some Familiar Illnesses
      Cancer
      Acquired Immune Deficiency Syndrome (AIDS)
      Pain Management
      Sleep Disorders
Cardiovascular Disease
      Typical Symptoms and Associated Features of Hypertension and CHD
      Classification of CVD
      Epidemiology of CVD
      Etiological Considerations and Research on CVD
      Prevention and Treatment of Cardiovascular Disease
Summary

OBJECTIVES

1. Explain the significance of stress factors in health and illness.
2. Describe the stages of the general adaptation syndrome.
3. Distinguish between several theories of stress and its impact on illness.
4. Define physiological toughness.
5. Distinguish between problem-focused and emotion-focused coping.
6. Describe the emotional, cognitive, and behavioral responses to stress.
7. Understand how stress is used in diagnostic classification.
8. Understand the role of psychological factors in cancer, AIDS, and pain.
9. Distinguish between primary and secondary hypertension.
10. Describe the major causes of primary hypertension.
11. Discuss the impact of low control, high demand job strain.
12. Discuss the relationship between depression, anxiety, and CHD.
13. Describe the major characteristics of Type A personality and its impact on health.
14. Describe the primary preventive, secondary preventive and tertiary preventive treatment approaches to cardiovascular disease.

MATCHING I

Answers are found at the end of this chapter. Match these terms and concepts with the definitions that follow:

a. Stress
b. Traumatic stress
c. Psychosomatic disorders
d. Behavioral medicine
e. Health psychologists
f. General adaptation syndrome
g. Primary appraisal
h. Secondary appraisal
i. Optimism
j. Fight or flight response
k. Sleep terror disorder
l. Sleepwalking disorder
m. Specificity hypothesis
n. Carcinogens
o. Cardiovascular disease (CVD)
p. Hypertension
q. Coronary heart disease (CHD)
r. Myocardial infarction (MI)
s. Systolic blood pressure

1. ____ an individual's cognitive evaluation of the challenge, threat, or harm posed by a particular event
2. ____ a challenging event that requires physiological, cognitive, or behavioral adaptation
3. ____ a disorder involving abrupt awakening and intense autonomic arousal but little memory of a dream and a quick return to sleep
4. ____ a group of diseases of the heart
5. ____ an individual's assessment of his or her abilities and resources for coping with a difficult event
6. ____ a general cognitive style of taking a positive attitude
7. ____ a three-stage model of reaction to stress involving alarm, resistance, and exhaustion
8. ____ a heart attack, the most deadly form of CHD, caused by oxygen deprivation and death of heart muscle tissue
9. ____ stress caused by exposure to catastrophic event involving actual or threatened death to oneself or others
10. ____ high blood pressure
11. ____ a multidisciplinary field including medical and mental health professionals who investigate psychological factors in the symptoms, etiology, and treatment of physical illness
12. ____ specific personality types cause specific psychosomatic diseases
13. ____ the highest blood pressure reading, it is the pressure that the blood exerts against the arteries when the heart is beating
14. ____ a response to threat in which psychophysiological reactions prepare the body to take action against danger
15. ____ a disorder involving rising during sleep and walking about in an unresponsive state with no later memory of the episode
16. ____ a term indicating that physical disease is a product of both the mind and body
17. ____ a group of disorders affecting the heart and circulatory system
18. ____ cancer-causing agents
19. ____ psychologists who specialize in behavioral medicine

MATCHING II

Answers are found at the end of this chapter. Match these terms and concepts with the definitions that follow:

1. Psychoneuroimmunology
2. Glucocorticoids
3. T cells
4. Lymphocytes
5. Antigens
6. Immunosuppression
7. Physiological toughness
8. Problem-focused coping
9. Emotion-focused coping
10. Diastolic blood pressure
11. Angina pectoris
12. Sudden cardiac death
13. Secondary hypertension
14. Essential hypertension
15. Myocardial ischemia
16. Atherosclerosis
17. Coronary occlusion
18. Cardiovascular reactivity
19. Type A behavior pattern
20. AIDS
21. HIV

a. _____ hypertension resulting from a known problem such as a diagnosed kidney or endocrine disorder
b. _____ the decreased production of immune agents, often a result of stress
c. _____ a competitive, hostile, urgent, impatient, achievement-striving style of responding to challenge
d. _____ sudden oxygen deprivation when arteries are completely blocked by fatty deposits or when blood clots make their way to the heart muscle
e. _____ internally oriented coping involving attempts to alter subjective distress
f. _____ a category of white blood cells that fight off antigens
g. _____ a form of high blood pressure where the hypertension is the principal disorder
h. _____ externally-oriented coping that involves attempts to change a stressor
i. _____ temporary oxygen deprivation that accompanies intermittent chest pains which causes no permanent damage
j. _____ a beneficial effect of stress under certain circumstances
k. _____ death within 24 hours of a coronary episode
l. _____ a measure of the intensity of an individual's cardiovascular reactions to stress in the laboratory which predicts future cardiovascular disease
m. _____ a major form of coronary heart disease involving intermittent chest pains brought on by some form of exertion
n. _____ adrenal hormones secreted in response to stress
o. _____ foreign substances like bacteria that invade the body
p. _____ the lowest blood pressure reading, it is the pressure that the blood exerts against the arteries between heartbeats
q. _____ research on the effects of stress on the functioning of the immune system
r. _____ one of the major types of white blood cells of the immune system
s. _____ the thickening of the coronary artery wall as a result of the accumulation of blood lipids with age
t. _____ the virus that causes AIDS
u. _____ an infectious disease which attacks the immune system

MATCHING III

Answers are found at the end of this chapter. Match these terms and concepts with the definitions that follow:

a. Health behavior
b. Primary sleep disorder
c. Dyssomnias
d. Parasomnias
e. Primary insomnia
f. Narcolepsy
g. Breathing-related sleep disorder
h. Circadian rhythm sleep disorder
i. Nightmare disorder
j. Longitudinal study
k. Cross-sectional approach
l. Social ecology
m. Antihypertensives
n. Beta blockers
o. Stress management
p. Biofeedback
q. Role playing
r. Primary hypersomnia
s. Sleep apnea

1. ____ activities essential to promoting good health, such as healthy eating, exercise, and avoidance of unhealthy activities like drug use
2. ____ a disorder involving frequent awakening to alertness by terrifying dreams
3. ____ disorders characterized by abnormal events that occur during sleep, like nightmares
4. ____ the interrelations between the individual and the social world
5. ____ the disruption of sleep due to breathing problems such as sleep apnea, the temporary obstruction of the respiratory airway
6. ____ a treatment to teach more effective coping skills, reduce adverse reactions to stress and improve health behavior
7. ____ medications effective in reducing high blood pressure
8. ____ a type of research design in which subjects are studied over time, allowing researchers to make inferences about causation
9. ____ drugs that reduce the risk of myocardial infarction of sudden coronary death
10. ____ irresistible attacks of refreshing sleep
11. ____ a mismatch between the patient's twenty four hour sleeping patterns and their 24-hour life demands
12. ____ a condition where sleeping disturbance is the primary complaint
13. ____ a technique used in therapy of improvisational play acting to teach patients how to respond to stressful interactions with less hostility
14. ____ problems in the amount, quality, or timing of sleep
15. ____ a treatment using equipment to monitor physiological processes and provide the patient with feedback about them to help patients gain conscious control over them
16. ____ research design in which subjects are studied at one point in time
17. ____ excessive sleepiness characterized by prolonged or daytime sleep which interferes with functioning
18. ____ difficulties initiating or maintaining sleep, or poor quality of sleeping
19. ____ a sleep disorder caused by temporary obstruction of the airway

MATCHING IV
Answers are found at the end of this chapter. Match these names with the descriptions of their contributions to the study of abnormal psychology:

    a. Richard Lazarus   b. Hans Selye   c. Walter Cannon

1. ____ defined stress in terms of the general adaptation syndrome; did research on animal analogue studies of the GAS
2. ____ argued that stress is not just a stimulus but also the individual's response to the stimulus, specifically their cognitive appraisal of the event as being potentially harmful and exceeding their coping resources
3. ____ one of the first researchers to conduct systematic studies of stress; interested in the fight or flight response

CONCEPT REVIEW
Answers are found at the end of this chapter. After you have read and reviewed the material, test your comprehension by filling in the blanks or circling the correct answer.

1. Stress can be produced by daily _____ as well as by traumatic events.
2. Scientists used to think that psychological factors were **important/irrelevant** in most physical illnesses; today they think they are **important/irrelevant**.
3. The Diagnostic and Statistical Manual no longer contains a list of psychosomatic disorders because _____.
4. Holmes and Rahe developed the Social Readjustment Rating Scale, an attempt to measure the amount of _____ caused by various life events.
5. List three criticisms of the Social Readjustment Rating Scale: _____, _____, and _____
6. What are the three stages of the GAS? _____, _____, and _____
7. One problem with Lazarus' approach to defining stress is that it runs the risk of being tautological, or _____.
8. The fight or flight response is _____ in the modern world.
9. Research indicates that optimism **is/is not** linked to better health habits and less illness.
10. An analogy for **Cannon's/Selye's** theory is a car in which the engine continues to race instead of idling down after running fast, and an analogy for **Cannon's/Selye's** theory is a car that has run out of gas and is damaged because stress keeps turning the key, trying to restart the engine.
11. Another mechanism whereby stress may cause physical illness is the stress response sapping _____ away from routine bodily functions.
12. Stress weakens immune functioning: **true**   **false**

13. In one study with newly married couples, partners who were more _____ during discussions of marital problems showed greater immunosuppression during the next 24 hours.
14. From an evolutionary perspective, heightened immune functioning is **adaptive/maladaptive** in response to immediate threat.
15. One theory indicates that the moderate release of **betablockers/epinephrine and norepinephrine** serves to protect the body from depletion under future, more intense stress, a process called physiological toughness.
16. People who repress their anxiety show fewer psychophysiological reactions to stress:
      true   false
17. Predictability of a stressor **improves/impairs** our ability to cope with it.
18. Rats who can stop a shock by pressing a bar experience a bigger stress response than rats who receive an identical shock but don't have to worry about stopping it: **true   false**
19. One pathway that may explain how stress and illness are linked is that stress can reduce people's _____.
20. The more a stressed monkey can interact with other monkeys, the less immunosuppression it demonstrates:
      true   false
21. Stress can cause illness, but illness can also cause _____.
22. Modern research supports the specificity hypothesis, that certain personality types are more prone to certain psychosomatic illnesses: **true   false**
23. Why does the DSM-IV-TR not include the rating system for severity of stressors that was included in DSM-III and DSM-III-R? _____.
24. Cancer deaths have risen substantially over the past 30 years: **true   false**
25. Cancer is the leading cause of death today: **true   false**
26. Stress can directly affect the body's ability to fight cancer cells: **true   false**
27. Psychological treatments, such as structured self-help groups, have unfortunately not been shown to be effective in reducing the death rate among cancer patients:
      true   false
28. The prevalence of HIV/AIDS is particularly high on which continent? _____.
29. Most users of injection drugs are **white/black**.
30. Needle sharing in poor urban neighborhoods is a substantial contributor to the spread of HIV among minorities: **true   false**
31. Programs to educate the public about the transmission of HIV are quite effective in changing risky behaviors related to transmission: **true   false**

32. A wide range of treatments, such as biofeedback, hypnosis, relaxation training, and cognitive therapy are quite useful in eliminating chronic pain: **true   false**

33. Cardiovascular disease is the third leading cause of death in the United States: **true   false**

34. Why is hypertension called the "silent killer?" _____

35. The rate of death due to CVD has decreased in the United States in recent years: **true   false**

36. Where has the rate of death due to CVD increased? _____

37. Who are more likely to suffer from CHD? **men   women**

38. Who are more likely to suffer from CHD? **whites   blacks**

39. Which of the following are not among the risk factors for CHD?
    drinking   smoking   obesity   a fatty diet

40. Hypertension is twice as common among blacks, but black men living in high-stress neighborhoods had four times the risk for hypertension: **true   false**

41. Rats with a genetic predisposition to develop hypertension do so only when exposed to salty diets or environmental stress: **true   false**

42. The Los Angeles earthquake was linked to **higher/lower** levels of cardiac deaths.

43. Job strain involves a situation with **high/low** psychological demand with **high/low** decisional control.

44. The number of _____ a woman has, increases her risk for heart disease if she works but not if she is a homemaker.

45. The key feature of the Type A behavior pattern in predicting CHD is _____.

46. Depression **is/is not** correlated with CHD.

47. People exposed to an experimental media campaign to improve knowledge and change behavior related to CHD risk factors changed their behaviors relating to _____ but not _____.

48. The only two treatment conditions that lowered blood pressure in a study comparing weight reduction, salt reduction, stress management, calcium supplement, magnesium supplement, potassium supplement, and fish oil supplement, were: _____.

CROSSWORD

Answers are found at the end of this chapter. Complete the following crossword puzzle to reinforce your understanding of this chapter's key terms and concepts:

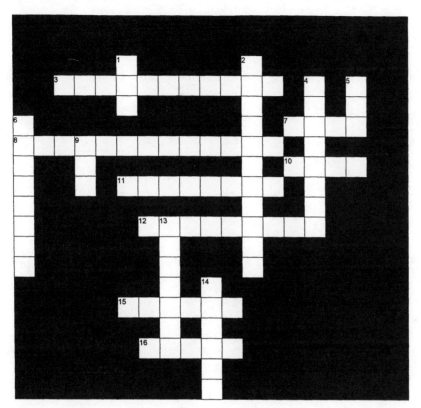

ACROSS

3. white blood cells
7. scale developed by Holmes and Rahe
8. disorders which are a product of the mind and body
10. caused by HIV
11. foreign substances, such as bacteria, which invade the body
12. cognitive evaluation
15. psychologists who specialize in behavioral medicine
16. behavior pattern characterized by hostility, impatience, sense of urgency

DOWN

1. axis within the brain which is activated by stress
2. responding to threat with social affiliation
4. stress hormone
5. consists of alarm, resistance, exhaustion
6. key to effective coping with stress
9. group of disorders that affect circulatory system
13. sleep disorders where difficulty in sleeping is the principle complaint
14. requires physiological, cognitive, behavioral adaptation

MULTIPLE CHOICE

Answers are found at the end of this chapter. The multiple choice questions listed will test your understanding of the material presented in the chapter. Read through each question and circle the letter representing the best answer.

1. All of the following are criticisms of the Holmes and Rahe Social Re-Adjustment Rating Scale except
    a. the inclusion of both positive and negative events as stressors
    b. failure to distinguish between transient and chronic life events
    c. a given stressor does not always produce the same number of life change units for all individuals in all situations
    d. all of the above are criticisms of this scale

2. Generally, hypertension is defined by a systolic blood pressure of above _____ and a diastolic blood pressure of above _____.
    a. 110; 60
    b. 120; 70
    c. 130; 80
    d. 140; 90

3. According to Walter Cannon, _____ is the mobilization of the body in reaction to a perceived threat.
    a. stage of alarm
    b. generalized arousal
    c. emergency response
    d. physiological toughness

4. Which of the following is not a reaction of the body to sympathetic nervous system arousal?
    a. heart rate increases
    b. blood pressure rises
    c. blood sugar lowers
    d. respiration rate increases

5. Although somewhat stressful, _____ decreases negative responding to an actual stressor.
    a. predictability
    b. anticipation
    c. control
    d. appraisal

6. Anxiety, depression, and _____ are considered to be the primary affective responses to stressors.
    a. anger
    b. tension
    c. an upset stomach
    d. aggression

7. Stress plays a role in
    a. all physical disorders
    b. some physical disorders
    c. only heart disease
    d. no physical disorders

122

8. _____ of all deaths from CHD occur within 24 hours of a coronary event.
   a. One-quarter
   b. One-half
   c. One-third
   d. Two-thirds

9. Which would have the greatest risk for suffering from high blood pressure?
   a. African-American male who is homeless
   b. White male who is a stock broker
   c. African-American female who is an attorney
   d. White female who is a homemaker

10. This uses laboratory equipment to monitor physiological processes that generally occur outside of conscious awareness to help individuals learn how to control their autonomic nervous system functions voluntarily.
    a. biofeedback
    b. stress management
    c. systematic desensitization
    d. flooding

11. _____ is the most important goal of intervention with cardiovascular disease.
    a. Medication
    b. Prevention
    c. Psychotherapy
    d. Education

12. According to the Social Re-Adjustment Rating Scale, _____ is the most significant life event that constitutes the greatest number of life change units.
    a. pregnancy
    b. divorce
    c. foreclosure of a mortgage or loan
    d. death of one's spouse

13. Psychoneuroimmunology refers to the study of
    a. decreased production of T cells and other immune agents
    b. inhibition and destruction of various immune agents
    c. the effects of stress on the functioning of the immune system
    d. white blood cells that fight off foreign substances that invade the body

14. Psychologists in this field define disease as "dis-ease," indicating that illness is a departure not only from adaptive biological functioning but also from adaptive social and psychological functioning.
    a. biopsychosocial psychology
    b. behavioral psychology
    c. health psychology
    d. dynamic psychology

15. Which is not a method of transmitting HIV?
    a. donating blood
    b. sharing needles
    c. sexual intercourse
    d. mother to fetus

16. According to the Framingham Study, which was reviewed in your textbook, which of the following is most likely to suffer from heart disease?
    a. a woman who is a homemaker and has two children
    b. a woman who is a homemaker and has four children
    c. a woman who is a sales manager and has two children
    d. a woman who is a waitress and has four children

17. This term indicates that physical disease is a product of both the mind and body.
    a. somatoform
    b. cognitive error
    c. dissociation
    d. psychosomatic

18. All of the following are examples of cognitive responses to stress with the exception of
    a. control
    b. repression
    c. appraisal
    d. predictability

UNDERSTANDING RESEARCH
Answers are found at the end of this chapter.

<u>Disclosure of Trauma and Immunity</u>: The text presents a detailed description of a study in the Research Close-Up. Finding the answers to these questions will provide an understanding of this study and why it is important.

1. Subjects were asked to write about _____ events in their lives for _____ consecutive days, especially things they _____. A control group wrote about _____ topics for four days. All writing took place in the _____. There was a total of _____ subjects.

2. Dependent variables included self-reported mood _____ and _____ writing, measures of _____ arousal, such as blood pressure and heart rate, and _____ assays of blood before the study, _____ afterwards, and _____ weeks later.

3. Evaluations by researchers of what the students wrote about confirmed that they had written about _____ experiences, such as serious _____ conflict. Immediately after writing, subjects in the experimental group were more _____ than those in the control group. However, they had significantly fewer visits to the _____ and better _____ responses over the next six weeks. No differences were found on the measures of _____. If they wrote about previously _____ events they showed better _____ pressure and immunological functioning.

SHORT ANSWER

Answer the following short answer questions. Compare your work to the material presented in the text.

1. Discuss Holmes and Rahe's Social Re-Adjustment Rating Scale. What is a life change unit? What are the strengths of this scale? What are the criticisms of this scale? How would you change this scale to address some of these criticisms?

2. Discuss Selye's and Cannon's approaches to studying stress. In what ways are they similar? In what ways do they differ?

3. Discuss the implications of considering cardiovascular disease a lifestyle disease. How has health psychology addressed this issue?

4. Discuss the characteristics of a longitudinal research design. What are its advantages and disadvantages?

ANSWER KEY

MATCHING I

1. g
2. a
3. k
4. q
5. h
6. i
7. f
8. r
9. b
10. p

11. d
12. m
13. s
14. j
15. l
16. c
17. o
18. n
19. e

MATCHING II

a. 13
b. 6
c. 19
d. 17
e. 9
f. 4
g. 14
h. 8
i. 15
j. 7
k. 12

l. 18
m. 11
n. 2
o. 5
p. 10
q. 1
r. 3
s. 16
t. 21
u. 20

MATCHING III

1. a	11. h
2. i	12. b
3. d	13. q
4. l	14. c
5. g	15. p
6. o	16. k
7. m	17. r
8. j	18. e
9. n	19. s
10. f	

MATCHING IV

1. b   2. a   3. c

MULTIPLE CHOICE

1.	d	4.	c	7.	a	10.	a	13.	c	16. d
2.	d	5.	a	8.	d	11.	b	14.	c	17. d
3.	c	6.	a	9.	a	12.	d	15.	a	18. b

CONCEPT REVIEW

1. hassles
2. irrelevant; important
3. all illnesses are now seen as psychosomatic
4. stress
5. doesn't account for different ages and backgrounds; includes positive life changes; doesn't consider different meanings for different people
6. alarm, resistance, exhaustion
7. circular
8. maladaptive
9. is
10. Cannon's; Selye's
11. energy
12. true
13. hostile or negative
14. maladaptive
15. epinephrine and norepinephrine
16. false
17. improves
18. false
19. health behaviors
20. true
21. stress
22. false
23. the ratings were unreliable
24. true
25. false
26. true
27. false
28. Africa
29. white
30. true
31. false
32. false
33. false
34. it has no symptoms
35. true
36. Eastern Europe
37. men
38. blacks
39. drinking
40. true
41. true
42. higher
43. high; low
44. children
45. hostility
46. is
47. diet; smoking
48. weight and salt reduction

UNDERSTANDING RESEARCH

1. traumatic; 4; had never told anyone about; trivial; laboratory; 50

2. before; after; autonomic; immunological; immediately; 6

3. upsetting; family; upset; student health center; immune; autonomic arousal; undisclosed; blood

CROSSWORD

ACROSS		DOWN	
3. white blood cells	16. behavior pattern characterized by hostility, impatience, sense of urgency	1. axis within the brain which is activated by stress	14. requires physiological, cognitive, behavioral adaptation
7. scale developed by Holmes and Rahe		2. responding to threat with social affiliation	
8. disorders which are a product of the mind and body		4. stress hormone	
10. caused by HIV		5. consists of alarm, resistance, exhaustion	
11. foreign substances, such as bacteria, which invade the body		6. key to effective coping with stress	
12. cognitive evaluation		9. group of disorders that affect circulatory system	
15. psychologists who specialize in behavioral medicine		13. sleep disorders where difficulty in sleeping is the principle complaint	

CHAPTER NINE

PERSONALITY DISORDERS

CHAPTER OUTLINE

Overview
Typical Symptoms and Associated Features
    Social Motivation
    Temperament and Personality Traits
    Context and Personality
Classification
    Cluster A: Paranoid, Schizoid, and Schizotypal Personality Disorders
    Cluster B: Antisocial, Borderline, Histrionic, and Narcissistic Personality Disorders
    Cluster C: Avoidant, Dependent, and Obsessive-Compulsive Personality Disorders
    Personality Disorders Not Otherwise Specified (PD NOS)
    A Dimensional Perspective on Personality Disorders
Epidemiology
    Prevalence in Community and Clinical Samples
    Gender Differences
    Stability of Personality Disorders Over Time
    Culture and Personality
Schizotypal Personality Disorder (SPD)
    Brief Historical Perspective
    Clinical Features and Comorbidity
    Etiological Considerations
    Treatment
Borderline Personality Disorder (BPD)
    Brief Historical Perspective
    Clinical Features and Comorbidity
    Etiological Considerations
    Treatment
Antisocial Personality Disorder (ASPD)
    Brief Historical Perspective
    Clinical Features and Comorbidity
    Etiological Considerations
    Treatment
Dependent Personality Disorder (DPD)
    Brief Historical Perspective
    Clinical Features and Comorbidity
    Etiological Considerations
    Treatment
Summary

OBJECTIVES

1. Distinguish between ego-syntonic and ego-dystonic and the implications for the assessment of personality disorders.
2. Define temperament and personality. Explain the relevance of these concepts to the study of personality disorders.
3. Discuss the categorization of personality disorders.
4. Distinguish between avoidant and dependent personality disorders.
5. Discuss prevalence rates for several personality disorders.
6. Describe the clinical features of schizotypal personality disorder, borderline personality disorder, and antisocial personality disorder.
7. Discuss treatment options for personality disorders.

MATCHING I

Answers are found at the end of this chapter. Match these terms and concepts with the definitions that follow:

a. Personality
b. Temperament
c. Extraversion
d. Openness to experience
e. Dependent personality disorder
f. Ego-dystonic
g. Ego-syntonic
h. Primary process thinking
i. Splitting
j. Impulse control disorders
k. Intermittent explosive disorder
l. Pyromania
m. Kleptomania
n. Schizophrenic phenotype

1. ____ characteristic styles of relating to the world; evident in first years of life
2. ____ enduring patterns of perceiving, relating to, and thinking about the environment and oneself; displayed in a wide range of important social and personal contexts
3. ____ the idea that the symptoms of schizotypal personality disorder is seen among people who possess the genotype that makes them vulnerable to schizophrenia
4. ____ out of proportion aggressive behaviors resulting in serious assault or destruction of property
5. ____ stealing objects even though they are not needed or beneficial
6. ____ a dimension of personality describing a person's willingness to consider and explore new ideas, feelings, and activities
7. ____ symptoms that the person is distressed by and uncomfortable with
8. ____ the tendency to see people and events alternatively as all good or all bad
9. ____ disorders characterized by failure to resist a temptation to perform some pleasurable or tension-relieving act that is harmful to self or others
10. ____ where the id relieves tensions by imagining the things it desires
11. ____ a dimension of personality describing a person's activity level, especially interest in interacting with others, and the ease of expressing positive emotions
12. ____ deliberate and purposive fire setting accompanied by fascination with fire; not for personal gain
13. ____ symptoms that are comfortable and acceptable to the person
14. ____ an enduring pattern of dependent and submissive behavior

MATCHING II

Answers are found at the end of this chapter. Match these terms and concepts with the definitions that follow:

1. Agreeableness
2. Conscientiousness
3. Culture
4. Cross-cultural psychology
5. Paranoid personality disorder
6. Schizoid personality disorder
7. Schizotypal personality disorder
8. Borderline personality disorder
9. Histrionic personality disorder
10. Avoidant personality disorder
11. Trichotillomania
12. Pathological gambling
13. Dialectical behavior therapy
14. Psychopathy
15. Adolescence-limited antisocial behavior
16. Life-course-persistent antisocial behavior
17. Adoptees
18. Affiliation

a. ___ an enduring pattern of thinking and behavior characterized by excessive emotionality and attention seeking
b. ___ the scientific study of ways that human behavior and mental processes are influenced by social and cultural factors
c. ___ an enduring pattern of thinking and behavior whose primary feature is a pervasive instability of mood, self-image, and interpersonal relationships
d. ___ another term for antisocial personality disorder
e. ___ the shared way of life of a group of people
f. ___ a common form of social behavior that is often adaptive and disappears by adulthood
g. ___ people separated from their biological parents at an early age and raised by adoptive parents
h. ___ an enduring pattern of thinking and behavior characterized by a pervasive tendency to be inappropriately suspicious of motives and behaviors of others
i. ___ an enduring pattern of thinking and behaving characterized by pervasive social discomfort, fear of negative evaluation, and timidity
j. ___ pulling out one's hair, resulting in noticeable hair loss
k. ___ an approach to psychotherapy with borderline patients
l. ___ an enduring pattern of thinking and behavior characterized by pervasive indifference to interacting with others and a diminished range of emotional experience and expression
m. ___ a dimension of personality describing willingness to cooperate and empathize with others
n. ___ antisocial behavior that spans a person's life
o. ___ desire for close relationships
p. ___ a dimension of personality describing the person's persistence in the pursuit of goals, ability to organize activities, and dependability
q. ___ repeated maladaptive gambling despite repeated efforts to stop
r. ___ an enduring pattern of discomfort with other people coupled with peculiar thinking and behavior, which takes the form of perceptual and cognitive disturbances

MATCHING III
Answers are found at the end of this chapter. Match these names with the descriptions of their contributions to the study of abnormal psychology:

a. Cleckley c. Gunderson e. Robins
b. Kernberg d. Akiskal f. Moffitt

1. ___ furthered the psychodynamic view of borderline personality disorder by developing reliable, descriptive terms to allow reliable diagnosis
2. ___ advocates a psychodynamic theory of borderline personality disorder focusing on the faulty development of ego structure
3. ___ proposed that there are two forms of antisocial behavior
4. ___ wrote early descriptions of psychopathy
5. ___ argued that borderline personality disorder is not a meaningful diagnostic category but a heterogeneous collection of symptoms that are associated with mild forms of brain dysfunction
6. ___ conducted a longitudinal study showing the stability of antisocial behavior of boys into adulthood

CONCEPT REVIEW
Answers are found at the end of this chapter. After you have read and reviewed the material, test your comprehension by filling in the blanks or circling the correct answer.

1. People with personality disorders are especially likely to seek psychological treatment:

    true   **false**

2. What are some reasons why personality disorders are controversial among professionals?
   _____

3. The personality disorders are listed on Axis ___ of DSM-IV-TR.

4. Personality disorders are usually ego-**syntonic/dystonic**.

5. Why are self-report measures limited in assessing personality disorders? _____

6. Which of the following is not a dimension of temperament?

    irritability   wealth   activity level   fearfulness

7. Under what circumstances could a difficult temperament be adaptive for an infant?
   _____

8. Cultures differ in displays of _____ and in how much they value individualism versus _____.

9. Typologies of personality are likely to be **limited to the culture in which they are developed/applicable across many different cultures.**

10. The behavior of people who fit Cluster ___ is typically anxious and fearful.

11. The behavior of people who fit Cluster ___ is typically odd, eccentric, or asocial.

12. The behavior of people who fit Cluster ___ is typically dramatic, emotional, or erratic.

13. Only criminals meet the diagnostic requirements for antisocial personality disorder:

    true   **false**

14. There may be an etiological link between histrionic and _____ personality disorders; both reflect a common, underlying tendency toward lack of inhibition and both form shallow, intense relationships with others.
15. One of the advantages of a categorical system over a dimensional system of personality diagnosis is that it provides a more complete description of each person: **true   false**
16. The DSM-IV-TR uses a **categorical/dimensional** system with personality disorders.
17. The overall lifetime prevalence for having any type of personality disorder is:

    1-2%   10-14%   25-30%   46-50%
18. Which personality disorder appears to be the least common? _____
19. Very few people who meet the criteria for one personality disorder also meet the criteria for another personality disorder: **true   false**
20. Which personality disorder is most likely to be represented in inpatient and outpatient treatment settings? _____
21. Borderline personality disorder is more common among **men/women**; antisocial personality disorder is more common among **men/women**; and dependent personality disorder is more common among **men/women**.
22. Some critics argue that criteria for personality disorders are unfairly biased against traditionally **masculine/feminine** traits.
23. People diagnosed with borderline personality disorder as a young adult are **more/less** likely to still qualify for the diagnosis in their fifties than people diagnosed with schizotypal or schizoid personality disorders.
24. Research indicates that schizotypal personality disorder is genetically related to schizophrenia:

    true   false
25. When people with personality disorders appear for psychological treatment, it is usually because _____.
26. Research has shown that low doses of antipsychotic medications are effective in alleviating symptoms of schizotypal personality disorder: **true   false**
27. The difference between impulsive and compulsive behavior is that the original goal for impulsive behavior is to experience _____ while for compulsive behavior it is to avoid _____.
28. Borderline personality disorder is often comorbid with what Axis I disorder? _____
29. Borderline personality disorder patients have often had problematic relationships with their _____.
30. Patients in dialectical behavior therapy for borderline personality disorder are less likely to _____.
31. There is no evidence that psychotropic medication is effective for borderline personality disorder:

    true   false
32. Which personality disorder has been studied the most? _____

33. The DSM-IV-TR category of antisocial personality disorder does not include traits relating to _____ that the Cleckley description included.

34. The expression of antisocial personality is likely to _____ as the person ages.

35. Research indicates that antisocial behavior is caused by both _____ and _____.

36. In one study of adoptees, being raised in an adverse home environment **did/did not** increase the likelihood of antisocial behavior among children with antisocial biological parents; being raised in an adverse home environment **did/did not** increase the likelihood of antisocial behavior among children with nonantisocial biological parents.

37. Children raised in families with inconsistent or absent _____ were more likely to be antisocial as adults.

38. Children with difficult temperaments due to genetic predisposition to antisocial behavior may induce their parents to _____.

39. There is research evidence that antisocial people lack _____, an emotion that normal people have.

40. Some researchers argue that lack of _____ and pathological egocentricity are more important than low anxiety in understanding antisocial personality disorder.

41. Research shows that experiencing physical abuse in childhood increases risk for _____ personality disorder in adulthood.

42. Research shows that experiencing sexual abuse in childhood increases risk for _____ personality disorder in adulthood.

43. Several forms of treatment have been shown to be effective with antisocial personality disorder:

                true   **false**

44. People with borderline personality disorder become enraged and manipulative and people with dependent personality disorder become clingy and submissive when threatened with _____.

45. What type of parents are likely to foster dependency in their children? _____

CROSSWORD

Answers are found at the end of this chapter. Complete the following crossword puzzle to reinforce your understanding of this chapter's key terms and concepts:

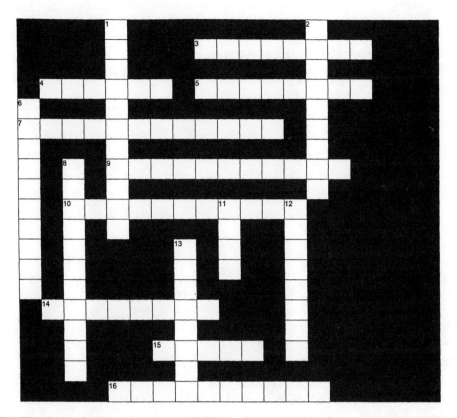

ACROSS

3. includes people who often appear dramatic, emotional, or erratic
4. refers to a person's desires or goals
5. includes people who often appear anxious or fearful
7. personality disorder characterized by pervasive pattern of grandiosity
9. a person's most basic style of relating to the world
10. perceiving one's feelings as natural part of one's self
14. personality disorder characterized by suspiciousness
15. desire for impact, prestige, dominance
16. personality disorder characterized by pervasive pattern of instability in mood and relationships

DOWN

1. desire for close relationships with others
2. personality disorder characterized by pattern of submissive and clinging behavior
6. personality disorder characterized by pattern of irresponsible and antisocial behavior
8. impulse control disorder involving the stealing of objects
11. personality disorder characterized by pattern of orderliness, perfectionism, and control
12. includes people who often appear odd or eccentric
13. personality disorder characterized by pervasive patterns of indifference

MULTIPLE CHOICE

Answers are found at the end of this chapter. The multiple choice questions listed will test your understanding of the material presented in the chapter. Read through each question and circle the letter representing the best answer.

1. John is always on the lookout for potential harm. He has difficulty trusting anyone, even family members, and is consistently suspicious of their motives. He is oversensitive to minor events, reading into them ulterior meanings. His manner of relating to people has caused him problems at work and home. What type of personality disorder does John likely have?
    a. schizoid
    b. obsessive-compulsive
    c. antisocial
    d. paranoid

2. The overall lifetime prevalence of personality disorders is approximately
    a. 5 - 9%
    b. 10-14%
    c. 15 - 19%
    d. 20 - 24%

3. Which is a criterion used in DSM-IV-TR to define personality disorders?
    a. the person must be aware of how his or her behavior is maladaptive
    b. the person's behavior must be rigid and inflexible
    c. the person's behavior must cause legal problems
    d. the person's behavioral difficulties must have started in childhood

4. Which of the following statements represents an approach that has been used to conceptualize personality disorders?
    a. they are types of personality styles that are closely associated with specific forms of adult psychopathology
    b. they result from problems in childhood development as conceptualized by psychodynamic theories
    c. they are manifestations of the presence of specific psychological deficits
    d. all of the above

5. The Axis I disorder most often diagnosed with borderline personality disorder is
    a. depression
    b. substance abuse
    c. anxiety
    d. sexual dysfunction

6. According to the DSM-IV-TR, an important characteristic of personality disorders is
    a. they are typically experienced as ego-syntonic
    b. the impairment associated with these disorders is more severe than is found in other forms of mental disorder
    c. there is considerable overlap across diagnostic categories
    d. obsessive-compulsive personality disorder demonstrates the greatest amount of overlap with other personality disorders

7. Research focusing on relationships among personality disorders suggests that
    a. there is little diagnostic overlap across all personality disorder categories
    b. histrionic personality disorder demonstrates the least amount of diagnostic overlap with other personality disorder categories
    c. there is considerable overlap across diagnostic categories
    d. obsessive-compulsive personality disorder demonstrates the greatest amount of overlap with other personality disorders

8. The most common personality disorder in both inpatient and outpatient settings is
    a. dependent
    b. antisocial
    c. borderline
    d. paranoid

9. Which statement is correct regarding treatment of personality disorders?
    a. people with personality disorders benefit most from insight-oriented therapy
    b. people with personality disorders who present for treatment often do so because they have another type of mental disorder such as depression
    c. people with personality disorders benefit most from antipsychotic drugs
    d. people with personality disorders who present for treatment usually remain in treatment until it is completed

10. The Axis I disorder most often diagnosed along with antisocial personality disorder is
    a. dissociative fugue
    b. depression
    c. schizophrenia
    d. substance abuse

11. Which is considered the primary feature of borderline personality disorder?
    a. consistent instability in self-image, mood, and interpersonal relationships
    b. extreme social anxiety
    c. consistent disregard for authority figures
    d. extreme fear of rejection from others

12. About _____ of people with personality disorders do not seek treatment.
    a. 40%
    b. 60%
    c. 80%
    d. 95%

13. Warren is definitely a loner. He has no close friends and appears to be indifferent to relationships. Other people would describe Warren as distant and aloof. In addition, Warren reports that he does not feel strongly about anything. He can't think of anything that really makes him excited, but he doesn't get upset or distressed about anything either. Warren might qualify for which of the following personality disorders?
    a. borderline
    b. schizoid
    c. paranoid
    d. narcissistic

14. Which of the following has not been a proposed explanation for the etiology of borderline personality disorder?
    a. early substance abuse
    b. negative consequences resulting from parental loss during childhood
    c. a history of physical and sexual abuse
    d. problematic relationships with parents

15. Personality disorders are listed on which axis of DSM-IV-TR?
    a. I
    b. II
    c. III
    d. IV

16. Which statement regarding gender differences in personality disorders is correct?
    a. antisocial personality disorder is more frequently diagnosed in women
    b. men seek treatment for their personality disorders more often than women
    c. the overall prevalence of personality disorders is about equal in men and women
    d. histrionic personality disorder is more likely to be diagnosed in men

17. Which of the following would not be considered a characteristic feature of antisocial personality disorder?
    a. emotional instability
    b. failure to conform to social norms
    c. deceitfulness
    d. irritability and aggressiveness

18. Mary reports that she feels lonely and isolated. Although she has good relations with family members, she is so afraid of negative criticism from others that she tends to distance herself from relationships. She desperately wants to make friends, but is afraid of being rejected. She constantly watches for even minimal signs of disapproval. Which personality disorder diagnosis is most appropriate for Mary?
    a. schizoid
    b. histrionic
    c. narcissistic
    d. avoidant

19. An advantage of a dimensional system of classifying personality disorders is
    a. it eliminates the need for diagnosis
    b. personality disorders are more reliably assessed
    c. it is more useful for those individuals whose symptoms and behaviors fall on the boundaries between different personality disorder diagnoses
    d. it requires less time to arrive at a diagnosis

20. Studies investigating the long-term course of antisocial personality disorder indicate that
    a. antisocial individuals tend to become more careless as they grow older, resulting in increasing numbers of arrests
    b. antisocial individuals continue their criminal activity well into middle age
    c. antisocial individuals reform their behavior after several incarcerations
    d. people exhibiting antisocial behavior tend to "burn out" when they reach middle age

21. According to the five-factor model of personality, the willingness to cooperate and empathize with other people is the trait referred to as
    a. conscientiousness
    b. affiliation
    c. agreeableness
    d. cooperativeness

22. Larry has extreme difficulty making decisions on his own. He tends to cling to other people and continually asks them for assistance in making even minor decisions. In addition, he constantly asks for his friends' advice and wants to be reassured about everything, even his ability to be a friend. A possible diagnosis for Larry is
    a. dependent personality disorder
    b. avoidant personality disorder
    c. narcissistic personality disorder
    d. borderline personality disorder

23. Individual psychotherapy with borderline patients can be difficult because
    a. borderline patients frequently cannot afford the cost of such treatment
    b. borderline patients are often so transient that it is difficult for them to remain in treatment for more than a brief period of time
    c. maintaining the type of concentration necessary for individual therapy is particularly difficult for such patients
    d. establishing and maintaining the type of close relationship necessary between therapist and patient is particularly difficult for borderlines

24. The personality disorders listed in DSM-IV-TR are divided into how many clusters?
    a. 2
    b. 3
    c. 4
    d. 5

25. Research on the genetics of antisocial personality disorder suggests which of the following statements?
    a. genetic and environmental factors combine to produce criminal behavior
    b. the presence of any type of genetic factor in the production of antisocial behavior is dubious
    c. without the presence of genetic factors, environmental factors alone can never predict the development of criminal behavior
    d. environmental factors are much more important than genetic factors in the production of criminal behavior

26. Sally takes pride in efficient performance and rational behavior. While others see her as rigid, perfectionistic, inflexible, and judgmental, Sally believes that others simply do not share the same standards and are not worthy of her high opinion. She does not show affection and finds 'mushy' feelings in others distasteful. Which personality disorder might Sally be diagnosed with?
    a. schizotypal
    b. antisocial
    c. obsessive-compulsive
    d. schizoid

27. Which statement regarding treatment of antisocial personalities is correct?
    a. treatment is usually successful if the individual does not have a history of legal difficulties
    b. currently the best treatment available for this disorder is family therapy
    c. approximately two-thirds of individuals with this disorder show clinical improvement if treated with psychodynamic therapy
    d. the presence of depression in people with this disorder may be associated with a better prognosis for treatment for this disorder

UNDERSTANDING RESEARCH
Answers are found at the end of this chapter.

<u>Stability of Personality Disorders in Adolescents:</u> The text presents a detailed description of a study in the Research Close-Up. Finding the answers to these questions will provide an understanding of this study and why it is important.

1. The researchers wanted to know how _____ adolescents had personality disorders and whether they kept them over time. The subjects were selected from a _____ sample of more than _____ families with one or more children between the ages of _____ and 21. _____ child from each family could participate. The families were representative of the general population in terms of _____. Half the subjects were _____ and the average age was _____. How many families were not intact? _____

2. Was the study cross-sectional or longitudinal? _____ Information was collected by asking _____ and _____ about the adolescent's behavior in interviews and _____. Based on this data, adolescents were diagnosed as having a moderate or severe form of _____. What percent had at least one personality disorder? _____ What percent had a severe one? _____ What was the most common moderate personality disorder? _____ What was the most common severe one? _____

3. What was the one significant sex difference? _____ Was this expected or unexpected? _____ What was the age that most adolescents had a personality disorder? _____ How many teens who had a diagnosis at Time I had one at Time II? _____ The most persistent types were paranoid, obsessive-compulsive, borderline, and _____.

4. What are the implications of this study? _____

SHORT ANSWER
Answer the following short answer questions. Compare your work to the material presented in the text.

1. Describe the five-factor model of personality. What are the five factors and their definitions? What would be characteristics of low and high scorers on these traits?

2. Discuss the problems associated with the treatment of individuals with personality disorders. Why is a poor prognosis for treatment associated with most of these disorders? What treatment approaches seem most promising to you?

3. Review the controversies that surround the issue of stability of personality. What methods have been used to demonstrate stable traits? What do you think are methodological limitations of these approaches?

4. Do you believe personality disorders should be classified using a dimensional or categorical approach? Why?

5. Discuss the importance of cross-cultural research. Provide an example.

ANSWER KEY

MATCHING I

1. b
2. a
3. n
4. k
5. m
6. d
7. f
8. i
9. j
10. h
11. c
12. l
13. g
14. e

MATCHING II

a. 9
b. 4
c. 8
d. 14
e. 3
f. 15
g. 17
h. 5
i. 10
j. 11
k. 13
l. 6
m. 1
n. 16
o. 18
p. 2
q. 12
r. 7

MATCHING III

1. c
2. b
3. f
4. a
5. d
6. e

CONCEPT REVIEW

1. false
2. difficult to diagnose reliably; etiology is poorly understood; little evidence they are treatable
3. II
4. syntonic
5. people with personality disorders have poor insight into their own behavior
6. wealth
7. during a famine, while being raised in an institution, in a busy daycare center
8. emotion, collectivism
9. limited to the culture in which they are developed
10. C
11. A
12. B
13. false
14. antisocial
15. false
16. categorical
17. 10-14%
18. narcissistic
19. false
20. borderline
21. women; men; women
22. feminine
23. less
24. true
25. have another mental disorder
26. true
27. pleasure; anxiety
28. depression
29. parents
30. leave treatment
31. true
32. antisocial
33. emotions and interpersonal behavior
34. change forms
35. genes; environment
36. did; did not
37. discipline
38. be inconsistent or give up in discipline
39. fear or anxiety
40. shame
41. antisocial
42. borderline
43. false
44. abandonment
45. overprotective or authoritarian

MULTIPLE CHOICE

1. d
2. b
3. b
4. d
5. a
6. a
7. c
8. c
9. b
10. d
11. a
12. c
13. b
14. a
15. b
16. c
17. a
18. d
19. c
20. d
21. c
22. a
23. d
24. b
25. a
26. c
27. d

UNDERSTANDING RESEARCH

1. many; random; 700; 11; One; socioeconomic status; boys; 16; 39%
2. longitudinal; adolescents; mothers; questionnaires; personality disorder; 31%; 17%; obsessive-compulsive; narcissistic
3. boys more likely to have a dependent personality disorder; unexpected; 12-13 years old; less than half; narcissistic
4. Personality disorders are relatively common among teens and are fairly, although not overwhelmingly, stable over time.

CROSSWORD

ACROSS

3. includes people who often appear dramatic, emotional, or erratic
4. refers to a person's desires or goals
5. includes people who often appear anxious or fearful
7. personality disorder characterized by pervasive pattern of grandiosity
9. a person's most basic style of relating to the world
10. perceiving one's feelings as natural part of one's self
14. personality disorder characterized by suspiciousness
15. desire for impact, prestige, dominance
16. personality disorder characterized by pervasive pattern of instability in mood and relationships

DOWN

1. desire for close relationships with others
2. personality disorder characterized by pattern of submissive and clinging behavior
6. personality disorder characterized by pattern of irresponsible and antisocial behavior
8. impulse control disorder involving the stealing of objects
11. personality disorder characterized by pattern of orderliness, perfectionism, and control
12. includes people who often appear odd or eccentric
13. personality disorder characterized by pervasive patterns of indifference

CHAPTER TEN

EATING DISORDERS

CHAPTER OUTLINE

Overview
Typical Symptoms and Associated Features of Anorexia Nervosa
    Refusal to Maintain a Normal Weight
    Disturbance in Evaluating Weight or Shape
    Fear of Gaining Weight
    Cessation of Menstruation
    Medical Complications
    Struggle for Control
    Comorbid Psychological Disorders
Typical Symptoms and Associated Features of Bulimia Nervosa
    Binge Eating
    Inappropriate Compensatory Behavior
    Excessive Emphasis on Weight and Shape
    Comorbid Psychological Disorders
    Medical Complications
Classification of Eating Disorders
    Brief Historical Perspective
    Contemporary Classification
Epidemiology of Eating Disorders
    Gender Differences and Standards of Beauty
    Age of Onset
Etiological Considerations and Research
    Social Factors
    Psychological Factors
    Biological Factors
    Integration and Alternative Pathways
Treatment of Anorexia Nervosa
    Course and Outcome of Anorexia Nervosa
Treatment of Bulimia Nervosa
    Antidepressant Medications
    Cognitive Behavior Therapy
    Interpersonal Psychotherapy
    Course and Outcome of Bulimia Nervosa
Summary

OBJECTIVES

1. Discuss the characteristics of eating disorders, anorexia nervosa, and bulimia nervosa.
2. Describe several ways in which those with anorexia have distorted perceptions of self.
3. Identify several medical complications associated with anorexia nervosa and bulimia nervosa.
4. Describe the symptoms of bulimia nervosa and the compensatory behavior that typifies the disorder.
5. Identify the two subtypes of anorexia nervosa and bulimia nervosa.
6. Discuss the gender differences involved in eating disorders.
7. Discuss introceptive awareness and its role in eating disorders.

8. Identify several social, psychological, and biological factors responsible for the development of eating disorders.
9. Discuss the concept of set point.
10. Discuss the techniques utilized in the treatment of anorexia nervosa and bulimia nervosa.
11. Describe the course and outcome associated with eating disorders.

MATCHING I

Answers are found at the end of this chapter. Match these terms and concepts with the definitions that follow:

a.	Eating disorders	l.	Binge eating disorder
b.	Anorexia nervosa	m.	Obesity
c.	Bulimia nervosa	n.	Incidence
d.	Body mass index	o.	Cohort effects
e.	Distorted body image	p.	Enmeshed families
f.	Amenorrhea	q.	Perfectionism
g.	Lanugo	r.	Introceptive awareness
h.	Electrolyte imbalance	s.	Effects of dietary restraint
i.	Binge eating	t.	Weight set points
j.	Purging	u.	Hypothalamus
k.	Rumination		

1. ____ a fine, downy hair on the face or trunk of the body
2. ____ number of new cases
3. ____ eating an amount of food in a fixed period of time that is clearly larger than most people would eat under similar circumstances
4. ____ the area of the brain that regulates routine biological functions like appetite
5. ____ absence of at least three consecutive menstrual cycles
6. ____ differences that distinguish one group, born during a particular time period, from another group born at a different time period
7. ____ a disturbance in the levels of potassium, sodium, calcium, and other vital elements found in bodily fluids that can lead to cardiac arrest or kidney failure
8. ____ families whose members are overly involved in one another's lives
9. ____ the endless pursuit of unrealistically high standards
10. ____ repeated episodes of binge eating followed by inappropriate compensatory behaviors with other symptoms related to eating and body image
11. ____ excess body fat; body weight over 20 percent above the expected weight
12. ____ an inaccuracy in how one perceives their body size and shape
13. ____ an intentional act designed to eliminate consumed food from the body
14. ____ severe disturbances in eating behavior that result from obsessive fear of gaining weight
15. ____ direct consequences of restricted eating
16. ____ a controversial diagnosis defined by repeated episodes of binge eating in the absence of compensatory behavior
17. ____ the body's preference for a fixed weight that may have biologically controlled homeostatic mechanisms
18. ____ refusal to maintain a minimally normal body weight along with other symptoms related to eating and body image
19. ____ the regurgitation and rechewing of food
20. ____ recognition of internal cues including emotional states as well as hunger
21. ____ a calculation derived from weight and height used to determine whether someone is significantly underweight

MATCHING II
Answers are found at the end of this chapter. Match these names with the descriptions of their contributions to the study of abnormal psychology.

        a. Hilde Bruch   b. Christopher Fairburn

1. ____ asserted that a struggle for control and perfectionism is the central psychological issue in the development of eating disorders
2. ____ developed a cognitive behavioral treatment for bulimia nervosa

CONCEPT REVIEW
Answers are found at the end of this chapter. After you have read and reviewed the material, test your comprehension by filling in the blanks or circling the correct answer.

1. People with anorexia nervosa suffer from a loss of appetite: **true**   **false**

2. Anorexia and bulimia are how much more common in women than in men:

   twice as common   **four times as common**   **ten times as common**

3. Males in our society see themselves as thin when they weigh 105 percent of their expected weight, while females see themselves as thin when they weight 90 percent of their expected weight: **true**   **false**

4. Female anorexics are likely to be proud of their emaciation, while male anorexics are likely to be stigmatized for it: **true**   **false**

5. Eating disorders are more common among men who are wrestlers and men who are gay:

       true   **false**

6. Often eating disorders begin with a _____.

7. What percent of people admitted to hospitals with anorexia nervosa die of starvation, suicide, or medical complications? _____

8. A person with anorexia often becomes more and more afraid of fat the thinner they become:

       true   **false**

9. It is likely that amenorrhea and lack of interest in sex common among anorexics are a result rather than a predisposition of the weight loss: **true**   **false**

10. Although anorexia is a serious mental disorder, it seldom involves medical complications:

        true   **false**

11. A person with anorexia can be seen as exceptionally successful in what area? _____

12. The study with World War II conscientious objectors found that obsessive-compulsive behaviors probably **precede/follow** the change in eating patterns.

13. Anorexia seldom co-occurs with symptoms of bulimia: **true   false**
14. Binge eating is often triggered by _____.
15. Lack of control is characteristic of _____ while excessive control is characteristic of _____.
16. Vomiting prevents the absorption of how many of the calories consumed during a binge?

    almost none   about half   almost all
17. The two subtypes of anorexia are the _____ type and the _____ type.
18. The two subtypes of bulimia are the _____ type and the _____ type.
19. Research indicates that obesity is primarily caused by lack of willpower in eating habits: **true   false**
20. Eating disorders have become somewhat less common since the 1960s and 1970s: **true   false**
21. Which type of eating disorder is more common? _____
22. In Third World countries, weighing more is a status symbol: **true   false**
23. Studies have shown that physical _____ predicts self-esteem among girls and physical _____ predicts self-esteem among boys.
24. People with which type of eating disorder are more likely to report that their families have high levels of conflict? _____
25. Clinicians note that enmeshed families are more characteristic of people with which type of eating disorder? _____
26. Perfectionism is characteristic of people with which type of eating disorder? _____
27. Negative evaluations of one's weight, shape, and appearance predict the subsequent development of eating disorders: **true   false**
28. There is evidence that diets can be the trigger for the development of an eating disorder:

    true   false
29. When food intake is reduced, there is an increase in the metabolic rate:

    true   false
30. There is strong evidence that eating disorders are genetic: **true   false**
31. There is evidence that family therapy is more effective than individual therapy in treating adolescents with anorexia: **true   false**
32. Current forms of treatment for anorexia are quite effective: **true   false**
33. Psychotherapy tends to be more effective than antidepressant medication in the treatment of bulimia:

    true   false
34. Interpersonal therapy was found to be as effective as cognitive behavior therapy in the treatment of bulimia: **true   false**
35. Bulimia is more likely to lead to death than anorexia: **true   false**

CROSSWORD

Answers are found at the end of this chapter. Complete the following crossword puzzle to reinforce your understanding of this chapter's key terms and concepts:

ACROSS	DOWN
1. type of anorexia which does not involve binge eating or purgation	2. awareness of internal cues
4. paramount struggle for many with anorexia	3. elimination of food from the body
5. group which shares some feature in common	6. absence of menstrual cycle
8. refusal to maintain a minimally normal body weight	7. negative mood state
12. type of medication shown to be effective in treating bulimia nervosa	9. type of bulimia which does not involve regular purgation
14. families which are overly involved in one another's lives	10. percentage of all people with anorexia who engage in episodes of binge eating, purging
	11. male athletes with high prevalence of eating disorders
	13. index derived from weight and height

MULTIPLE CHOICE

Answers are found at the end of this chapter. The multiple choice questions listed will test your understanding of the material presented in the chapter. Read through each question and circle the letter representing the best answer.

1. Both bulimia and anorexia nervosa are characterized by which of the following?
    a. struggle for control
    b. considerable shame
    c. obsessive-compulsive disorder
    d. the absence of menstruation

2. All of the following are compensatory behaviors of bulimia nervosa except
    a. misuse of laxatives
    b. complete avoidance of food
    c. intense exercise
    d. misuse of enemas

3. All of the following are symptoms of anorexia nervosa except
    a. an intense fear of gaining weight
    b. refusal to maintain weight at or above minimally normal weight for age and height
    c. acknowledgment of the seriousness of low body weight, but refusal to change eating behavior
    d. amenorrhea

4. Which of the following theories offers the most promising explanations for eating disorders?
    a. biological
    b. social
    c. psychological
    d. all of the above equally offer promising explanations of eating disorders

5. All of the following are symptoms of bulimia nervosa except
    a. recurrent episodes of binge eating that involve large amounts of food
    b. occurs solely during episodes of anorexia nervosa
    c. recurrent inappropriate compensatory behavior, especially purging
    d. undue influence of weight and body shape on self-evaluation

6. Both bulimia and anorexia nervosa are approximately _____ times more common among women than among men.
    a. 10
    b. 15
    c. 20
    d. 25

7. Many professionals agree that anorexia is a source of which of the following?
    a. shame
    b. pride
    c. gratification
    d. resentment

8. Bulimia nervosa is most prevalent among which of the following groups?
    a. women born after 1960
    b. women born before 1960
    c. girls ages 10-15
    d. women born in the 1950s

9. Which of the following is not a finding that provides evidence that social factors are very important in eating disorders?
    a. eating disorders have recently become much more common
    b. eating disorders are much more common among women working in fields that emphasize weight and appearance, such as modeling and ballet
    c. eating disorders are more common among middle- and upper-class whites
    d. eating disorders have a higher concordance rate in MZ rather than DZ twins

10. Medical complications from anorexia can include all but
    a. growth of downy hair on the face
    b. dry, cracked skin
    c. hallucinations
    d. kidney failure

UNDERSTANDING RESEARCH
Answers are found at the end of this chapter.

<u>Using the Internet to Prevent Eating Disorders</u>: The text presents a detailed description of a study in the Research Close-Up. Finding the answers to these questions will provide an understanding of this study and why it is important.

1. This study involved _____ subjects who were _____ . The subjects _____ an eating disorder. Investigators assigned the women _____ to _____ groups. The investigators assessed _____ about eating among the women.

2. At the _____ assessments, the _____ group showed significantly more improvement than the _____ group on measures of dysfunctional eating attitudes. Several factors were critical, accounting for the positive effect. These included _____.

3. The combination of _____, _____, and _____ may produce positive benefits, especially for those at high risk for developing eating disorders.

SHORT ANSWER
Answer the following short answer questions. Compare your work to the material presented in the text.

1. Discuss the differences between anorexia nervosa and bulimia nervosa in terms of symptomatology, prevalence, etiology, and treatment.

2. Which social factors play a role in the etiology of eating disorders? Provide examples.

3. If you were a therapist and a young woman entered therapy for an eating disorder, what would your treatment plan entail? Would your treatment for a male patient differ from treatment for a female patient? Explain.

4. Discuss the role of placebo control groups in psychological research. What are the challenges in using such groups?

ANSWER KEY

MATCHING I

1. g	8. p	15. s
2. n	9. q	16. l
3. i	10. c	17. t
4. u	11. m	18. b
5. f	12. e	19. k
6. o	13. j	20. r
7. h	14. a	21. d

MATCHING II

1. a   2. b

CONCEPT REVIEW

1. false
2. ten times as common
3. true
4. true
5. true
6. diet
7. 10 percent
8. true
9. true
10. false
11. self-control
12. follow
13. false
14. an unhappy mood
15. bulimia; anorexia
16. about half
17. restricting; binge-eating/purging
18. purging; nonpurging
19. false
20. false
21. bulimia
22. true
23. attractiveness; competence
24. bulimia
25. anorexia
26. anorexia
27. true
28. true
29. false
30. false
31. true
32. false
33. true
34. true
35. false

MULTIPLE CHOICE

1. a   4. b   7. b   10. c
2. b   5. b   8. a
3. c   6. a   9. d

UNDERSTANDING RESEARCH

1. 76; female undergraduates; did not have; randomly; three; dysfunctional attitudes

2. post-treatment; SB internet; WLC; women in SB group were required to complete homework assignments related to body image, SB group was more engaged, SB group received social support

3. education, support from peers, structured exercises

CROSSWORD

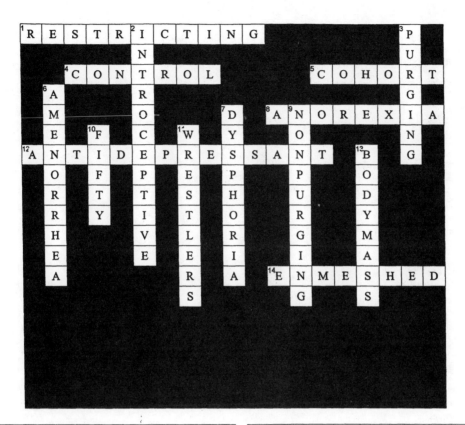

ACROSS	DOWN
1. type of anorexia which does not involve binge eating or purgation	2. awareness of internal cues
4. paramount struggle for many with anorexia	3. elimination of food from the body
5. group which shares some feature in common	6. absence of menstrual cycle
8. refusal to maintain a minimally normal body weight	7. negative mood state
12. type of medication shown to be effective in treating bulimia nervosa	9. type of bulimia which does not involve regular purgation
14. families which are overly involved in one another's lives	10. percentage of all people with anorexia who engage in episodes of binge eating, purging
	11. male athletes with high prevalence of eating disorders
	13. index derived from weight and height

CHAPTER ELEVEN

SUBSTANCE USE DISORDERS

CHAPTER OUTLINE

Overview
Typical Symptoms and Associated Features
    The Concept of Substance Dependence
    Alcohol
    Nicotine
    Amphetamine and Cocaine
    Opiates
    Barbiturates and Benzodiazepines
    Cannabis
    Hallucinogens and Related Drugs
Classification
    Brief History of Legal and Illegal Substances
    DSM-IV-TR
    Proposed Subtypes
    Course and Outcome
    Other Disorders Commonly Associated With Addictions
Epidemiology
    Prevalence of Alcohol Abuse and Dependence
    Prevalence of Drug and Nicotine Dependence
    Risk for Addiction Across the Life Span
Etiological Considerations and Research
    Social Factors
    Biological Factors
    Psychological Factors
    Integrated Systems
Treatment
    Detoxification
    Medications During Remission
    Self-Help Groups: Alcoholics Anonymous
    Cognitive Behavior Therapy
    Outcome Results and General Conclusions
Summary

OBJECTIVES

1. Distinguish between substance abuse, substance dependence, and polysubstance abuse.
2. Define tolerance and withdrawal.
3. Discuss several short-term effects and consequences of prolonged abuse of alcohol.
4. Describe several properties, short-term effects, and consequences of abusing benzodiazepines, opiates, nicotine, amphetamines, cocaine, cannabis, and hallucinogens.
5. Discuss the classification system utilized to differentiate between substance abuse and dependence.
6. Describe the typical course and outcome of alcoholism.
7. Discuss the epidemiology of alcoholism.
8. Explain how social factors influence initial experimentation with drugs and alcohol.

9. Discuss several research findings regarding the genetics of alcoholism.
10. Explain the endorphin and serotonin hypotheses.
11. Describe the role of cognitive expectations on perceived effects of alcohol consumption.
12. Discuss the integrated systems approach to substance use and abuse.
13. Describe the use of detoxification, self-help groups, controlled drinking training, and relapse prevention training in the treatment of alcoholism.

MATCHING I
Answers are found at the end of this chapter. Match these terms and concepts with the definitions that follow:

a.	Substance dependence		n.	Alcohol withdrawal delirium
b.	Substance abuse		o.	Delirium tremens
c.	Polysubstance abuse		p.	Tranquilizers
d.	Addiction		q.	Barbiturates
e.	Psychoactive substance		r.	Benzodiazepines
f.	Hypnotics		s.	Cocaine
g.	Sedatives		t.	Opiates
h.	Narcotic analgesics		u.	Morphine
i.	Craving		v.	Codeine
j.	Psychological dependence		w.	Heroin
k.	Physiological dependence		x.	Methadone
l.	Tolerance		y.	Psychomotor stimulants
m.	Withdrawal			

1. ____ CNS depressants that are used for relieving anxiety
2. ____ a less severe pattern of drug use defined in terms of interference with a person's ability to fulfill major role obligations, the recurrent use of a drug in dangerous situations, or the experience of legal problems associated with the drug use
3. ____ drugs with properties similar to opium, often used to relieve pain
4. ____ convulsions, hallucinations, and a sudden disturbance of consciousness with changes in cognitive processes during withdrawal from alcohol
5. ____ the process through which the nervous system becomes less sensitive to the effects of a substance with repeated exposure to that substance
6. ____ a synthetic opiate often injected, inhaled, or smoked
7. ____ physical symptoms related to drug use, including tolerance and withdrawal
8. ____ a class of drugs, discovered in the early twentieth century, used widely for many years to treat anxiety, prevent seizures, and relieve pain
9. ____ drugs which produce their effects by simulating the actions of certain neurotransmitters
10. ____ also known as drug of abuse; a chemical substance that alters mood, level of perception, or brain functioning
11. ____ a synthetic opiate sometimes used therapeutically as an alternative to heroin
12. ____ used to decrease anxiety or agitation
13. ____ CNS depressants that are used to help people sleep
14. ____ the abuse of several types of drugs
15. ____ opiates that can be used clinically to decrease pain
16. ____ a forceful urge to use drugs
17. ____ symptoms experienced when a person stops using a drug
18. ____ a more severe pattern of repeated self-administration often resulting in tolerance, withdrawal, or compulsive drug-taking behavior
19. ____ one of the active ingredients of opium, very similar to heroin

20. _____ one of the active ingredients of opium, available in small quantities in Canada in over-the-counter medications
21. _____ an older term used to describe substance use problems such as alcoholism
22. _____ feeling compelled to use a drug to control one's feelings or to prepare for certain activities
23. _____ an older term for alcohol withdrawal delirium
24. _____ synthetic drugs whose therapeutic effects were discovered in the 1950s which have largely replaced barbiturates in medical practice
25. _____ a naturally occurring stimulant drug extracted from the leaf of a small tree that grows at high elevations

MATCHING II
Answers are found at the end of this chapter. Match these terms and concepts with the definitions that follow:

1. Amphetamines
2. Naltrexone
3. Amphetamine psychosis
4. Cannabis
5. Marijuana
6. Hashish
7. Temporal disintegration
8. Reverse tolerance
9. Hallucinogens
10. LSD
11. Psilocybin
12. Mescaline
13. Peyote
14. PCP
15. Acamprosate
16. Flashbacks
17. Endorphins
18. Balanced placebo design
19. Risk
20. Relative risk
21. High-risk research design
22. Vulnerability indicators
23. Alcohol myopia
24. Detoxification
25. Antabuse
26. Abstinence violation effect

a. _____ the dried leaves and flowers of the hemp plant
b. _____ a medication used in Europe to treat alcoholism; not yet approved by the FDA
c. _____ a newly approved medication to treat alcoholism which has been demonstrated to be effective in reducing relapse rates
d. _____ synthetically produced psychomotor stimulants such as dexedrine or methamphetamine
e. _____ a procedure that allows the investigator to separate the direct, biological effects of the drug from the subjects' expectations about how the drug should affect their behavior
f. _____ drugs that cause people to experience hallucinations at relatively low doses
g. _____ a drug that can block the chemical breakdown of alcohol which will make the person taking it violently ill if he or she consumes alcohol
h. _____ brief visual aftereffects that can occur at unpredictable intervals long after a hallucinogen has cleared the body
i. _____ a technique where subjects are selected from the general population based on some identified risk factor that has a fairly high risk ratio
j. _____ auditory or visual hallucinations as well as delusions of persecution or grandeur that can occur with high doses of amphetamines or cocaine and usually disappears after the drug is metabolized
k. _____ manifestations of the genotype associated with a mental disorder
l. _____ a hallucinogen found in certain mushrooms which bears a chemical resemblance to serotonin
m. _____ a synthetic hallucinogen which bears a strong chemical resemblance to serotonin
n. _____ a condition often accompanying cannabis intoxication in which people have trouble retaining and organizing information
o. _____ becoming more sensitive to a drug with prolonged use; reported by users but not yet documented in laboratory studies

p. ____ a synthetic drug that can induce psychotic behavior at high doses
q. ____ the probability that a certain outcome will occur
r. ____ the probability that someone with a certain characteristic will develop a disorder divided by the probability that someone without the same characteristic will develop the same disorder
s. ____ the guilt and perceived loss of control that a person feels whenever he or she slips and takes a drug after an extended period of abstinence
t. ____ the removal of a drug on which a person has become dependent
u. ____ a drug with the active ingredient called THC, derived from the hemp plant
v. ____ a type of hallucinogen that resembles norepinephrine
w. ____ the dried resin from the top of the female hemp plant
x. ____ a marked tendency to engage in shortsighted information processing when intoxicated
y. ____ a cactus that contains mescaline
z. ____ endogenous opioids that are naturally synthesized in the brain and are closely related to morphine

MATCHING III
Answers are found at the end of this chapter. Match these names with the descriptions of their contributions to the study of abnormal psychology:

a. George Vaillant   c. Robert Cloninger
b. Alan Marlatt

1. ____ proposed that there were two types of alcoholism, Type I, which has a later onset, psychological dependence, and the absence of antisocial personality traits, and Type II, which is predominantly among men, has an earlier onset, and co-occurs with antisocial behaviors
2. ____ conducted a longitudinal study of alcoholism among inner-city adolescents and college students
3. ____ developed a cognitive behavioral view of the relapse process and a relapse prevention model for treatment of substance use

CONCEPT REVIEW
Answers are found at the end of this chapter. After you have read and reviewed the material, test your comprehension by filling in the blanks or circling the correct answer.

1. Most researchers have moved toward a view of substance abuse that emphasizes common causes, behaviors, and consequences of using the substance rather than a focus on the particular drug used:

    true   **false**

2. One of the best indices for defining alcoholism is the amount of alcohol a person consumes:

    true   **false**

3. A crucial feature of alcoholism is diminished _____.

4. The most substantial tolerance effects are found among people who use which drugs? _____

5. What drugs have not been shown to have tolerance effects? _____

6. _____ is the most widely used psychoactive substance in the world.

7. What organ metabolizes alcohol? _____

8. Blood alcohol levels are only weakly correlated with intoxicating effects:

true   false

9. When blood alcohol levels go too high, the person will become unconscious and can always sleep off the effects of the alcohol with no acute dangers:

    true   false

10. There is a strong correlation between crime and alcohol: **true**   **false**

11. The abuse of alcohol has more negative health consequences over an extended period of time than any other drug: **true**   **false**

12. Sedatives and hypnotics can lead to a state of arousal similar to that of cocaine:

    true   **false**

13. When used to reduce anxiety, barbiturates and benzodiazepines produce a calm, relaxed feeling:

    true   **false**

14. Barbiturates may not be helpful because a return in symptoms occurs when a person stops taking them:

    true   **false**

15. Opiates produce _____.

16. Heroin addicts suffer from few health problems and are not more likely to die than non-addicts.

    true   **false**

17. Nicotine may mimic the effects of _____ drugs.

18. Nicotine produces CNS **arousal/depression.**

19. The FDA decided to regulate cigarettes as a **drug/medical device.**

20. At what age does addiction to nicotine almost always begin? _____

21. From a psychological point of view, withdrawal from nicotine is just as difficult as withdrawal from _____.

22. Cocaine and amphetamines activate the sympathetic nervous system:

    true   **false**

23. Amphetamine psychosis is a permanent condition: **true**   **false**

24. The most common reaction to discontinuing stimulant drugs is _____

25. Marijuana and hashish show strong tolerance effects: **true**   **false**

26. Hallucinogens may trigger persistent psychosis in people vulnerable to that type of disorder:

    true   **false**

27. A typical American during colonial times never consumed alcohol:

    true   **false**

28. Most alcoholics go through repeated periods of _____.

29. In Vaillant's study, relapse to alcohol abuse was unlikely if the period of abstinence was how many years?

    _____

30. What three types of disorders are commonly associated with alcohol abuse?
    _____, _____, and _____
31. Cannabis is used almost exclusively in North America: **true**   **false**
32. Among all men and women who have ever used alcohol, about _____ percent will develop serious problems with drinking sometime during their lives.
33. Men outnumber women in chronic abuse of alcohol by a ratio of about:

    3 to 1   **5 to 1**   **10 to 1**
34. Women who drink experience more social _____ than men.
35. Women metabolize alcohol more slowly than men, even when differences in body weight are controlled:

    true   **false**
36. The lifetime prevalence for addiction to nicotine is:

    4 percent   **14 percent**   **24 percent**
37. The lifetime prevalence for addiction to drugs (illegal and prescription) other than nicotine or alcohol is:

    4.5 percent   **7.5 percent**   **14.5 percent**
38. The elderly are more likely to be addicted to alcohol than are younger people:

    true   **false**
39. Parents have a greater influence over their children's decision to use _____ and peers seem to play a more important role in the decision to use _____.
40. Adolescents with alcoholic parents are less likely to drink than those whose parents are not alcoholic:

    true   **false**
41. A flushing response to even a small amount of alcohol, including flushed skin, nausea, and an abnormal heartbeat occurs in 30 to 50 percent of people of what ethnic ancestry? _____
42. There is an elevated risk for alcoholism among first-degree relatives of alcoholics:

    true   **false**
43. Twin studies indicate that genetic factors alone are responsible for the increased risk for alcoholism among relatives of alcoholics: **true**   **false**
44. The Indians of South America who produce coca leaves to sell typically have severe dependence problems: **true**   **false**
45. Rates of cigarette smoking among young adults declined over the 1990s:

    true   **false**
46. There is evidence that a deficiency in the activity of what type of neurotransmitter is related to vulnerability to alcoholism? _____

47. The tension-reduction hypothesis suggests that people drink alcohol in an effort to reduce the impact of a

_____ environment.

48. In one study, people who believed they consumed alcohol, but really did not, showed increased _____ and _____ arousal.

49. _____ expectancies about effects of alcohol predict drinking problems.

50. Detoxification from alcohol is typically accomplished by abruptly discontinuing consumption of alcohol:

    true   **false**

51. Many patients using Antabuse have poor compliance with treatment, that is they stop taking the Antabuse:

    true   **false**

52. There is no research evidence that Alcoholics Anonymous is an effective form of treatment:

    true   **false**

53. The heritability estimates for men and women in risk for alcoholism due to genetic factors are about:

    1/10   **2/3**   **9/10**

54. The relapse prevention model of treatment teaches patients to interpret slips in abstinence as _____.

55. Research suggests that a person's coping skills, social support, and stress are **better/worse** predictors of successfully stopping drinking than the particular type of treatment received.

56. The medication _____ works by making a person feel sick if they drink, and the medication _____ works by reducing the rewarding effects of alcohol.

57. Motivational interviewing takes a **confrontational/nonconfrontational** approach.

CROSSWORD

Answers are found at the end of this chapter. Complete the following crossword puzzle to reinforce your understanding of this chapter's key terms and concepts:

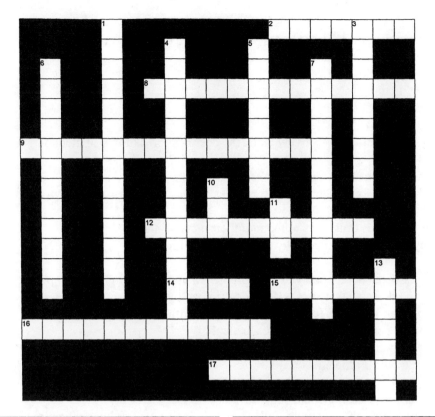

ACROSS	DOWN	
2. sometimes called opioids	1. dopamine, serotonin, and norepinephrine are examples	11. most common active ingredient in cannabis
8. cause people to experience hallucinations	3. process through which the nervous system becomes less sensitive to effects of a drug	13. a psychomotor stimulant
9. Xanax and Valium are examples	4. tolerance occuring when receptors in the brain adapt to continued presence of drug	
12. a nervous system aroused by nicotine	5. active ingredient in tobacco	
14. known as a "club drug"	6. high doses of these may lead to psychosis	
15. affects virtually every organ and system in the body	7. abuse of several types of drugs	
16. substance which alters a person's mood	10. a synthetic drug often classified with the hallucinogens	
17. endogenous opioids		

MULTIPLE CHOICE

Answers are found at the end of this chapter. The multiple choice questions listed will test your understanding of the material presented in the chapter. Read through each question and circle the letter representing the best answer.

1. The two terms included in the DSM-IV-TR to describe substance use disorders are
    a. substance dependence and substance abuse
    b. substance abuse and addiction
    c. tolerance and addiction
    d. substance abuse and polysubstance abuse

2. Although disulfiram (Antabuse) can effectively block the chemical breakdown of alcohol, people resist using this drug because
    a. it is an extremely expensive drug to administer
    b. the effect of the drug is very short-lived; it reduces alcohol intake for only a few hours after its ingestion
    c. individuals who use this drug have to monitor their dietary intake
    d. use of the drug produces a dramatically adverse physical reaction

3. Because alcoholism is associated with many diverse problems, distinguishing between people who are dependent on alcohol and those who are not is often determined by which of the following?
    a. the presence of legal problems (e.g., driving under the influence)
    b. whether or not the person reports tolerance to alcohol
    c. the number of problems that the person experiences
    d. the presence of medical problems

4. Research on the long term course of alcohol suggests that
    a. the typical individual is able to successfully stop drinking only after hospitalization
    b. the typical individual cycles through periods of alcohol consumption, cessation, and relapse
    c. the typical individual rarely experiences relapse after making the decision to stop drinking
    d. the typical individual spends approximately 10 years in the alcohol consumption period before making the decision to quit

5. Which of the following is an example of a CNS stimulant?
    a. alcohol
    b. cocaine
    c. morphine
    d. hashish

6. Results from adoption studies focusing on the genetic transmission of alcohol indicate that
    a. the familial nature of alcoholism appears to be at least partially determined by genes; that is, having an alcoholic biological parent increases risk for alcoholism
    b. if a person does not have an alcoholic biological parent, having an adopted parent with alcohol problems greatly increases risk for alcoholism
    c. having the personality trait of "behavioral overcontrol" increases risk for alcoholism
    d. only people with at least one alcoholic biological parent are at risk for alcoholism

7. Sam currently drinks large amounts of alcohol on a daily basis. He plans his day around when alcohol will be available to him. He drives a certain route home from work that passes two liquor stores to ensure that liquor will be available each evening. His weekend activities are planned around availability of alcohol, and he will not attend social functions where alcohol is absent. Which term best describes his condition?
   a. binge drinker
   b. controlled drinker
   c. psychological dependence
   d. pre-alcoholic drinker

8. In most states, the current legal limit of alcohol concentration for driving is
   a. 50 mg percent
   b. 100 mg percent
   c. 150 mg percent
   d. 200 mg percent

9. A person who has a compelling need to use a drug and cannot control or regulate his drug use is commonly described as
   a. in withdrawal
   b. a recreational drug user
   c. intoxicated
   d. addicted

10. One reason that risk for substance dependence is increased in elderly people is
    a. the elderly demonstrate a reduced sensitivity to drug toxicity and therefore require higher drug dosages
    b. adult children often encourage their elderly parents to use drugs to control their nerves
    c. the elderly use prescribed psychoactive drugs more frequently than compared to other age groups
    d. in fact, there is little risk for substance dependence in the elderly

11. A principal assumption of Alcoholics Anonymous (AA) is
    a. people need to relapse several times before they will learn to take their alcohol problem seriously
    b. individuals cannot recover on their own
    c. individuals need to remove themselves from the stressful situations that trigger alcohol use
    d. with enough help, people can develop effective methods of controlled drinking

12. Which of the following statements is accurate regarding the definition of substance dependence in the DSM-IV-TR?
    a. evidence of tolerance and withdrawal is required
    b. the individual must exhibit several characteristics that describe a pattern of compulsive use
    c. the person must exhibit characteristics of problematic substance use for at least two years
    d. a prior diagnosis of substance abuse is required before the diagnosis of substance dependence may be considered

13. Which would not be considered an example of a common alcohol expectancy?
    a. alcohol decreases power and aggression
    b. alcohol enhances social and physical pleasure
    c. alcohol enhances sexual performance
    d. alcohol increases social assertiveness

14. Aerosol spray, glue, and paint thinner are all examples of which class of psychoactive drugs?
    a. CNS depressants
    b. over the counter drugs
    c. solvents
    d. hallucinogens

15. What percentage of men in the United States develop problems resulting from prolonged alcohol consumption?
    a. 10 percent
    b. 20 percent
    c. 30 percent
    d. 40 percent

16. Which of the following statements is true regarding alcohol expectancies?
    a. negative expectancies appear to be less powerful than positive expectancies in influencing alcohol use
    b. adolescents do not appear to have strong beliefs about alcohol prior to taking their first drink
    c. expectations regarding alcohol do not predict drinking behaviors
    d. portrayal of alcohol in the mass media does not appear to influence individuals' alcohol expectancies

17. Which of the following statements regarding tolerance is true?
    a. individuals can develop tolerance to all psychoactive drugs over time
    b. certain hallucinogens may not lead to the development of tolerance
    c. the most substantial tolerance effects are found among cannabis users
    d. heroin and CNS stimulants do not lead to the development of tolerance

18. Rates of alcohol abuse are significantly lower among
    a. Jews
    b. Catholics
    c. Native Americans
    d. Protestants

19. Which of the following statements is true regarding the presence of alcohol dependence over a long period of time?
    a. alcohol dependence always results in Korsakoff's psychosis
    b. alcohol dependence follows opiate dependence and cocaine dependence in terms of potential negative health consequences
    c. nutritional disturbances caused by alcohol dependence can be controlled through appropriate medication
    d. alcohol dependence has more negative health consequences than does abuse of any other substance

20. Which of the following symptoms are side effects of alcohol withdrawal?
    a. hand tremors, sweating, and nausea
    b. anxiety and insomnia
    c. convulsions and hallucinations
    d. all of the above

21. The most promising neurochemical explanation of alcoholism currently focuses on which of the following neurotransmitters?
    a. serotonin
    b. dopamine
    c. epinephrine
    d. norepinephrine

22. Considering all the direct and indirect ways that alcohol use contributes to death (e.g., suicides, accidents, medical disorders), alcohol is considered:
    a. the first leading cause of death in this country
    b. the second leading cause of death in this country
    c. the third leading cause of death in this country
    d. the fourth leading cause of death in this country

23. Which of the following statements reflects a difference between men and women in their use of alcohol?
    a. the average age of onset for alcoholism is higher among men
    b. women are less likely to develop hepatic disorders even after drinking heavily for many years
    c. women are more likely to report additional symptoms of depression and anxiety, while antisocial personality traits are more likely to be displayed in men
    d. men are more likely to drink if their partners drink

24. Which of the following factors is a predictor of long-term successful treatment outcome for alcoholism?
    a. the availability of residential alcohol treatment programs in the area
    b. the alcoholic's participation in AA
    c. the presence of environmental stress
    d. the availability of social support

25. Which class of drugs is least associated with severe withdrawal effects?
    a. stimulants
    b. alcohol
    c. sedatives and anxiolytics
    d. opiates

26. One reason that it is difficult to gather epidemiological information on substance use is that
    a. the definition of substance abuse and dependence has been clearly restricted in the past
    b. this type of research is expensive and therefore has not been adequately funded
    c. drug users are often reluctant to accurately report their drug use because of the illegal status of many drugs
    d. all of the above

UNDERSTANDING RESEARCH
Answers are found at the end of this chapter.

The Swedish Adoption Studies: The text presents a detailed description of a study in the Research Close-Up. Finding the answers to these questions will provide an understanding of this study and why it is important.

1. What are the two types of alcoholism that were evaluated in this study? _____ and _____. What were the two cities where subjects were collected? _____ and _____. Did the findings from the two sites agree?

_____ How old were the men at the time of the study? Between the ages of _____ and _____. How were these men selected? _____
_____

2. The information was gathered from the records of local _____ boards, hospital and _____ records, and the national _____ register. It was felt that this approach would identify _____ percent of those who had a serious drinking problem. What two types of background were evaluated? _____ and _____. Which type of alcoholism is characterized by criminal activity and an early age of onset? Type _____.

3. For those with a genetic background of Type 1 alcoholism, a significant increase in the risk of alcoholism was evident in those people with what type of genetic and environmental background? _____
_____.

For those with a genetic background of Type 2 alcoholism, which was a stronger predictor of alcoholism, environmental factors or genetic factors? _____
Females with a genetic predisposition to Type 1 alcoholism were _____ times more likely to abuse alcohol. Females with a genetic predisposition to Type 2 alcoholism were _____ more likely to abuse alcohol. What is one criticism of this study? _____
_____.

SHORT ANSWER
Answer the following short answer questions. Compare your answers to the material presented in the text.

1. Explain the theory of Type 1 and Type 2 alcoholism. What do you believe to be the weaknesses of this model? What further type of research is necessary to support or disconfirm this theory?

2. Describe the balanced placebo design. Why is it a useful research design to study of the effects of alcohol on behavior?

3. Review the attention-allocation model of alcohol, as proposed by Steele and Josephs. What are the two factors on which this model is based? How does the theory predict such behaviors as drunken excess, drunken self-inflation, and drunken relief?

4. Discuss the issue of risk and risk factors in research.

ANSWER KEY

MATCHING I

1. g
2. b
3. t
4. n
5. l
6. w
7. k
8. q
9. y
10. e
11. x
12. p
13. f
14. c
15. h
16. i
17. m
18. a
19. u
20. v
21. d
22. j
23. o
24. r
25. s

MATCHING II

a. 5
b. 15
c. 2
d. 1
e. 18
f. 9
g. 25
h. 16
i. 21
j. 3
k. 22
l. 11
m. 10
n. 7
o. 8
p. 14
q. 19
r. 20
s. 26
t. 24
u. 4
v. 12
w. 6
x. 23
y. 13
z. 17

MATCHING III

1. c
2. a
3. b

MULTIPLE CHOICE

1. a
2. d
3. c
4. b
5. b
6. a
7. c
8. b
9. d
10. c
11. b
12. b
13. a
14. c
15. a
16. a
17. b
18. a
19. d
20. d
21. a
22. d
23. c
24. d
25. a
26. c

UNDERSTANDING RESEARCH

1. Type 1; Type 2; Stockholm; Gothenburg; yes; 23; 43; They were born out of wedlock and placed for adoption at a young age.

2. temperance; insurance; criminal; 70; genetic; environmental; two

3. Both genetic and environmental predispositions to alcoholism were necessary; genetic; three; were not; the measure of environmental factors was limited to social class, which is a crude measure

CONCEPT REVIEW

1. true
2. false
3. control over drinking
4. alcohol, nicotine, heroin, cocaine, amphetamines
5. hallucinogens
6. caffeine
7. the liver
8. false
9. false
10. true
11. true
12. false
13. true
14. true
15. euphoria
16. false
17. antidepressant
18. arousal
19. medical device
20. adolescence
21. heroin
22. true
23. false
24. depression
25. false
26. true
27. false
28. abstinence
29. six
30. antisocial personality disorder, mood disorder; anxiety disorder
31. false
32. 20
33. 5 to 1
34. disapproval
35. true
36. 24 percent
37. 7.5 percent
38. false
39. alcohol; marijuana
40. false
41. Asian
42. true
43. false
44. false
45. false
46. serotonin
47. stressful
48. aggression; sexual
49. positive
50. false
51. true
52. false
53. 2/3
54. temporary
55. better
56. Antabuse; Naltrexone
57. nonconfrontational

CROSSWORD

ACROSS	DOWN	
2. sometimes called opioids	1. dopamine, serotonin, and norepinephrine are examples	11. most common active ingredient in cannabis
8. cause people to experience hallucinations	3. process through which the nervous system becomes less sensitive to effects of a drug	13. a psychomotor stimulant
9. Xanax and Valium are examples		
12. a nervous system aroused by nicotine	4. tolerance occuring when receptors in the brain adapt to continued presence of drug	
14. known as a "club drug"		
15. affects virtually every organ and system in the body	5. active ingredient in tobacco	
16. substance which alters a person's mood	6. high doses of these may lead to psychosis	
17. endogenous opioids	7. abuse of several types of drugs	
	10. a synthetic drug often classified with the hallucinogens	

CHAPTER TWELVE

SEXUAL AND GENDER IDENTITY DISORDERS

CHAPTER OUTLINE

Overview
    Brief Historical Perspective
Sexual Dysfunctions
    Typical Symptoms and Associated Features
    Classification
    Epidemiology
    Etiology
    Treatment
Paraphilias
    Typical Symptoms and Associated Features
    Classification
    Epidemiology
    Etiology
    Treatment
Gender Identity Disorders
    Typical Symptoms and Associated Features
    Epidemiology
    Etiology
    Treatment
Summary

OBJECTIVES

1. Discuss the role of cultural and religious values in the examination of sexual disorders.
2. Discuss the contributions of Freud, Ellis, Kinsey, and Masters and Johnson in the study of human sexuality.
3. Distinguish hypoactive sexual desire from sexual aversion disorder.
4. Define male erectile disorder, female arousal disorder, premature ejaculation, dyspareunia, and female orgasmic disorder.
5. Discuss the prevalence of sexual disorders.
6. Discuss the biological and psychological causes of sexual disorders.
7. Describe sensate focus as a treatment technique for sexual disorders.
8. Identify the major forms of paraphilias.
9. Describe the etiology of paraphilias.
10. Discuss differences between sexual disorders and disorders of gender identity.

MATCHING I

Answers are found at the end of this chapter. Match these terms and concepts with the definitions that follow:

a. Sexual dysfunctions
b. Paraphilias
c. Gender identity
d. Gender identity disorder
e. Excitement
f. Orgasm
g. Resolution
h. Refractory period
i. Probability sampling
j. Convenience sampling
k. Hypoactive sexual desire disorder
l. Sexual aversion disorder
m. Erectile dysfunction
n. Impotence
o. Female sexual arousal disorder
p. Male erectile disorder
q. Inhibited sexual arousal
r. Hypothetical construct
s. Operational definition

1. _____ sudden intensely pleasurable release of sexual tension
2. _____ a strong and persistent identification with the opposite sex coupled with a sense of discomfort with one's anatomical sex
3. _____ a disorder in which a person has an extreme aversion to and avoidance of genital sexual contact with a partner
4. _____ persistent or recurrent erectile dysfunction
5. _____ sampling in which every member of a clearly specified population has a known probability of selection
6. _____ forms of sexual disorder that involve inhibitions of sexual desire or interference with the physiological responses leading to orgasm
7. _____ a procedure used to measure a theoretical construct
8. _____ sampling from a readily available group of participants
9. _____ forms of sexual disorder that involve sexual arousal in association with unusual objects and situations
10. _____ persistent or recurrent inability to attain or maintain an adequate lubrication-swelling response of sexual excitement even in the presence of sexual desire
11. _____ a person's sense of being male or female
12. _____ third stage of Masters and Johnson's human sexual response cycle where the body returns to its resting state
13. _____ disorder characterized by diminished desire for sexual activity and reduced frequency of sexual fantasies
14. _____ first stage of Masters and Johnson's human sexual response cycle involving physiological responses and subjective feelings
15. _____ inability to attain or maintain an adequate lubrication-swelling response of sexual excitement
16. _____ an older term for erectile dysfunction that is no longer used because of its negative implications
17. _____ events or states that reside within a person and are proposed to explain that person's behavior
18. _____ difficulty in obtaining an erection that is sufficient to accomplish intercourse or to satisfy self or partner during intercourse
19. _____ period of time after orgasm the person is unresponsive to further sexual stimulation

MATCHING II

Answers are found at the end of this chapter. Match these terms and concepts with the definitions that follow:

1. Penile plethysmograph
2. Vaginal photometer
3. Construct validity
4. Premature ejaculation
5. Female orgasmic disorder
6. Genital anesthesia
7. Dyspareunia
8. Vaginismus
9. Excessive sexual drive
10. Performance anxiety
11. Sensate focus
12. Scheduling
13. Fetishism
14. Partialism
15. Transvestite
16. Transvestic fetishism
17. Drag queens
18. Transvestic fetishism with gender dysphoria
19. Sexual masochism
20. Sexual sadism

a. _____ the extent that a measure produces results consistent with the theoretical construct it is purported to assess
b. _____ a procedure for measuring male sexual arousal
c. _____ a diagnosis included in the ICD but not the DSM
d. _____ a person who dresses in the clothing of the other gender
e. _____ a paraphilia in which sexual arousal is associated with the actual act of being humiliated, beaten, bound, or otherwise made to suffer
f. _____ cross-dressing for sexual arousal with eventual persistent discomfort with gender identity
g. _____ involuntary muscular spasm preventing sexual intercourse
h. _____ setting aside specific time for sexual activity
i. _____ a treatment for sexual dysfunction that involves a series of simple exercises in which the couple spends time in a quiet, relaxed setting, learning to touch each other
j. _____ a paraphilia in which sexual arousal is associated with desires to inflict physical or psychological suffering or humiliation on another person
k. _____ absence of genital sensations during sexual activity
l. _____ a procedure for measuring female sexual arousal
m. _____ association of sexual arousal with nonliving objects
n. _____ persistent genital pain during or after intercourse
o. _____ gay men who engage in cross-dressing for reasons other than sexual arousal
p. _____ inability to achieve orgasm even though a person experiences uninhibited sexual arousal
q. _____ intense sexual attraction to specific, nonsexual body parts
r. _____ fear of failure
s. _____ cross-dressing for the purpose of sexual arousal
t. _____ a disorder in which a man is unable to delay ejaculation long enough to accomplish intercourse

MATCHING III

Answers are found at the end of this chapter. Match these terms and concepts with the definitions that follow:

a. Exhibitionism
b. Voyeurism
c. Frotteurism
d. Pedophilia
e. Incest
f. Rape
g. Acquaintance rape
h. Sadistic rapists
i. Nonsadistic rapists
j. Vindictive rapists
k. Opportunistic rapists
l. Lovemap
m. Aversion therapy
n. Community notification laws
o. Sexual predator laws
p. Sex roles
q. Transexualism (gender dysphoria)
r. Pseudohermaphroditism
s. Sex-reassignment surgery

1. _____ a paraphilia characterized by distress over, or acting on, urges to expose one's genitals to an unsuspecting stranger
2. _____ rape committed by someone known to the victim
3. _____ sexual activity between close blood relatives
4. _____ a category of rapist who is preoccupied with sadistic sexual fantasies whose actions are brutal and violent
5. _____ a paraphilia characterized by distress over or acting on urges involving sexual activity with a prepubescent child
6. _____ discomfort with one's anatomical sex
7. _____ characteristics, behaviors, and skills that are defined within a culture as being either masculine or feminine
8. _____ surgery in which the person's genitals are changed to match his or her gender identity
9. _____ a category of rapist whose actions are intended to degrade and humiliate the victim
10. _____ being genetically male but lacking a hormone responsible for shaping the penis and scrotum, resulting in ambiguous external genitalia
11. _____ a paraphilia characterized by recurrent, intense sexual urges involving touching and rubbing against a nonconsenting person
12. _____ a paraphilia in which a person becomes sexually aroused by observing unsuspecting people while they are undressing or involved in sexual activity
13. _____ a category of rapist with distorted views of sexuality and women, feelings of inferiority, and poor social skills
14. _____ a treatment where the therapist repeatedly presents the stimulus that elicits inappropriate sexual arousal in association with an aversive stimulus
15. _____ acts involving nonconsensual sexual penetration obtained by physical force, threat of bodily harm, or when the victim is incapable of giving consent
16. _____ a mental picture representing a person's ideal sexual relationship
17. _____ laws designed to keep some criminals in custody indefinitely
18. _____ a category of rapist with impulsive, unplanned actions who seeks immediate gratification
19. _____ laws which require the distribution of information to the public regarding the presence of child molesters and sexually violent offenders when they are released from prison

MATCHING IV
Answers are found at the end of this chapter. Match these names with the descriptions of their contributions to the study of abnormal psychology:

    a. Alfred Kinsey   b. William Masters and Virginia Johnson   c. John Money

1. ____ proposed a model of the human sexual response cycle and developed treatments for sexual dysfunctions
2. ____ applied scientific methods to the study of sexuality
3. ____ studied the etiology of paraphilias; developed the concept of lovemaps

CONCEPT REVIEW
Answers are found at the end of this chapter. After you have read and reviewed the material, test your comprehension by filling in the blanks or circling the correct answer.

1. Male and female orgasm have different numbers of stages: **true**   **false**
2. Women typically have a longer refractory period than men: **true**   **false**
3. Women are capable of multiple orgasms while men are typically not: **true**   **false**
4. Sexual problems are best seen as problems of the individual: **true**   **false**
5. Early scientific approaches to sexual behavior were strongly influenced by the idea that the exclusive goal of sexuality was _____.
6. Kinsey rejected the distinction between _____ and _____ sexual behavior and saw differences as quantitative rather than qualitative.
7. Men report that their sexual partners have orgasms more often than women report having orgasms:

         true   **false**

8. The only factor important to sexual satisfaction, especially among women, is experiencing an orgasm:

         true   **false**

9. Failure to reach orgasm is not considered a disorder unless it is _____ and results in _____.
10. Viagra has been documented to be effective in the treatment of erectile dysfunction:

         true   **false**

11. Viagra has been associated with some deaths: **true**   **false**
12. Hypoactive Sexual Desire Disorder can be diagnosed by comparing a person's interest level with a chart of normal levels of sexual interest: **true**   **false**
13. People with low sexual desire often have _____ disorders.

14. There are high correlations between subjective and physiological measures of arousal in normal women:

    true   false

15. Almost all clinicians will identify the response of ejaculating before or upon_____ as indicative of premature ejaculation.

16. Dyspareunia is more common in **men/women.**

17. What is the most frequent form of male sexual dysfunction? _____

18. There is a cultural prejudice against sexual activity among older_____.

19. Older men achieve erections **more quickly/more slowly.**

20. The subjective experience of the intensity of orgasm **increases/decreases** with age.

21. Frequency of sexual dysfunction among men typically **increases/decreases** with age.

22. Frequency of sexual dysfunction among women typically **increases/decreases** with age.

23. The influence of male sex hormones on sexual behavior is thought to be on sexual _____ rather than on sexual _____.

24. Men who smoke cigarettes are more likely to have problems with _____.

25. Antidepressants can include the side-effect of orgasm problems: **true   false**

26. Women born in more recent decades are less likely to be orgasmic: **true   false**

27. Changing the way people think about sex is a major aspect of sex therapy:

    true   false

28. Paraphilias are only diagnosed if the person has _____ the urges or is _____ by them.

29. Most of the people in treatment for sexual disorders are people with paraphilias:

    true   false

30. The central feature of paraphilia is that sexual arousal is dependent on images that are detached from _____ relationships with another adult.

31. Paraphilias are similar to the _____.

32. Masochists tend to be disproportionately represented among poorer groups of people:

    true   false

33. Most exhibitionists are women: **true   false**

34. A voyeur is not aroused by watching people who know they are being observed:

    true   false

35. Most pedophiles are homosexual: **true   false**

36. Rape is not included as a paraphilia because it is not always motivated by _____.

37. Many rapists in one study had a history of paraphilias: **true   false**

38. Most people with a paraphilia exhibit other paraphilias as well: **true   false**

39. About what percent of people with paraphilias are men?

    60%   **75%**   **95%**

40. Damage to what part of the brain can lead to unusual sexual behaviors? _____

41. _____ skills may play as important a role in paraphilias as sexual arousal.

42. A surprising number of people involved in masochism had what type of experience as children? _____

43. Most people in treatment for paraphilias are there _____.

44. Cognitive-behavioral treatment was found to be **more/less** effective than aversion therapy in treating paraphilia.

45. Gender identity disorders are relatively **rare/common**.

46. Pseudohermaphrodites typically make a quick and fairly easy transition from a childhood female to an adult male gender identity: **true**   **false**

47. Results of sex-reassignment surgery have mostly been negative: **true**   **false**

CROSSWORD

Answers are found at the end of this chapter. Complete the following crossword puzzle to reinforce your understanding of this chapter's key terms and concepts:

ACROSS	DOWN
1. persistent genital pain associated with sexual intercourse	2. device which measures male sexual arousal
5. also referred to as "indecent exposure"	3. procedure developed by Masters and Johnson; cornerstone of sex therapy
7. sexually arousing urges involving being humiliated	4. device inserted into vagina; used to measure sexual arousal
10. involves sexually arousing urges or behaviors involving sex with prepubescent child	6. persistent involuntary spasm of musculature of vagina
12. sexual arousal from rubbing one's genitals against other, nonconsenting person	8. sexual desire disorder marked by recurrently deficient desire for sexual activity
13. refers to association of sexual arousal with nonliving objects	9. conditions marked by sexual arousal associated with unusual things or situations
15. involves sexually arousing fantasies involving suffering	11. sexual arousal from observing an unsuspecting person
16. dysfunction marked by difficulty obtaining or maintaining an erection	14. sexual activity between close blood relatives

MULTIPLE CHOICE

Answers are found at the end of this chapter. The multiple choice questions listed will test your understanding of the material presented in the chapter. Read through each question and circle the letter representing the best answer.

1. All of the following types of medication have been used to treat paraphilias except
    a. antipsychotic medications
    b. antidepressants
    c. antianxiety medications
    d. all of the above

2. According to Freund and Blanchard, all of the following factors may increase the probability that a person might experiment with unusual types of sexual stimulation or employ maladaptive sexual behaviors except
    a. ignorance and poor understanding of human sexuality
    b. lack of diverse sexual experiences
    c. lack of self-esteem
    d. lack of confidence and ability in social interactions

3. With regard to the context of occurrence, which of the following terms indicates that the sexual dysfunction is not limited only to certain situations or partners
    a. situational
    b. lifelong
    c. acquired
    d. generalized

4. Recent revisions of the DSM reflect the following important changes in society's attitudes toward sexual behavior except
    a. growing acceptance of women of their own sexuality
    b. tolerance for greater variety in human sexuality
    c. society's complete acceptance of organized groups that represent specific forms of sexual orientation and expression
    d. increased recognition that the main purpose of sexual behavior need not be reproduction

5. _____ disorders are more common among women while _____ disorders are more common among men.
    a. Orgasm; arousal
    b. Arousal; orgasm
    c. Aversion; desire
    d. Desire; aversion

6. Studies show that most women seeking treatment for hypoactive sexual desire report all of the following except
    a. negative perceptions of their parents' attitudes regarding sexual behavior
    b. a history of physical and sexual abuse
    c. negative perceptions of their parents' demonstration of affection
    d. feeling less close to their husbands and having fewer romantic feelings

7. This involves the use of nonliving objects for the purpose of sexual arousal.
    a. frotteurism
    b. pedophilia
    c. fetishism
    d. sexual masochism

8. Sex-reassignment surgery is the process whereby a person's genitals are changed to match his or her
    a. gender identity
    b. sex role
    c. sexual identity
    d. gender role

9. According to your text, _____ may be the most common neurologically-based cause of impaired erectile responsiveness among men.
    a. depression
    b. coronary heart disease
    c. diabetes
    d. cancer

10. All of the following are treatment options for sexual dysfunctions except
    a. sensate focus
    b. cognitive restructuring
    c. communication training
    d. aversion therapy

11. _____ of those who seek treatment for paraphilia disorders are men.
    a. Forty percent
    b. Sixty percent
    c. Seventy-five percent
    d. Ninety-five percent

12. _____ and _____ have undoubtedly been the best-known sex therapists and researchers in the United States since the late 1960s.
    a. William Masters; Virginia Johnson
    b. Alfred Kinsey; Havelock Ellis
    c. Sigmund Freud; Richard von Krafft-Ebing
    d. Robert Spitzer; Helen Singer Kaplan

13. The sense of being either male or female is known as
    a. sexual identity
    b. gender dysphoria
    c. gender identity
    d. sex roles

14. Premature ejaculation may be the most frequent form of sexual dysfunction, affecting nearly 1 in every
    a. five adult men
    b. ten adult men
    c. fifteen adult men
    d. twenty adult men

15. The treatment approach used for paraphilias in which the therapist repeatedly presents a stimulus eliciting inappropriate sexual arousal in association with an aversive stimulus is called
    a. counterconditioning
    b. aversion therapy
    c. flooding
    d. systematic desensitization

16. Research on sexual behavior across the life span shows that
    a. younger men have difficulty regaining an erection if it is lost before orgasm, while older men can only maintain erections for a short period of time
    b. older adults are not as interested in, or capable of, performing sexual behaviors as younger adults
    c. differences between younger and older people are mostly a matter of degree
    d. as women get older, the clitoris becomes more responsive

17. Men with this problem may report feeling aroused, but the vascular reflex mechanism fails, and sufficient blood is not pumped to the penis.
    a. sexual aversion disorder
    b. premature ejaculation
    c. male orgasmic disorder
    d. erectile dysfunction

18. In order to meet diagnostic criteria, all categories of sexual dysfunction require all of the following except
    a. the sexual dysfunction is associated with atypical stimuli and the person is preoccupied with, or consumed by, these activities
    b. the disturbance causes marked distress or interpersonal difficulty
    c. the sexual dysfunction is not better accounted for by another Axis I disorder (such as major depression)
    d. the sexual dysfunction is not due to direct physiological effects of a substance or a general medical condition

19. Perhaps as many as _____ of females seeking treatment for hypoactive sexual desire report other forms of sexual dysfunction.
    a. 25 percent
    b. 40 percent
    c. 60 percent
    d. 75 percent

20. According to your text, sexual desire remains a controversial topic because
    a. it is so difficult to define
    b. there is very little empirical research on sexual desire
    c. it is a different construct for men than it is for women
    d. all of the above

21. The unresponsiveness of most men to further engage in sexual stimulation for a period of time after reaching orgasm is called
    a. sensation of suspension
    b. pulsation
    c. sexual aversion
    d. refractory period

22. Premature ejaculation might be present if a man is unable to delay ejaculation until his partner reaches orgasm at least _____ of the time.
    a. 25 percent
    b. 50 percent
    c. 75 percent
    d. 100 percent

23. Studies have shown that all of the following are important factors contributing to failure to reach orgasm among anorgasmic women except
    a. failure to engage in effective behaviors during foreplay
    b. negative attitudes toward masturbation
    c. feelings of guilt about sex
    d. failure to communicate effectively with their partner about sexual activities involving direct stimulation of the clitoris

24. All of the following refer to a sense of discomfort with one's anatomical sex except
    a. gender identity disorder
    b. transvestic fetishism
    c. gender dysphoria
    d. transsexualism

25. Research suggests that _____ of men over age 75 report experiencing erectile dysfunction.
    a. 30 percent
    b. 40 percent
    c. 50 percent
    d. 60 percent

26. This involves the act of observing an unsuspecting person who is naked, in the process of disrobing, or engaging in sexual activity
    a. sexual sadism
    b. voyeurism
    c. exhibitionism
    d. fetishism

27. Which of the following characterizes an individual who is genetically male, but is unable to produce a hormone that is responsible for shaping the penis and scrotum in the fetus, and is therefore born with external genitalia that are ambiguous in appearance?
    a. transsexualism
    b. secondary sexual characteristic disorder
    c. transvestic fetishism
    d. pseudohermaphroditism

28. Which of the following is not one of the reasons for opposition to the proposed diagnostic category of excessive sexual drive?
    a. it is very rare
    b. its definition is circular
    c. problems controlling sexual impulses can be characteristic of several other disorders
    d. it is unclear whether it represents a meaningful diagnostic category

UNDERSTANDING RESEARCH
Answers are found at the end of this chapter.

Sexual Activity in the General Population: The text presents a detailed description of a study in the Research Close-Up. Finding the answers to these questions will provide an understanding of this study and why it is important.

1. This study was the first large-scale follow up to the _____ reports. How many men and women participated? _____ What ages were the subjects? _____ to _____. What was the most important element of the research design? The study used _____. During the year of the survey, _____ percent of the participants had more than one sexual partner, and _____ percent had no partner. What percent of people born between 1963 and 1974 have had premarital sex? _____ percent of men and _____ percent of women.

2. People without _____ affiliation felt less guilty about masturbating. Which was more prevalent, masturbation or anal sex? _____ Younger, better-educated people were more likely to use _____. When were people most reluctant to use condoms? _____

SHORT ANSWER
Answer the following short answer questions. Compare your work to the material presented in the text.

1. Compare and contrast the treatment of paraphilias with the treatment of sexual dysfunction. Select two types of paraphilias and two types of sexual dysfunctions. Discuss which type of treatment would be most effective for each.

2. Discuss Barlow's studies comparing sexually dysfunctional men with control subjects in laboratory settings. What were his findings? What are several limitations to these studies? Discuss several applications of his findings?

3. Compare and contrast different perspectives regarding the etiology of paraphilias. Which perspectives do you believe best explain the etiology of paraphilias? Why?

4. Discuss what is meant by a hypothetical construct. Why is sexual arousal considered a hypothetical construct?

ANSWER KEY

MATCHING I

1. f
2. d
3. l
4. p
5. i
6. a
7. s
8. j
9. b
10. o

11. c
12. g
13. k
14. e
15. q
16. n
17. r
18. m
19. h

MATCHING II

a. 3
b. 1
c. 9
d. 15
e. 19
f. 18
g. 8
h. 12
i. 11
j. 20

k. 6
l. 2
m. 13
n. 7
o. 17
p. 5
q. 14
r. 10
s. 16
t. 4

MATCHING III

1. a
2. g
3. e
4. h
5. d
6. q
7. p
8. s
9. j
10. r

11. c
12. b
13. i
14. m
15. f
16. l
17. o
18. k
19. n

MATCHING IV

1. b
2. a

3. c

MULTIPLE CHOICE

1.	a	6.	b	11.	d	16.	c	21.	d	26.	b
2.	b	7.	c	12.	a	17.	d	22.	b	27.	d
3.	d	8.	a	13.	c	18.	a	23.	a	28.	a
4.	c	9.	c	14.	a	19.	d	24.	b		
5.	a	10.	d	15.	b	20.	a	25.	c		

CONCEPT REVIEW

1. true
2. false
3. true
4. false
5. reproduction
6. normal; abnormal
7. true
8. false
9. persistent; distress
10. true
11. true
12. false
13. mood
14. false
15. insertion
16. women
17. premature ejaculation
18. women
19. more slowly
20. decreases
21. increases
22. decreases
23. appetite; performance
24. erection
25. true
26. false
27. true
28. acted on; distressed
29. false
30. loving
31. addictions
32. false
33. false
34. true
35. false
36. sexual arousal
37. true
38. true
39. 95 %
40. temporal lobe
41. Interpersonal
42. traumatic disease and painful medical procedures
43. involuntarily
44. more
45. rare
46. true
47. false

UNDERSTANDING RESEARCH

1. Kinsey; 3,500; 18; 59; probability sampling; 16; 11; 84; 80

2. religious; masturbation; condoms; in new sexual relationships

CROSSWORD

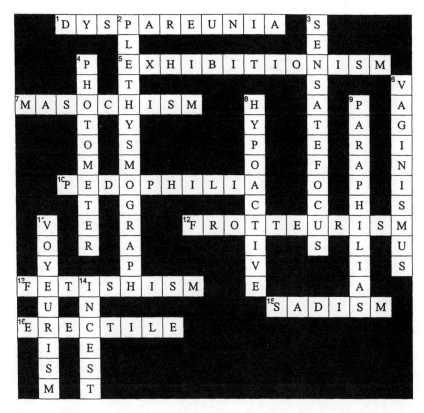

ACROSS	DOWN
1. persistent genital pain associated with sexual intercourse	2. device which measures male sexual arousal
5. also referred to as "indecent exposure"	3. procedure developed by Masters and Johnson; cornerstone of sex therapy
7. sexually arousing urges involving being humiliated	4. device inserted into vagina; used to measure sexual arousal
10. involves sexually arousing urges or behaviors involving sex with prepubescent child	6. persistent involuntary spasm of musculature of vagina
12. sexual arousal from rubbing one's genitals against other, nonconsenting person	8. sexual desire disorder marked by recurrently deficient desire for sexual activity
13. refers to association of sexual arousal with nonliving objects	9. conditions marked by sexual arousal associated with unusual things or situations
15. involves sexually arousing fantasies involving suffering	11. sexual arousal from observing an unsuspecting person
16. dysfunction marked by difficulty obtaining or maintaining an erection	14. sexual activity between close blood relatives

CHAPTER THIRTEEN

SCHIZOPHRENIC DISORDERS

CHAPTER OUTLINE

Overview
Typical Symptoms and Associated Features
    Positive Symptoms
    Negative Symptoms
    Disorganization
Classification
    Brief Historical Perspective
    DSM-IV-TR
    Subtypes
    Related Psychotic Disorders
    Course and Outcome
Epidemiology
    Gender Differences
    Cross-Cultural Comparisons
Etiological Considerations and Research
    Biological Factors
    Social Factors
    Psychological Factors
    Integration and Multiple Pathways
    The Search for Markers of Vulnerability
Treatment
    Antipsychotic Medication
    Psychosocial Treatment
Summary

OBJECTIVES

1. Distinguish between positive symptoms, negative symptoms, and disorganization.
2. Discuss the phases of schizophrenia.
3. Define and describe hallucinations, delusional beliefs, and disorganized speech.
4. Provide examples of motor disturbances, affective and emotional disturbances, and avolition.
5. Discuss the contributions of Kraepelin and Bleuler in defining schizophrenia.
6. Distinguish between disorganized, catatonic, paranoid, undifferentiated, and residual types of schizophrenia.
7. Describe characteristics of schizoaffective, delusional, and brief psychotic disorder.
8. Discuss the epidemiology of schizophrenia.
9. Discuss the diathesis-stress model as it relates to schizophrenia.
10. Describe current brain research regarding the etiology of schizophrenia.
11. Explain the dopamine hypothesis and current beliefs about the role of dopamine in schizophrenia.
12. Identify several social and psychological factors which may contribute to the development and maintenance of schizophrenia.
13. Discuss the identification of attentional, cognitive, and eye-tracking dysfunctions in schizophrenics and biological relatives.

14. Describe the effectiveness of medications in the treatment of schizophrenia.
15. Describe family-oriented aftercare programs, social skills training, and the use of token economies in the treatment of those with schizophrenia.

MATCHING I

Answers are found at the end of this chapter. Match these terms and concepts with the definitions that follow:

a	Negative symptoms		n.	Perseveration
b.	Positive symptoms		o.	Alogia
c.	Disorganization		p.	Poverty of speech
d.	Schizophreniform disorder		q.	Thought blocking
e.	Active phase		r.	Catatonia
f.	Prodromal phase		s.	Delusions
g.	Residual phase		t.	Blunted affect
h.	Hallucinations		u.	Anhedonia
i.	Disorganized speech		v.	Inappropriate affect
j.	Stuporous state		w.	Avolition
k.	Incoherent		x.	Dementia praecox
l.	Loose associations		y.	Catatonic type
m.	Tangentiality		z.	Disorganized type

1. _____ the patient's train of speech is interrupted before a thought is completed
2. _____ when hallucinations, delusions, and disorganized speech are evident
3. _____ after positive symptoms; continued deterioration of role functioning
4. _____ reflect loss of normal functions
5. _____ immobility and marked muscular rigidity, or excitement and overactivity
6. _____ extremely disorganized speech which conveys little meaning
7. _____ an early grouping of several types of psychosis now seen as schizophrenia
8. _____ reflect a distortion of normal functions, like psychosis
9. _____ inability to experience pleasure
10. _____ remarkable reductions in the amount of speech
11. _____ schizophrenia characterized by disorganized speech, disorganized behavior, and flat or inappropriate affect
12. _____ shifting topics too abruptly
13. _____ schizophrenia characterized by symptoms of motor immobility or excessive and purposeless motor activity
14. _____ psychotic symptoms lasting between 1 and 6 months
15. _____ idiosyncratic beliefs that are rigidly held despite their preposterous nature
16. _____ indecisiveness, ambivalence, and loss of willpower
17. _____ generally reduced responsiveness
18. _____ persistently repeating the same word or phrase over and over again
19. _____ prior to positive symptoms, marked by deterioration in role functioning
20. _____ a flattening or restriction of a person's nonverbal display of emotion
21. _____ incongruity and lack of adaptability in emotional expression
22. _____ severe disruptions of verbal communication involving the form of speech
23. _____ replying to a question with an irrelevant response
24. _____ impoverished thinking marked by non fluent or barren speech
25. _____ verbal communication problems and bizarre behavior
26. _____ sensory experiences not caused by actual external stimuli

MATCHING II

Answers are found at the end of this chapter. Match these terms and concepts with the definitions that follow:

1. Paranoid type
2. Undifferentiated type
3. Residual type
4. Schizoaffective disorder
5. Delusional disorder
6. Brief psychotic disorder
7. Lifetime morbid risk
8. Lateral ventricles
9. Magnetic resonance imaging
10. Hemispheric asymmetry
11. Treatment resistance
12. Assertive community treatment
13. Positron emission tomography
14. Dopamine hypothesis
15. Social causation hypothesis
16. Social selection hypothesis
17. Communication deviance
18. Expressed emotion
19. Case control design
20. Schizotaxia
21. Threshold model
22. Vulnerability marker
23. Neuroleptic drugs
24. Extrapyramidal symptoms
25. Tardive dyskinesia
26. Atypical antipsychotics

a. _____ harmful events associated with membership in lowest social classes play a causal role in the development of schizophrenia
b. _____ subtle neurological defect in people predisposed to schizophrenia
c. _____ an imaging technique that allows identification of specific, small brain structures
d. _____ comparisons between groups of people with a disorder and groups of people who do not have the disorder
e. _____ side effects including muscular rigidity, tremors, restless agitation, peculiar involuntary postures, and motor inertia
f. _____ the cavities on each side of the brain that are filled with cerebrospinal fluid
g. _____ an imaging technique that reflects changes in brain activity as the person performs various tasks
h. _____ focuses on the function of specific dopamine pathways in the limbic area of the brain as having a role in the etiology of schizophrenia
i. _____ schizophrenia characterized by psychotic symptoms but that does not fit any one subtype
j. _____ antipsychotic medications that induce side effects that resemble the motor symptoms of Parkinson's disease
k. _____ an intervention combining psychological treatments with medication
l. _____ schizophrenia characterized by systematic delusions with persecutory or grandiose content
m. _____ a specific measure that might be useful in identifying people who are vulnerable to a disorder
n. _____ an episode of symptoms of both schizophrenia and a mood disorder
o. _____ people with schizophrenia experience downward social mobility
p. _____ peculiar statements, difficulty in completing answers, and other types of disruptive verbal behavior in parents of schizophrenics
q. _____ does not meet the criteria of schizophrenia but are preoccupied for at least one month with delusions that are not bizarre
r. _____ the proportion of a specific population that will be affected by a disorder at some point during their lives
s. _____ negative or intrusive attitudes displayed by relatives of schizophrenics
t. _____ a syndrome caused by prolonged treatment with neuroleptic drugs consisting of involuntary movements of the mouth and face as well as spasmodic movements of the limbs and trunk of the body
u. _____ people who exhibit psychotic symptoms for at least a day but less than a month
v. _____ new forms of antipsychotic medication that do not produce extrapyramidal symptoms or tardive dyskinesia

w. ____ a structure being larger in one hemisphere of the brain than the other
x. ____ liability to have a disorder lies along a continuum, but the probability that certain symptoms will be present changes dramatically as the person crosses a certain point on the continuum
y. ____ failure to improve on three types of medication after six weeks of treatment
z. ____ schizophrenia in partial remission, with no active phase symptoms

MATCHING III
Answers are found at the end of this chapter. Match these names with the descriptions of their contributions to the study of abnormal psychology:

a. Emil Kraeplin
b. Eugen Bleuler
c. Lyman Wynne & Margaret Singer
d. Kurt Schneider
e. Irving Gottesman
f. Leonard Heston
g. Paul Meehl

1. ____ one of the world's leading experts on genetic factors and schizophrenia
2. ____ grouped together several psychotic disorders into the category of dementia praecox, an early term for schizophrenia
3. ____ proposed a theory of schizophrenia involving schizotaxia
4. ____ conducted the first adoption study of schizophrenia
5. ____ developed a diagnostic system for schizophrenia which emphasized first-rank symptoms
6. ____ coined the term schizophrenia, which means splitting of mental associations
7. ____ explored communication deviance among parents of schizophrenics

CONCEPT REVIEW
Answers are found at the end of this chapter. After you have read and reviewed the material, test your comprehension by filling in the blanks or circling the correct answer.

1. What are the three categories of symptoms of schizophrenia? _____, _____, and _____
2. What is the period of risk for the development of a first episode of schizophrenia? _____ years old to _____ years old
3. After the onset of schizophrenia, most people return to their previous levels of functioning:

    true   **false**

4. What is the most common type of hallucination? _____
5. Delusions are typically shared by the patient's family: **true**   **false**
6. Disorganized speech breaks all the rules of grammar: **true**   **false**
7. During a state of stupor, schizophrenic patients remain aware of what is happening around them:

    true   **false**

8. Many people with schizophrenia evidence social withdrawal: **true**   **false**
9. Schizophrenia is a sort of multiple personality disorder: **true**   **false**
10. Schizophrenia follows a predictable course among most patients: **true**   **false**
11. What is the lifetime morbid risk of schizophrenia? _____ percent
12. Women typically have an earlier age of onset than men: **true**   **false**

13. Men typically have more negative symptoms than women: **true**   **false**
14. Women typically respond better to treatment than men: **true**   **false**
15. Schizophrenia is very rare in non industrialized countries: **true**   **false**
16. People with schizophrenia have a better outcome if they live in a developing country rather than a developed country: **true**   **false**
17. What is the lifetime risk of developing schizophrenia if your identical twin has the disorder? ____ percent
18. What is the lifetime risk of developing schizophrenia if your fraternal twin has the disorder? ____ percent
19. Genetic factors do not play a role in the etiology of schizophrenia: **true**   **false**
20. Adoption studies indicate that environmental factors cause schizophrenia:

    true   **false**
21. The data suggest that multiple genes are responsible for vulnerability to schizophrenia:

    true   **false**
22. People with schizophrenia are more likely to have experienced difficulties during and prior to their birth:

    true   **false**
23. Severe _____ of the mother during the early part of pregnancy increases the child's later risk for schizophrenia.
24. People with schizophrenia were more likely to be born during what season? _____
25. People with schizophrenia have been found to have _____ lateral ventricles in the brain.
26. People with schizophrenia are more likely to show a decrease in the size of what brain structure? _____
27. One MZ twin pair discordant for schizophrenia involved one brother who was a successful businessman and another who was severely impaired with schizophrenia. Whose lateral ventricles were five times larger? _____
28. What other neurotransmitter besides dopamine may be involved in schizophrenia? _____
29. Which hypothesis has received support in the research literature, the social causation hypothesis or the social selection hypothesis? _____
30. Parents of schizophrenic children who show communication deviance in their conversations with their ill children **do/do not** show CD in their conversations with their well children.
31. Men with schizophrenia were **more/less** likely to return to the hospital if they were discharged to live with their wives or parents rather than their siblings or strangers.
32. What seems to be the important component of expressed emotion? _____
33. Lots of contact with relatives high on EE **helps/hurts** patients with schizophrenia; and lots of contact with relatives low on EE **helps/hurts** patients with schizophrenia.
34. High EE is **more/less** common in Western countries.

35. Schizophrenic patients are **more/less** accurate than normal people in the Continuous Performance Task.
36. Relatives of schizophrenic patients are **more/less** accurate than normal people in the Continuous Performance Task.
37. _____-tracking performance may be associated with a predisposition to schizophrenia.
38. Neuroleptic medications take _____ to have an effect.
39. All people with schizophrenia respond to neuroleptic medications given in the correct dose:

    true   **false**

40. What percent of patients develop tardive dyskinesia after long-term treatment with neuroleptic drugs? _____ percent
41. Continued maintenance on neuroleptic drugs after recovery significantly reduces relapse:

    true   **false**

42. Why is Clozaril not used with all schizophrenic patients? _____
43. Patients who do not respond to neuroleptic medication do not improve with any type of treatment:

    true   **false**

CROSSWORD

Answers are found at the end of this chapter. Complete the following crossword puzzle to reinforce your understanding of his chapter's key terms and concepts:

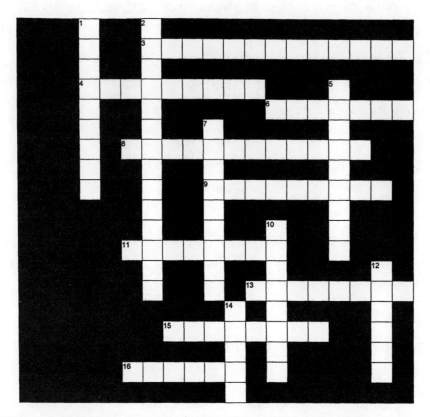

ACROSS	DOWN
3. medications used to reduce the severity of psychotic symptoms	1. immobility and marked muscular rigidity
4. lack of will	2. sensory experiences not caused by actual external stimuli
6. affective flattening	5. inability to experience pleasure
8. type of schizophrenia characterized by disorganized speech and behavior	7. phase which precedes active phase of schizophrenia
9. idiosyncratic beliefs which are rigidly held	10. symptoms which include lack of initiative and social withdrawal
11. neurotransmitter which figures prominently in understanding of schizophrenia	12. area which plays a role in emotional processing within the brain
13. type of schizophrenia marked by systematic delusions with persecutory content	14. infections which may play a role in development of schizophrenia
15. symptoms which include hallucinations and delusions	
16. impoverished thinking	

MULTIPLE CHOICE

Answers are found at the end of this chapter. The multiple choice questions listed will test your understanding of the material presented in the chapter. Read through each question and circle the letter representing the best answer.

1. Research on the relationship between expressed emotion (EE) and schizophrenia supports which of the following?
    a. the presence of expressed emotion is only associated with the onset of an individual's initial episode of schizophrenia
    b. among the various types of comments that contribute to a high EE rating, criticism is typically most associated with the likelihood of relapse
    c. the influence of expressed emotions is unique to schizophrenia
    d. all of the above

2. The trend in the DSM-IV-TR diagnosis of schizophrenia over time has been which of the following?
    a. include more affective symptoms
    b. omit subtyping of the disorder
    c. move from a broader to narrower definition of schizophrenia
    d. move from a more restrictive to less restrictive duration criterion

3. Which of the following would not be considered a positive symptom of schizophrenia?
    a. hallucinations
    b. blunted affect
    c. delusions
    d. disorganized speech

4. The distribution of schizophrenia within families is probably best explained by which of the following genetic models?
    a. polygenic
    b. single dominant gene
    c. single recessive gene
    d. linked genes

5. A difference between schizophrenia and delusional disorder is that
    a. patients with schizophrenia display less impairment in their daily functioning than patients with delusional disorder
    b. patients with delusional disorder display more negative symptoms during the active phase of their illness
    c. the behavior of patients with schizophrenia is considerably less bizarre
    d. patients with delusional disorder are preoccupied with delusions that are not necessarily bizarre

6. In the search to identify people who are vulnerable to schizophrenia, several potential vulnerability markers have been considered. Which of the following would not be considered a good criterion for a vulnerability marker?
    a. the marker should be able to distinguish between people who are already schizophrenic and people who are not
    b. the marker should be a characteristic which is stable over time
    c. the marker should be able to identify more people who are relatives of schizophrenics than people in the general population
    d. the marker should be able to predict the likelihood of relapse for people who have already experienced their first episode of schizophrenia

7. Individuals who exhibit psychotic symptoms for no more than a month and that cannot be attributed to other disorders such as substance abuse or mood disorder usually receive the diagnosis of
    a. delusional disorder
    b. schizophreniform disorder
    c. brief psychotic disorder
    d. schizoaffective disorder

8. Tangentiality is an example of which type of disturbance?
    a. motor disturbance
    b. affective disturbance
    c. disorganized speech
    d. delusional belief

9. Which of the following statements is true regarding the use of neuroleptic medication?
    a. beneficial effects are noticed within 24 hours after beginning the medication
    b. they appear to be particularly effective for relief of the positive symptoms associated with schizophrenia
    c. almost all schizophrenic patients are considered to be complete responders to this type of medication
    d. schizophrenic patients with the most severe symptoms respond best to them

10. Research on schizophrenic twins and adopted-away offspring of schizophrenics suggests which of the following?
    a. vulnerability to schizophrenia is consistently manifested by the same symptoms of this disorder across relatives
    b. vulnerability to schizophrenia is expressed through a variety of different symptom patterns, including depressive and anxiety syndromes
    c. vulnerability to schizophrenia is consistently manifested by the same symptoms of this disorder only when male relatives are affected
    d. vulnerability to schizophrenia is sometimes manifested by schizophrenic-like personality traits and non-schizophrenic psychotic disorders

11. Which of the following is not a possible explanation for the relationship between the presence of familial communication problems and schizophrenia?
    a. parental communication problems may cause the child's disorder
    b. the child's adjustment problems may cause the parents' problems
    c. the child's disorder and the parent communication problems reflect a common genetic influence
    d. all of the above are possible explanations for the presence of this relationship

12. Which of the following reflects a change in the DSM-IV-TR's definition of schizophrenia?
    a. negative symptoms assume a more prominent role
    b. positive symptoms assume a more prominent role
    c. the person must display active symptoms of the illness for at least one year
    d. a decline in the person's functioning is no longer required

13. A restriction of an individual's nonverbal display of his or her emotional responses is referred to as
    a. blunted affect
    b. affective loosening
    c. anhedonia
    d. inappropriate affect

14. An interesting and consistent result across numerous MRI studies is that some people with schizophrenia have
    a. an enlarged hypothalamus
    b. enlarged lateral ventricles
    c. enlarged temporal lobes
    d. less cerebrospinal fluid

15. Studies investigating the relationship between social class and schizophrenia indicate that risk for the disorder
    a. is associated with adverse social and economic circumstances
    b. is not associated by circumstances most likely to be present in the lives of people who are economically disadvantaged
    c. is associated with the unique types of circumstances most frequently affiliated with high social class
    d. is most associated with recent immigration to a country

16. Which statement about the course of schizophrenia is true?
    a. a significant amount of individuals experience their first episode between 35-50 years of age
    b. the onset of the disorder typically occurs during adolescence or early adulthood
    c. the active phase of illness is always the longest of the three phases
    d. the premorbid phase of illness usually lasts no longer than six months

17. Inconsistencies associated with the dopamine model of schizophrenia include which of the following?
    a. dopamine blockage begins immediately when medication is administered but the drugs often take several days to become effective
    b. some patients do not respond positively to drugs that block dopamine receptors
    c. studies investigating the byproducts of dopamine in cerebrospinal fluid are inconsistent and inconclusive
    d. all of the above

18. Which of the following is not included in the DSM-IV-TR as a subtype of schizophrenia?
    a. paranoid
    b. residual
    c. undifferentiated
    d. negative

19. Joshua's behavior has been observed in the hospital ward for several hours. He has been sitting perfectly still in one position. Furthermore, he has been completely mute (has not spoken a single word) since admission. Which subtype of schizophrenia best represents Joshua's behavior?
    a. disorganized
    b. paranoid
    c. catatonic
    d. undifferentiated

20. The Danish High-Risk Project has supported which of the following hypotheses?
    a. families with individuals who develop the positive symptoms of the disorder appear to be at higher genetic risk
    b. children who experience head injuries before age five appear to be at greater risk for schizophrenia
    c. neurodevelopmental problems in schizophrenia are antecedents rather than consequences of the disorder
    d. problems in delivery at birth do not appear to be associated with vulnerability to schizophrenia

21. A criticism of twin studies and their persuasive evidence for the role of genetic factors in schizophrenia is that
    a. DZ and MZ twin concordance rates are approximately equal, suggesting that genetic factors are less important than environmental factors
    b. MZ twins, because of their physical similarity, are probably treated more similarly by their parents than even DZ twins, which confounds environmental with genetic factors
    c. the studies determining concordance rates are flawed because they do not take into account the birth order of the MZ twins
    d. the concordance rates for MZ twins for schizophrenia has fluctuated dramatically across studies

22. The potentially exciting part of eye-tracking dysfunction and the possibility of this characteristic being a vulnerability marker for schizophrenia is that
    a. eye-tracking dysfunction appears to be influenced by genetic factors and is apparently a stable trait
    b. eye-tracking dysfunction appears to be present only in patients with schizophrenia
    c. approximately 90 percent of the first-degree relatives of schizophrenic individuals show this characteristic
    d. the eye-tracking dysfunction only appears during episodes of schizophrenia

23. Research suggests that the outcome of schizophrenia may be best described by which of the following statements?
    a. fifty percent of the individuals continue to deteriorate after their first episode, 10 percent completely recover, and 40 percent experience intermittent episodes
    b. thirty percent of the individual recover fairly well after their initial episode, 30 percent continue to deteriorate, and 40 percent continue to experience intermittent episodes
    c. approximately 60 percent of the individuals recover fairly well after their initial episode, while 40 percent continue to deteriorate
    d. approximately 60 percent of the individuals continue to deteriorate after their initial episode, while 40 percent continue to experience intermittent episodes

24. When Samuel grins as he talks about the loss of his father in a traumatic accident, he is displaying
    a. disorganized affect
    b. avolition
    c. catatonia
    d. inappropriate affect

25. The theory that harmful events associated with being a member of the lowest social class (e.g., poor nutrition, social isolation) play a role in the development of schizophrenia is called
    a. the social class hypothesis
    b. the social causation hypothesis
    c. the social impairment hypothesis
    d. the social selection hypothesis

26. The usefulness of subtyping schizophrenia has been criticized because
    a. some individuals do not fit the traditional subtype descriptions
    b. some individuals display the symptoms of more than one subtype simultaneously
    c. the symptoms of some individuals change from one episode to the next, reflecting subtype instability
    d. all of the above

27. The average concordance rate for monozygotic twins for schizophrenia is
    a. 22 percent
    b. 36 percent
    c. 48 percent
    d. 72 percent

28. Perhaps the most unpleasant side effect of neuroleptics is
    a. the fact that the drugs must be taken for two to four months before the patient experiences relief from symptoms
    b. potentially toxic reactions to the drugs if the patient's diet is not carefully monitored
    c. the presence of extrapyramidal symptoms
    d. acute gastrointestinal symptoms (e.g., nausea, vomiting) during the first few weeks of use

29. Research on gender differences in schizophrenia supports that
    a. men experience their first episode of schizophrenia about five years later than women
    b. women typically display better premorbid social competence prior to their first episode of schizophrenia
    c. men typically display a less chronic course compared to women
    d. women display more negative symptoms

30. Bleuler's definition of schizophrenia emphasized which of the following?
    a. signs and symptoms of the disorder
    b. course and outcome
    c. genetic vulnerability markers
    d. impairment in social roles

UNDERSTANDING RESEARCH
Answers are found at the end of this chapter.

<u>The Danish High-Risk Project</u>: The text presents a detailed description of a study in the Research Close-Up. Finding the answers to these questions will provide an understanding of this study and why it is important.

1. What was the high-risk group used in this study? _____ What percent of the sample was expected to develop schizophrenia? _____ percent How many subjects were there all together? _____ The children in the comparison group came from families that had been free of mental illness for at least _____ generations. Data came from _____ records at the time of birth, structured _____ interviews, and _____ scans.

2. How many of the high-risk offspring have developed schizophrenia? _____ What percent of the high-risk offspring have developed schizotypal personality disorder? _____ percent Rates of mood disorders were _____ in the high-risk and the control groups. Delivery complications and enlarged ventricles were _____ in the high-risk but not the low-risk group. The members of the high-risk group who did develop schizophrenia had _____ pregnancy and birth complications than those who did not develop the disorder.

SHORT ANSWER
Answer the following short answer questions. Compare your work with the material presented in the text.

1. You are on a committee that will be responsible for developing the diagnostic criteria for schizophrenia for DSM-V. What would you consider to be the most appropriate criteria to be included? Explain.

2. Discuss the diathesis-stress model of schizophrenia. Which factors would represent the diathesis? Which factors would represent stress?

3. What issues must be addressed as a researcher designs a research project in psychopathology? What are the issues involved in the selection of subjects?

4. Describe and compare several forms of psychosocial approaches shown to be effective for the treatment of schizophrenia. What are their advantages and disadvantages?

ANSWER KEY

MATCHING I

1. q
2. e
3. g
4. a
5. r
6. k
7. x
8. b
9. u
10. p
11. z
12. l
13. y

14. d
15. s
16. w
17. j
18. n
19. f
20. t
21. v
22. i
23. m
24. o
25. c
26. h

MATCHING II

a. 15
b. 20
c. 9
d. 19
e. 24
f. 8
g. 13
h. 14
i. 2
j. 23
k. 12
l. 1
m. 22

n. 4
o. 16
p. 17
q. 5
r. 7
s. 18
t. 25
u. 6
v. 26
w. 10
x. 21
y. 11
z. 3

MATCHING III

1. e
2. a
3. g
4. f
5. d
6. b
7. c

MULTIPLE CHOICE

1.	b	7.	c	13.	a	19.	c	25.	b
2.	c	8.	c	14.	b	20.	c	26.	d
3.	b	9.	b	15.	a	21.	b	27.	c
4.	a	10.	d	16.	b	22.	a	28.	c
5.	d	11.	d	17.	d	23.	b	29.	b
6.	d	12.	a	18.	d	24.	d	30.	a

CONCEPT REVIEW

1. positive symptoms; negative symptoms; disorganization
2. 15; 35
3. false
4. auditory
5. false
6. false
7. true
8. true
9. false
10. false
11. 1
12. false
13. true
14. true
15. false
16. true
17. 48
18. 17
19. false
20. false
21. true
22. true
23. malnutrition
24. winter
25. larger
26. left temporal lobe
27. the businessman
28. serotonin
29. both
30. do not
31. more
32. criticism
33. hurts; helps
34. more
35. less
36. less
37. Eye
38. several weeks
39. true
40. 20
41. true
42. causes fatal agranulocystosis in 1 percent
43. false

UNDERSTANDING RESEARCH

1. children of schizophrenic patients; 13; 311; three; hospital; diagnostic; CT

2. 31; 18; similar; correlated; more

CROSSWORD

ACROSS	DOWN
3. medications used to reduce the severity of psychotic symptoms	1. immobility and marked muscular rigidity
4. lack of will	2. sensory experiences not caused by actual external stimuli
6. affective flattening	5. inability to experience pleasure
8. type of schizophrenia characterized by disorganized speech and behavior	7. phase which precedes active phase of schizophrenia
9. idiosyncratic beliefs which are rigidly held	10. symptoms which include lack of initiative and social withdrawal
11. neurotransmitter which figures prominently in understanding of schizophrenia	12. area which plays a role in emotional processing within the brain
13. type of schizophrenia marked by systematic delusions with persecutory content	14. infections which may play a role in development of schizophrenia
15. symptoms which include hallucinations and delusions	
16. impoverished thinking	

CHAPTER FOURTEEN

DEMENTIA, DELIRIUM, AND AMNESTIC DISORDERS

CHAPTER OUTLINE

Overview
Typical Symptoms and Associated Features
    Delirium
    Dementia
    Amnestic Disorder
Classification
    Brief Historical Perspective
    Specific Disorders Associated with Dementia
Epidemiology of Delirium and Dementia
    Prevalence of Dementia
    Prevalence by Subtypes of Dementia
    Cross-Cultural Comparisons
Etiological Considerations and Research
    Delirium
    Dementia
Treatment and Management
    Medication
    Environmental and Behavioral Management
    Support for Caregivers
Summary

OBJECTIVES

1. Describe the characteristics of dementia, delirium, and amnestic disorders.
2. Distinguish between retrograde and anterograde amnesia.
3. Describe the primary symptoms of aphasia, apraxia, and agnosia.
4. Discuss the role of neuropsychological assessment in the diagnosis of dementia.
5. Identify the contributions of Pinel, Broca, Wernicke, Korsakoff, Alzheimer, and Kraepelin in the diagnosis and understanding of cognitive disorders.
6. Distinguish between primary from secondary dementia.
7. Describe the features of Alzheimer's, Pick's, Huntington's, Parkinson's, and vascular diseases.
8. Describe the role of genetics, neurotransmitters, viral infections, and environmental factors in the development of cognitive disorders.
9. Discuss the importance of an accurate diagnosis in the treatment of dementia.
10. Discuss the importance of environmental and behavioral management, caregiver support, and respite programs in treatment patients with cognitive disorders.

MATCHING I
Answers are found at the end of this chapter. Match these terms and concepts with the definitions that follow:

a. Dementia
b. Delirium
c. Amnestic disorders
d. Neurologists
e. Neuropsychologists
f. Mechanics
g. Pragmatics
h. Retrograde amnesia
i. Anterograde amnesia
j. Aphasia
k. Apraxia
l. Agnosia
m. Neuropsychological assessment
n. Dyskinesia
o. Korsakoff's syndrome
p. Primary dementia
q. Secondary dementia

1. ____ a gradually worsening loss of memory and related cognitive functions
2. ____ inability to learn or remember new material after a particular point in time
3. ____ a disorder caused by chronic alcoholism characterized by memory impairment
4. ____ problems identifying stimuli in the environment
5. ____ cognitive impairment is produced by the direct effect of a disease on brain tissue
6. ____ a confusional state that develops over a short period of time and is often associated with agitation and hyperactivity
7. ____ involuntary movements such as tics and tremors
8. ____ fluid intelligence, the "hardware" of the mind
9. ____ psychologists with expertise in the assessment of specific types of cognitive impairment
10. ____ various types of loss or impairment in language caused by brain damage
11. ____ evaluation of performance on psychological tests to indicate whether a person has a brain disorder
12. ____ physicians who deal primarily with diseases of the brain and nervous system
13. ____ a cognitive disorder characterized by limited memory impairments
14. ____ difficulty performing purposeful movements in response to verbal commands
15. ____ cognitive impairment is a by-product or side effect of some other type of biological or psychological dysfunction
16. ____ loss of memory for events prior to the onset of an illness or traumatic event
17. ____ crystallized intelligence, the "software" of the mind

MATCHING II
Answers are found at the end of this chapter. Match these terms and concepts with the definitions that follow:

1. Alzheimer's disease
2. Tauproteins
3. Neurofibrillary tangles
4. Senile plaques
5. Beta-amyloid
6. Pick's disease
7. Pick's bodies
8. Huntington's disease
9. Chorea
10. Parkinson's disease
11. Infarct
12. Vascular dementia
13. Pseudodementia
14. Autosomal dominant trait
15. Genetic linkage
16. Creutzfeldt-Jakob disease
17. Respite programs
18. Lewy bodies

a. _____ a protein material
b. _____ caused by a dominant gene not located on one of the sex chromosomes
c. _____ a lesion consisting of a central core of homogenous protein material surrounded by clumps of debris left over from destroyed neurons
d. _____ a distinctive ballooning of nerve cells
e. _____ reinforce microtubules; lacking in patients with Alzheimer's Disease
f. _____ a form of dementia associated with atrophy in the frontal and temporal lobes of the brain
g. _____ a close association between two genes on a chromosome
h. _____ disorder of the motor system caused by a degeneration of the substantia nigra and loss of dopamine but rarely including dementia
i. _____ provide caregivers with temporary periods of relief from caring for a demented patient
j. _____ symptoms of dementia actually produced by a major depressive disorder
k. _____ a form of dementia characterized by the presence of unusual involuntary muscle movements as well as personality changes
l. _____ a form of dementia in which cognitive impairment appears gradually and deterioration is progressive
m. _____ a form of dementia produced by a slow-acting virus
n. _____ the area of dead tissue produced by a stroke
o. _____ a form of dementia associated with strokes
p. _____ when the structural network of some neurofibrils becomes highly disorganized
q. _____ unusual involuntary muscle movements
r. _____ deposits found in neurons of patients with Parkinson's disease and dementia

CONCEPT REVIEW

Answers are found at the end of this chapter. After you have read and reviewed the material, test your comprehension by filling in the blanks or circling the correct answer.

1. Delirium can fluctuate throughout the day: **true   false**
2. Delirium is less common among the elderly: **true   false**
3. Dementia can be cured: **true   false**
4. Changes in cognitive processes are not a normal part of aging: **true   false**
5. Which of the following typically show a decline with age?

   mechanics   pragmatics

6. Neuropsychological tests can sometimes be used to infer the location of a brain lesion:

   true   false

7. Hallucinations and delusions are seen in what percent of dementia cases?: _____
8. Korsakoff's syndrome may be caused in part by a _____ deficiency.
9. Which types of dementia are most common?

   differentiated   undifferentiated

10. A definitive diagnosis of Alzheimer's disease can only be made after _____.

11. Huntington's disease is caused by _____.
12. Vascular dementia often results in **unilateral/bilateral** impairment.
13. Almost _____ percent of people over ninety years of age exhibit symptoms of moderate or severe dementia: **20**   **40**   **60**
14. Average time between the onset of Alzheimer's disease and death is _____ years.
15. Genetic factors have been shown to play a role in dementia: **true   false**
16. Alzheimer's disease has been linked to what birth defect? _____.
17. Alzheimer's disease may involve dysfunction of the _____ system.
18. There is a controversial link between Alzheimer's disease and levels of what metal in the water system? _____
19. People who smoke cigarettes are **more/less** likely to develop Alzheimer's disease.
20. People with higher educational levels are less likely to develop Alzheimer's disease:
    true   false
21. Patients with dementia benefit from _____ environments.
22. Patients with dementia who remain active have less _____.
23. Dementia with Lewy bodies show fluctuations in cognitive performance:
    true   false
24. Prevalence rates for dementia may be **lower/higher** in developing countries.
25. Elderly people who have been knocked unconscious as adults have a **higher/lower** risk of developing Alzheimer's disease.

CROSSWORD

Answers are found at the end of this chapter. Complete the following crossword puzzle to reinforce your understanding of this chapter's key terms and concepts:

ACROSS
3. involuntary movements
4. condition that can be associated with symptoms of dementia
5. may be the second most common form of dementia
7. physicians who deal primarily with diseases of the brain
10. confusional state which develops over short period of time
13. disorder of the motor system
14. area of dead tissue produced by stroke

DOWN
1. amnesia marked by inability to learn new material
2. disease marked by chorea
5. gradual loss of memory and related cognitive functions
6. disease of which definite diagnosis may only be determined by autopsy
8. neurotransmitter of importance in the understanding of Parkinson's
9. amnesia marked by loss of memory for events prior to illness
11. "perception without meaning"
12. difficulty performing purposeful movements in response to verbal commands

MULTIPLE CHOICE
Answers are found at the end of this chapter. The multiple choice questions listed will test your understanding of the material presented in the chapter. Read through each question and circle the letter representing the best answer.

1. All of the following are goals in designing an environment conducive to patients with dementia except
    a. keep the patients relatively inactive in order to prevent them from hurting themselves
    b. facilitate the patient's knowledge of the environment through labeled rooms, hallways, etc.
    c. keep the environment negotiable (i.e., keep areas that a person will use often visible from their room if they cannot be remembered)
    d. stay abreast of safety and health issues

2. The _____ is probably the best known neuropsychological assessment procedure that involves the examination of performance on psychological tests to indicate whether a person has a brain disorder.
    a. Halstead-Reitan
    b. Weschler
    c. Symptoms Checklist-90 (SCL-90)
    d. Minnesota Multiphasic Personality Inventory-2 (MMPI-2)

3. _____ is a type of motor dysfunction that involves jerky, semi-purposeful movements of the person's face and limbs
    a. Anoxia
    b. Myotonia
    c. Chorea
    d. Lipofuscin

4. Which of the following appears to be the most common type of dementia?
    a. Pick's disease
    b. Huntington's disease
    c. Alzheimer's disease
    d. Vascular dementia

5. All of the following are typical symptoms of Parkinson's disease except
    a. tremors
    b. postural abnormalities
    c. gradual dementia
    d. reduction in voluntary movements

6. A _____ deals primarily with diseases of the brain and the nervous system.
    a. neurologist
    b. psychiatrist
    c. psychologist
    d. cardiologist

7. Which of the following diagnoses depends on the presence of a positive family history for the disorder?
    a. Parkinson's disease
    b. Alzheimer's disease
    c. Pick's disease
    d. Huntington's disease

8. According to Baltes, _____ is to fluid intelligence as _____ is to crystallized intelligence.
    a. wisdom; knowledge
    b. knowledge; wisdom
    c. cognitive mechanics; cognitive pragmatics
    d. cognitive pragmatics; cognitive mechanics

9. The DSM-IV-TR currently classifies dementia and related clinical phenomena as
    a. organic mental disorders
    b. biological mental disorders
    c. psychological disorders with organic etiology
    d. cognitive disorders

10. Betty's physician handed her a hairbrush and said "Show me what you do with this object." She took the brush and brushed her hair with it, but was unable to name the object. She is most likely suffering from which of the following?
    a. agnosia
    b. aphasia
    c. apraxia
    d. ataxia

11. Hallucinations and delusions are seen in about _____ of dementia cases.
    a. 10 percent
    b. 20 percent
    c. 30 percent
    d. 40 percent

12. The most effective form of treatment for improving cognitive functioning in dementia of the Alzheimer's type is
    a. cognitive therapy
    b. cognitive-behavioral therapy
    c. rational-emotive therapy (RET)
    d. no form of treatment is presently capable of improving cognitive functioning in dementia of the Alzheimer's type

13. One theory regarding Korsakoff's syndrome suggests that lack of _____ leads to atrophy of the medial thalamus.
    a. zinc
    b. vitamin C
    c. vitamin B1 (thiamin)
    d. potassium

14. Which of the of the following is a state of confusion which develops over a short period of time and is often associated with agitation and hyperactivity?
    a. delirium
    b. amnesia
    c. dementia
    d. Alzheimer's disease

15. All of the following are frequently associated with dementia except
    a. personality changes
    b. emotional difficulties
    c. a high frequency of drug abuse
    d. motivational problems

16. A definite diagnosis of Alzheimer's disease requires the observation of
    a. neurofibrillary tangles and senile plaques
    b. degeneration of the substantia nigra
    c. enlargement of the hypothalamus
    d. all of the above

17. Dementia with Lewy bodies is not associated with
    a. hallucinations
    b. variations in performance
    c. a slow, gradual course
    d. muscular rigidity

18. In order to qualify for a diagnosis of dementia, the person must exhibit memory impairment and which of the following?
    a. aggressive behavior
    b. problems in abstract thinking
    c. a previous episode of delirium
    d. age of at least 65 years

19. All of the following are true of delirium except
    a. it usually has a rapid onset
    b. speech is typically confused
    c. the person usually remains alert and responsive to the environment
    d. it can be resolved

20. Parkinson's disease is primarily a disorder of the motor system that is caused by a loss of dopamine and a degeneration of this specific area of the brain stem:
    a. substantia nigra
    b. thalamus
    c. fomix
    d. superior colliculi

21. Although controversial epidemiologic investigations have discovered that some types of dementia, especially Alzheimer's disease, may be related to all of the following except
    a. aluminum
    b. cigarette smoking
    c. level of educational experience
    d. lead

22. The incidence of dementia will be much greater in the near future because
    a. diagnostic criteria are more loosely defined
    b. the average age of the population is increasing steadily
    c. more people are being exposed to the environmental factors that have been shown to cause dementia
    d. dementia is now striking people at a much earlier age

23. Which of the following can be distinguished from other types of dementia listed in the DSM-IV-TR on the basis of speed of onset (i.e., cognitive impairment appears gradually, and the person's cognitive deterioration is progressive)?
    a. vascular dementia
    b. Huntington's disease
    c. Alzheimer's disease
    d. substance-induced persisting dementia

24. Which of the following is an example of a differentiated dementia?
    a. Huntington's disease
    b. Alzheimer's disease
    c. vascular dementia
    d. HIV

25. Some studies have confirmed an association between Alzheimer's disease and
    a. dependent personality disorder
    b. vascular dementia
    c. Korsakoff's syndrome
    d. Down syndrome

26. _____ is a disorder that is frequently associated with dementia.
    a. Bipolar disorder
    b. Depression
    c. Schizophrenia
    d. Multiple personality disorder

27. Which of the following are treatment options for patients with dementia??
    a. behavioral strategies
    b. cognitive strategies
    c. insight-oriented strategies
    d. all of the above

28. Almost _____ of people over 90 years of age exhibit symptoms of moderate or severe dementia.
    a. 25 percent
    b. 40 percent
    c. 65 percent
    d. 80 percent

29. All of the following are true of delirium except
    a. it typically fluctuates throughout the day and is usually worse at night
    b. the delirious person loses the ability to learn new information or becomes unable to recall previously learned information
    c. the delirious person is likely to be disoriented with relation to time or place
    d. the primary symptom is clouding of consciousness, which might also be described as a person's reduced awareness of his or her surroundings

UNDERSTANDING RESEARCH
Answers are found at the end of this chapter.

Japanese Culture and Reduced Risk for Cognitive Decline: The text presents a detailed description of a study in the Research Close-Up. Finding the answers to these questions will provide an understanding of this study and why it is important.

1. Prevalence rates for Alzheimer's disease are _____ in Japan than in North America and Europe. However, studies examining people living in each country are _____. One study examined 1604 _____ Americans in Washington. Elderly people without dementia were included and _____ percent had been tested for genetic vulnerability. Involvement in _____ culture was assessed with general _____ ability.

2. Two _____ later, participants' abilities were reassessed and 144 _____ were identified. Greater involvement with Japanese culture was associated with _____ levels of decline. This finding could not be attributed to diet. It may be that learning the Japanese _____ early in life is protective because of its inclusion of _____, which may build a cognitive _____.

SHORT ANSWER
Answer the following short answer questions. Compare your work to the material in your text.

1. Discuss how the behavioral effects of a stroke are different from those of dementia.

2. Discuss several environmental factors linked to dementia. What do you see as problematic with these findings? Why must we be cautious when interpreting this data?

3. Discuss the similarities and differences of dementia and depression. Provide an example of when it may be difficult to distinguish these apart.

4. Review the characteristics of delirium, Korsakoff's syndrome, Alzheimer's disease, and Huntington's disease.

5. What is a genetic linkage? Provide an example.

ANSWER KEY

MATCHING I

1. a
2. i
3. o
4. l
5. p
6. b
7. n
8. f
9. e
10. j
11. m
12. d
13. c
14. k
15. q
16. h
17. g

MATCHING II

a. 5
b. 14
c. 4
d. 7
e. 2
f. 6
g. 15
h. 10
i. 17
j. 13
k. 8
l. 1
m. 16
n. 11
o. 12
p. 3
q. 9
r. 18

CONCEPT REVIEW

1. true
2. false
3. false
4. false
5. mechanics
6. true
7. 20 percent
8. vitamin
9. undifferentiated
10. death
11. a gene
12. unilateral
13. 40
14. eight
15. true
16. Down Syndrome
17. immune
18. aluminum
19. less
20. true
21. structured
22. depression
23. true
24. lower
25. higher

MULTIPLE CHOICE

1.	a	9.	d	17.	c	25.	d
2.	a	10.	b	18.	b	26.	b
3.	c	11.	b	19.	c	27.	d
4.	c	12.	d	20.	a	28.	b
5.	c	13.	c	21.	d	29.	b
6.	a	14.	a	22.	b		
7.	d	15.	c	23.	c		
8.	c	16.	d	24.	a		

UNDERSTANDING RESEARCH

1. lower; confounded; Japanese; 70; Japanese; cognition

2. years; decliners; lower; language; pictographs; reserve

CROSSWORD

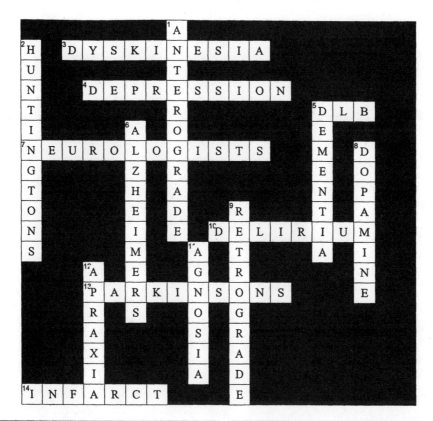

ACROSS	DOWN
3. involuntary movements	1. amnesia marked by inability to learn new material
4. condition that can be associated with symptoms of dementia	2. disease marked by chorea
5. may be the second most common form of dementia	5. gradual loss of memory and related cognitive functions
7. physicians who deal primarily with diseases of the brain	6. disease of which definite diagnosis may only be determined by autopsy
10. confusional state which develops over short period of time	8. neurotransmitter of importance in the understanding of Parkinson's
13. disorder of the motor system	9. amnesia marked by loss of memory for events prior to illness
14. area of dead tissue produced by stroke	11. "perception without meaning"
	12. difficulty performing purposeful movements in response to verbal commands

CHAPTER FIFTEEN

MENTAL RETARDATION AND PERVASIVE DEVELOPMENTAL DISORDERS

CHAPTER OUTLINE

Overview
Mental Retardation
    Typical Symptoms and Associated Features
    Classification
    Epidemiology
    Etiological Considerations and Research
    Treatment: Prevention and Normalization
Autistic Disorder and Pervasive Development Disorders
    Typical Symptoms and Associated Features
    Classification
    Epidemiology
    Etiological Considerations and Research
    Treatment
Summary

OBJECTIVES

1. Describe the defining characteristics of mental retardation and autism.
2. Distinguish between practical intelligence and social intelligence.
3. Identify the classification of mental retardation in DSM-IV-TR.
4. Discuss the biological causes of mental retardation.
5. Distinguish between primary, secondary, and tertiary prevention efforts as they relate to mental retardation.
6. Describe the types of difficulties autistic children have with social interactions.
7. Define dysprosody, echolalia, and pronoun rehearsal as they apply to impaired communication in autism.
8. Discuss the epidemiology of autism.
9. Discuss evidence pertaining to the biological basis of autism.
10. Discuss the advantages and disadvantages of behavior modification in the management of children with autism.

MATCHING I

Answers are found at the end of this chapter. Match the following terms and concepts with the definitions that follow:

a.	Mental retardation	n.	Phenylketonuria (PKU)
b.	Intelligence quotient (IQ)	o.	Tuberous sclerosis
c.	Normal distribution	p.	Tay-Sachs disease
d.	Standard deviation	q.	Hurler syndrome
e.	Mild mental retardation	r.	Lesch-Nyhan syndrome
f.	Moderate mental retardation	s.	Cytomegalovirus
g.	Severe mental retardation	t.	Toxoplasmosis
h.	Profound mental retardation	u.	Rubella
i.	Down syndrome	v.	Syphillis
j.	Fragile-X syndrome	w.	Genital herpes
k.	Klinefelter syndrome	x.	Encephalitis
l.	XYY syndrome	y.	Meningitis
m.	Turner syndrome	z.	Fetal alcohol syndrome

1. ____ an infection of the membranes that line the brain which can lead to inflammation that can damage the brain
2. ____ a relatively common and usually harmless infection that can be passed to the fetus that can cause mental retardation
3. ____ a chromosomal abnormality transmitted genetically which sometimes leads to mental retardation or learning disabilities
4. ____ characterized by mental retardation and self-mutilation
5. ____ substantial limitations in present functioning characterized by significantly subaverage intellectual functioning, concurrent limitations in adaptive skills, and an onset before age 18
6. ____ motor skills, communication, and self-care are severely limited; constant supervision required
7. ____ a bacterial sexually transmitted disease which, if untreated, can be passed to the fetus and can result in physical and sensory handicaps in the fetus, including mental retardation
8. ____ a protozoan infection caused by ingestion of infected raw meats or from contact with infected cat feces which can cause brain damage to a fetus
9. ____ an intelligence test's rating of an individual's intellectual ability
10. ____ can generally function at the second grade level academically, require close training and supervision in work activities, and need family or group home supervision
11. ____ a very rare dominant-gene disorder characterized by white growths in the ventricles of the brain
12. ____ also called German measles, a viral infection that can cause severe mental retardation or death in a fetus
13. ____ caused by a recessive gene, this disorder involves the absence of an enzyme that metabolizes phenylalanine, an amino acid in certain foods, which leads to brain damage that results in mental retardation
14. ____ once thought to increase criminality but now recognized to be linked with social deviance and a mean IQ 10 points lower than average
15. ____ a measure of dispersion of scores around the mean

16. ____ an extra X chromosome in males that leads to low normal to mildly mentally retarded intellectual functioning
17. ____ results in gross physical abnormalities, including dwarfism, humpback, bulging head, and clawlike hands
18. ____ a bell-shaped frequency distribution
19. ____ a rare recessive-gene disorder that eventually results in death during the infant or preschool years which is particularly common among Jews of Eastern European heritage
20. ____ can be transmitted to the baby at birth and cause mental retardation, blindness, or death
21. ____ a missing X chromosome in females that leads to failure to develop sexually and intelligence near or within the normal range
22. ____ a disorder characterized by retarded physical development, a small head, narrow eyes, cardiac defects, and cognitive impairment
23. ____ can generally function at the sixth grade level academically, acquire vocational skills, and live in the community without special supports
24. ____ typically have abnormal motor development, sharply limited communicative speech, and require close supervision for community living
25. ____ a brain infection that can cause permanent brain damage in about 20 percent of cases
26. ____ a chromosomal disorder characterized by a distinctively abnormal physical appearance and mental retardation typically in the moderate to severe range

MATCHING II

Answers are found at the end of this chapter. Match the following terms and concepts with the definitions that follow:

1. Mercury poisoning
2. Lead poisoning
3. Rh incompatibility
4. Premature birth
5. Anoxia
6. Epilepsy
7. Cultural-familial retardation
8. Heritability ratios
9. Reaction range
10. Amniocentesis
11. Normalization
12. Mainstreaming
13. Pervasive developmental disorders
14. Autism
15. Gaze aversion
16. Dysprosody
17. Echolalia
18. Pronoun reversal
19. Self-stimulation
20. Apparent sensory deficit
21. Self-injurious behavior
22. Savant performance
23. Asperger's disorder
24. Childhood disintegrative disorder
25. Rett's disorder

a. ____ a diagnostic procedure in which fluid is extracted from the amniotic sac that protects the fetus during pregnancy and genetic tests are run on the fluid to identify genetic abnormalities
b. ____ proposes that heredity determines the upper and lower limits of IQ, and experience determines the extent to which people fulfill their genetic potential
c. ____ a person's repetition of phrases that are spoken to them
d. ____ oxygen deprivation that can lead to brain damage
e. ____ can produce severe physical, emotional, and intellectual impairments

f. ____ disturbance in rate, rhythm, and intonation of speech production
g. ____ indices to measure the extent of genetic contribution to a characteristic
h. ____ a disorder similar to autism but which does not involve language delay
i. ____ at least five months of normal development followed by a deceleration in head growth, loss of purposeful hand movements, loss of social engagement, and language delay
j. ____ profound problems in social interaction, communication, and stereotyped behavior, interests, and activities
k. ____ confusion of pronouns, such as between "you" and "I"
l. ____ active avoidance of eye contact
m. ____ an exceptional ability in a highly specialized area of functioning
n. ____ cases of mental retardation with no known etiology that run in families and is linked with poverty
o. ____ seizure disorder that can result in mental retardation
p. ____ at toxic levels can produce behavioral and cognitive impairments, including mental retardation
q. ____ means that people with mental retardation are entitled to live as much as possible like other members of society
r. ____ unresponsiveness to auditory, tactile, or visual sensations even though there is no impairment in the sensory organ
s. ____ unusual psychological problems that begin early in life and involve severe impairments in a number of areas of functioning
t. ____ keeping mentally retarded children in regular classrooms as much as possible
u. ____ problems in social interaction and communication, as well as stereotyped behavior, with an onset following at least two years of normal development
v. ____ poses a risk for subsequent pregnancies because the mother's body produces antibodies which attack the developing fetus unless treated with an antibiotic
w. ____ ritual actions such as flapping a string or spinning a top that seem to serve no other purpose than to provide sensory feedback
x. ____ can result in sensory impairments, poor physical development, and mental retardation; worse outcomes are typically associated with lower birth weights
y. ____ often repeated head-banging or biting of fingers

MATCHING III

Answers are found at the end of this chapter. Match these names with the descriptions of their contributions to the study of abnormal psychology.

a. Alfred Binet   c. Langdon Down   e. Hans Asperger
b. Jean Marc Itard   d. Leo Kanner   f. O. Ivar Lovaas

1. ____ first described autism
2. ____ first described a subgroup of children with a chromosomal disorder later named after him
3. ____ described a subgroup of people with a disorder similar to autism but not involving mental retardation
4. ____ worked extensively with a feral child found living in the woods
5. ____ developed the first successful IQ test
6. ____ applied behavioral techniques to the management of people with autism

CONCEPT REVIEW

Answers are found at the end of this chapter. After you have read and reviewed the material, test your comprehension by filling in the blanks or circling the correct answer.

1. Which type of disorder is more common: **mental retardation   pervasive developmental disorders**

2. Intelligence is _____ distributed in the general population.

3. Intelligence tests have a mean of _____ and a standard deviation of _____.

4. The IQ of a particular person changes significantly over time: **true   false**

5. IQ tests measure potential for _____.

6. Adaptive skills include both _____ and _____ intelligence.

7. The physician who worked with Victor, the feral child of Aveyron, had great success in educating and socializing him: **true   false**

8. More people fall into the **lower/upper** range of the curve of IQs than would be predicted by a normal distribution.

9. What are the two categories of etiology of mental retardation? _____ and _____

10. The incidence of Down syndrome is related to maternal and paternal _____.

11. Intensive intervention with people with Down syndrome has been shown to be beneficial to their achievement: **true   false**

12. People with Down syndrome typically die in their 40s: **true   false**

13. Fragile-X syndrome is more likely to lead to mental retardation in boys than in girls: **true   false**

14. There is no known treatment for phenylketonuria: **true   false**

15. Pregnant women who drink one ounce of alcohol per day or less are not putting their fetus at risk for fetal alcohol syndrome: **true   false**

16. Babies exposed to crack-cocaine during the prenatal stage are more likely to be born _____.

17. Children living in dilapidated housing are at increased risk for ingesting paint chips containing _____.

18. Rh incompatibility is only a potential danger to children of mothers who are Rh **negative/positive**.

19. The IQs of adopted children are more highly correlated to the IQs of their **adoptive/biological** parents.

20. What is the most impoverished age group in the United States? _____

21. Environment has been shown to have little effect on IQ: **true   false**

22. Children who participate in Head Start are less likely to _____.

23. The use of neuroleptics to manage aggression and uncontrolled behavior among mentally retarded patients in institutions is recommended: **true   false**
24. People with autism have unusual physical appearances: **true   false**
25. Autism is not usually identified until the child reaches kindergarten:

    true   false
26. Children with autism tend to be very affectionate: **true   false**
27. Many children with autism remain mute: **true   false**
28. People with autism have problems in their capacity for social _____.
29. People with autism **resist/require** routine.
30. People with autism have superior intelligence: **true   false**
31. Some brain injured patients demonstrate savant abilities: **true   false**
32. Autism is more common among the upper social classes: **true   false**
33. Autism is more common among **boys/girls**.
34. Siblings of people with autism are likely to have autism: **true   false**
35. Autism is likely caused by some combination of poor parenting and biological factors:

    true   false
36. MZ twins show higher concordance for autism than DZ twins: **true   false**
37. Most people grow out of autism: **true   false**
38. A number of teens with autism develop _____ disorders.
39. A number of medications show promise in improving functioning of autistic patients:

    true   false
40. Behavioral treatments to reduce self-injurious behavior in autistic patients are controversial because they involve _____.
41. The only form of treatment found to be effective in increasing the functioning of autistic patients is _____ operant behavior therapy.

CROSSWORD

Answers are found at the end of this chapter. Complete the following crossword puzzle to reinforce your understanding of this chapter's key terms and concepts:

ACROSS	DOWN
1. tests which contain material equally familiar to people who differ in ethnicity	2. XO configuration in females
5. diagnostic procedure	3. infection of the meninges
7. caused by abnormally high levels of phenylalanine	4. marked by symptoms of autism without major problems in communication
8. providing least restrictive environment	6. dedicated to "genetic improvement" of human stock
10. oxygen deprivation	8. midpoint
11. score yielded by intelligence tests	9. seizure disorder
13. most frequent score	12. syndrome caused by chromosomal disorder

MULTIPLE CHOICE

Answers are found at the end of this chapter. The multiple choice questions listed will test your understanding of the material presented in the chapter. Read through each question and circle the letter representing the best answer.

1. Which of the following teratogens presents the greatest threat to a fetus?
    a. nicotine
    b. alcohol
    c. lead
    d. mercury

2. In all but which of the following are central symptoms of autism?
    a. impaired communication abilities
    b. impairments in social interaction
    c. abnormalities of the eyes, nose, and ears
    d. stereotyped patterns of behavior, interests, and activities

3. Mild mental retardation is designated for individual with IQ scores between which of the following?
    a. 20-25 and 40
    b. 35-40 and 50
    c. 50-55 and 70
    d. 65-70 and 90

4. As outlined in your text, which of the following has been suggested as an interpretation for pronoun reversal as documented in some cases of autism?
    a. pronoun reversal demonstrates a lack of understanding of speech
    b. pronoun reversal is a result of faulty neurotransmitters
    c. pronoun reversal results from damage to specific areas in the frontal lobe
    d. pronoun reversal is due to the autistic child's disinterest in other people

5. Autism is considered to be a _____ disorder, with approximately _____ out of every 10,000 children qualifying for the diagnosis.
    a. rare; 4-5
    b. rare; 20-25
    c. common; 1,000-1,500
    d. common; 3,000-3,500

6. Which of the following is one of the most important current secondary prevention efforts in preventing cultural-familial retardation?
    a. amniocentesis
    b. prenatal care
    c. Head Start
    d. prenatal evaluation

7. Treatment for self-injurious behavior that is sometimes seen in autistic children is controversial because
    a. there is no empirical support to back up the treatment
    b. the treatment typically involves punishment (e.g., slap or mild electric shock)
    c. the treatment has been relatively ineffective
    d. the treatment has been used without guardian consent

8. The reaction range concept of IQ proposed that (the) _____ determines the upper and lower limits of IQ, and (the) _____ determines the extent to which people fulfill their genetic potential.
    a. heredity; experience
    b. experience; heredity
    c. parents' IQ; age
    d. age; parents' IQ

9. Mental retardation with a specific, known organic cause
    a. is typically more common among families living in poverty
    b. generally is more common among Hispanics and African-Americans
    c. is most prevalent among the upper class
    d. generally has an equal prevalence among all social classes

10. Which of the following was the original developer of IQ tests?
    a. Biklin
    b. Binet
    c. Kanner
    d. Lovaas

11. In all but which of the following is true of autistic children?
    a. most are normal in physical appearance
    b. physical growth and development is generally normal
    c. their body movements are typically grossly uncoordinated
    d. they sometimes have unusual actions and postures

12. Premature birth is defined either as a birth weight of less than 5 ½ pounds or as birth before _____ weeks of gestation.
    a. thirty-five
    b. thirty-six
    c. thirty-seven
    d. thirty-eight

13. The most common form of self-injury that can accompany autism and other pervasive developmental disorders is:
    a. head-banging
    b. repetitive hitting of objects with one's fists
    c. dare-devil behaviors (i.e., skydiving, bungee jumping, etc.)
    d. cutting of oneself with sharp objects

14. All but which of the following is a diagnostic criterion for autism?
    a. lack of social or emotional reciprocity
    b. a prior diagnosis of Rett's disorder
    c. apparently compulsive adherence to specific, nonfunctional routines or rituals
    d. lack of varied spontaneous make-believe play or social imitative play appropriate to developmental level

15. Autism is believed to be caused by
    a. poor parenting
    b. an abusive environment
    c. neurological abnormalities
    d. there is no known etiology for autism

16. Almost _____ of all children in the United States are born to teenage mothers.
    a. 8 percent
    b. 12 percent
    c. 16 percent
    d. 20 percent

17. Savant performance is not typical in which of the following areas?
    a. artistic
    b. mathematical
    c. musical
    d. athletic

18. According to the text, which of the following interpretations of self-stimulation is most plausible?
    a. it is a way for the autistic child to feel like he or she is similar to others
    b. it serves the purpose of increasing stimulation to the autistic child who receives too little sensory input
    c. it serves the function of making a terrifying world more constant and predictable and therefore less frightening
    d. it is merely a repetitive behavior that serves no function

19. According to the American Association of Mental Retardation's (AAMR) definition, mental retardation manifests before age
    a. five
    b. eight
    c. thirteen
    d. eighteen

20. Which of the following is an infectious disease that is the result of infection of the brain and produces inflammation and permanent damage in approximately 20 percent of all cases?
    a. meningitis
    b. rubella
    c. encephalitis
    d. cytomegalovirus

21. Which of the following is caused by the presence of an extra chromosome and is characterized by a distinctively abnormal physical appearance, which includes slanting eyes, small head and stature, protruding tongue, and a variety of organ, muscle, and skeletal abnormalities?
    a. Down syndrome
    b. fetal alcohol syndrome
    c. Phenylketonuria (PKU)
    d. multiple sclerosis

22. Severe mental retardation accounts for approximately _____ of the mentally retarded.
    a. 1-2 percent
    b. 3-4 percent
    c. 8-10 percent
    d. 12-15 percent

23. Which of the following is the most promising approach to treating autism?
    a. intensive behavior modification using operant conditioning techniques
    b. antidepressant medication
    c. psychodynamic therapy that focuses on providing a nurturing, supportive environment
    d. none of the above have been effective in treating autism

24. Both mental retardation and pervasive developmental disorders include all of the following except
    a. either are present at birth or begin early in life
    b. serious disruptions in many areas of functioning, often including an inability to care for oneself independently
    c. gross physical abnormalities
    d. often, but not always, associated with a below-average IQ

25. Autism is usually first noticed
    a. early in life
    b. in adolescence
    c. in adulthood
    d. late in life

26. Which of the following terms was used for several years to classify autism together with other severe forms of childhood psychopathology?
    a. childhood dissociation
    b. disruptive childhood behaviors
    c. psychopathology first evident in childhood
    d. childhood schizophrenia

27. Which of the following developmental periods is particularly important to the course of autism?
    a. birth to six months
    b. six to thirty-six months
    c. early school years
    d. early adulthood

28. Allen is a six-year-old boy who has been diagnosed with autism. Frequently, when asked "would you like a drink," Allen will repeat the question over and over again. This is an example of
   a. pronoun reversal
   b. dysprosody
   c. echolalia
   d. self-stimulation

UNDERSTANDING RESEARCH
Answers are found at the end of this chapter.

<u>A Study of Facilitated Communication:</u> The text presents a detailed description of a study in the Research Close-Up. Finding the answers to these questions will provide an understanding of this study and why it is important.

1. Facilitated communication involves a facilitator who supports the hand and arm of a disabled person to allow them to _____. The technique was hailed as a _____, and purported to allow people with autism who never had communicated to express themselves and display insight and awareness. Biklin advocated a _____ approach to evaluating the technique. One systematic study was conducted with _____ adolescents with autism and _____ adult facilitators who were _____ about the technique.

2. There were four procedures in this study. The first, the _____ condition, involved asking the autistic adolescent questions and letting them type or communicate to the best of their abilities. The second, the pretest, the adolescents answered the same questions with the aid of the _____, who was _____ from hearing or seeing the questions being asked. The third, the _____, involved the adolescents answering with the full help of the facilitator after 20 hours of training. In the fourth, the _____, the adolescents were asked to respond to the identical questions as in the first and second conditions with the aid of the facilitator, who was again _____.

3. Results indicated that the responses during the pretest were _____ than during the baseline. The answers were phenomenal during the free response, with adolescents typing things like "EMOTION ZOMETHIN _____ EXPREZ." However, during the posttest, when the facilitators couldn't _____ or _____ again, they again did _____ than on baseline. However, some treatment providers still use the technique despite the lack of evidence that it is _____.

SHORT ANSWER
Answer the following short answer questions. Compare your work to the material presented in the text.

1. Despite the value of IQ tests in predicting academic performance, one controversial question is whether intelligence tests are culturally fair. Discuss your views on this topic.

2. Currently, mental retardation is classified according to the American Association on Mental Retardation and by the DSM-IV-TR. Discuss the similarities and differences in classification of these two approaches.

3. Discuss several etiological considerations regarding autism. Which hypotheses seem most plausible to you. Why? What research supports these hypotheses?

4. Discuss the ethical debate regarding the use of behavior modification techniques to reduce self-injurious behaviors in children with autism. Do you believe these treatments to be unethical? What may be several alternatives to this behavioral approach?

5. Discuss what is meant by a measure of central tendency. Provide an example. Why is this type of measure of importance in research?

ANSWER KEY

MATCHING I

1. y
2. s
3. j
4. r
5. a
6. h
7. v
8. t
9. b
10. f
11. o
12. u
13. n

14. l
15. d
16. k
17. q
18. c
19. p
20. w
21. m
22. z
23. e
24. g
25. x
26. i

MATCHING II

- a. 10
- b. 9
- c. 17
- d. 5
- e. 1
- f. 16
- g. 8
- h. 23
- i. 25
- j. 14
- k. 18
- l. 15
- m. 22
- n. 7
- o. 6
- p. 2
- q. 11
- r. 20
- s. 13
- t. 12
- u. 24
- v. 3
- w. 19
- x. 4
- y. 21

MATCHING III

1. d
2. c
3. e
4. b
5. a
6. f

MULTIPLE CHOICE

1. b
2. c
3. c
4. a
5. a
6. c
7. b
8. a
9. d
10. b
11. c
12. d
13. a
14. b
15. c
16. a
17. d
18. c
19. d
20. c
21. a
22. b
23. a
24. c
25. a
26. d
27. c
28. c

CONCEPT REVIEW

1. mental retardation
2. normally
3. 100; 15
4. false
5. school achievement
6. practical; social
7. false
8. lower
9. organic; familial
10. age
11. true
12. true
13. true
14. false
15. false
16. premature
17. lead
18. negative
19. biological
20. children
21. false
22. repeat a grade
23. false
24. false
25. false
26. false
27. true
28. imitation
29. require
30. false
31. true
32. false
33. boys
34. true

35. false
36. true
37. false
38. seizure
39. false
40. punishment
41. intensive

UNDERSTANDING RESEARCH

1. type on a keyboard; breakthrough; case study; 21; 10; enthusiastic

2. baseline; facilitator; screened; free response; posttest; screened

3. worse; FEEL; see; hear; worse; effective

CROSSWORD

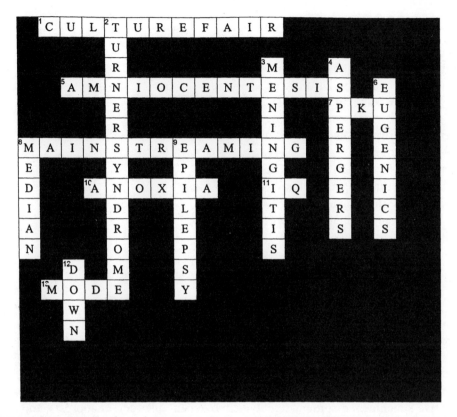

ACROSS	DOWN
1. tests which contain material equally familiar to people who differ in ethnicity	2. XO configuration in females
5. diagnostic procedure	3. infection of the meninges
7. caused by abnormally high levels of phenylalanine	4. marked by symptoms of autism without major problems in communication
8. providing least restrictive environment	6. dedicated to "genetic improvement" of human stock
10. oxygen deprivation	8. midpoint
11. score yielded by intelligence tests	9. seizure disorder
13. most frequent score	12. syndrome caused by chromosomal disorder

CHAPTER SIXTEEN

PSYCHOLOGICAL DISORDERS OF CHILDHOOD

CHAPTER OUTLINE

Overview
Externalizing Disorders
      Typical Symptoms of Externalizing Disorders
      Classification of Externalizing Disorders
      Epidemiology of Externalizing Disorders
      Etiology of Externalizing Disorders
      Treatment of Externalizing Disorders
Internalizing and Other Disorders
      Typical Symptoms of Internalizing and Other Disorders
      Classification of Internalizing and Other Disorders
      Epidemiology of Internalizing and Other Disorders
      Etiology of Internalizing and Other Disorders
      Treatment of Internalizing Disorders
Summary

OBJECTIVES

1. Distinguish between externalizing and internalizing disorders of childhood.
2. State several factors considered in the evaluation of externalizing symptoms.
3. Compare separation anxiety with separation anxiety disorder.
4. Differentiate between children's psychological problems and adult disorders.
5. Describe the characteristics of pica, rumination disorder, Tourette's disorder, selective autism, reactive attachment disorder, stereotypic movement disorder, encopresis, and enuresis.
6. Describe the defining characteristics of conduct disorder, oppositional defiant disorder, and attention deficit hyperactivity disorder.
7. Understand how attachment theory attempts to explain disorders of childhood.
8. State and describe the four parenting styles and explain how inconsistent parenting leads to externalizing symptoms in children.
9. List and describe genetic and biological evidence, both positive and negative, concerning the etiology of childhood disorders.
10. Describe the ways in which behavioral family therapy is utilized in the treatment of externalizing disorders.
11. Identify the common course and outcome of the primary childhood disorders.

MATCHING I

Answers are found at the end of this chapter. Match these terms and concepts with the definitions that follow:

a. Externalizing disorders
b. Attention deficit-hyperactivity disorder
c. Oppositional-defiant disorder
d. Conduct disorder
e. Internalizing disorders
f. Learning disorders
g. Continuous performance test
h. Separation anxiety
i. Separation anxiety disorder
j. School refusal
k. Peer sociometrics
l. Pica
m. Rumination disorder
n. Tourette's disorder
o. Stereotypic movement disorder
p. Selective autism
q. Reactive attachment disorder
r. Encopresis
s. Enuresis
t. Hyperkinesis
u. Index offenses
v. Juvenile delinquency
w. Status offenses
x. Representative sample
y. Attachment theory
z. Anaclitic depression

1. ____ crimes against people or property that are illegal at any age
2. ____ consistent failure to speak in certain social situations, while speech is unrestricted in other situations
3. ____ a set of proposals about the normal development of attachments and the adverse consequences of troubled attachment relationships
4. ____ a legal classification determined by a judge
5. ____ a disorder of childhood characterized by persistent and excessive worry for the safety of an attachment figure, fears of separation, nightmares with separation themes, and refusal to be alone
6. ____ an outdated term for hyperactivity
7. ____ the lack of social responsiveness found among infants who do not have a consistent attachment figure
8. ____ normal distress following separation from an attachment figure which peaks at about 15 months of age
9. ____ repeated motor and verbal tics
10. ____ acts that are illegal only because of the youth's status as a minor
11. ____ an empirically derived category of disruptive child behavior problems that create problems for the external world
12. ____ the repeated regurgitation and rechewing of food
13. ____ a disorder defined primarily by behavior that is illegal as well as antisocial
14. ____ characterized by severely disturbed and developmentally inappropriate social relationships
15. ____ a sample that accurately represents some larger group of people
16. ____ an extreme reluctance to go to school, accompanied by symptoms of anxiety
17. ____ a laboratory task that requires the subject to monitor and respond to numbers or letters presented on a computer screen
18. ____ a group of educational problems characterized by academic performance that is notably below academic aptitude
19. ____ a method of assessing children's social relationships and categorizing children's social standing by obtaining information on who is "liked most" And who is "liked least" from a group of children who know each other
20. ____ self-stimulation or self-injurious behavior that is serious enough to require treatment

21. ____ inappropriately controlled defecation
22. ____ a disorder characterized by hyperactivity, inattention, and impulsivity
23. ____ the persistent eating of nonnutritive substances
24. ____ inappropriately controlled urination
25. ____ a disorder characterized by negative, hostile, and defiant behavior
26. ____ an empirically derived category of psychological problems of childhood that affect the child more than the external world

MATCHING II

Answers are found at the end of this chapter. Match these terms and concepts with the definitions that follow:

1. Secure attachments
2. Anxious attachments
3. Anxious avoidant attachments
4. Anxious resistant attachments
5. Disorganized attachments
6. Resilience
7. Authoritative parenting
8. Authoritarian parenting
9. Indulgent parenting
10. Neglectful parenting
11. Coercion
12. Time-out
13. Temperament
14. Salicylates
15. Delay of gratification
16. Emotion regulation
17. Psychostimulants
18. Dose-response effects
19. Behavioral family therapy
20. Parent training
21. Negotiation
22. Multisystemic therapy
23. Recidivism
24. Rehabilitation
25. Parens patrial
26. Diversion

a. ____ an anxious attachment where the infant is wary of exploration, not easily soothed by the attachment figure, and angry or ambivalent about contact
b. ____ an anxious attachment where the infant responds inconsistently because of conflicting feelings toward an inconsistent caregiver who is the potential source of either reassurance or fear
c. ____ a food additive that was thought to be related to ADHD but which controlled research has found to be unrelated
d. ____ the response to different dosages of medications
e. ____ parenting that is unconcerned with both the child's emotional needs and needs for discipline
f. ____ repeat offending
g. ____ learning to identify, evaluate, and control one's feelings based on the reactions, attitudes, and advice of others in the social world
h. ____ combines family treatment with coordinated interventions in other important contexts of the troubled child's life
i. ____ teaching parents discipline strategies
j. ____ parenting that is affectionate but lax in discipline
k. ____ parenting that is strict, often harsh and undemocratic, as well as lacking in warmth
l. ____ keeping problem youths out of the juvenile justice system
m. ____ a technique of briefly isolating a child following misbehavior
n. ____ infants with these attachments are fearful about exploration and are not easily comforted by their attachment figures, who respond inadequately or inconsistently to the child's needs

o. ____ infants with these attachments separate easily and explore away from their attachment figure but seek comfort when threatened
p. ____ a child's inborn behavioral characteristics, such as activity level, emotionality, and sociability
q. ____ a form of family treatment which trains parents to use the principles of operant conditioning to improve child discipline
r. ____ a system of interaction in which parents and children reciprocally reinforce child misbehavior and parent capitulation
s. ____ an anxious attachment where the infant is generally unwary of strange situations and shows little preference for the attachment figure over others
t. ____ the adaptive ability to defer smaller but immediate rewards for larger long-term benefits
u. ____ the goal of treatment for delinquent youths
v. ____ a process in which young people are actively involved in defining rules
w. ____ the ability to bounce back from adversity
x. ____ the state as parent
y. ____ medications used to treat children with ADHD
z. ____ parenting that is both loving and firm

MATCHING III

Answers are found at the end of this chapter. Match these names with the descriptions of their contributions to the study of psychology:

a. Mary Ainsworth   c. John Bowlby   e. Gerald Patterson
b. Michael Rutter   d. Lawrence Kohlberg   f. Benjamin Feingold

1. ____ developed the family adversity index
2. ____ conducted many empirical studies on attachment theory
3. ____ developed the concept of coercion
4. ____ proposed that food additives caused hyperactivity
5. ____ studied moral development in children
6. ____ developed attachment theory

CONCEPT REVIEW

Answers are found at the end of this chapter. After you have read and reviewed the material, test your comprehension by filling in the blanks or circling the correct answer.

1. Which of the following disorders involves violations of laws?

    oppositional defiant disorder   **conduct disorder**

2. What percent of arrests for index offenses are of juveniles under 18 years of age?

    7 percent   **29 percent**   **63 percent**

3. Adult antisocial behavior is better predicted by information about the person during **childhood/adolescence**.

4. In adolescence, violations of rules is _____.

5. Impulsivity is acting before _____.
6. Where is hyperactivity often first noticed? _____
7. The behavioral problems that characterize ADHD are largely **intentional/unintentional**.
8. Assessment of children's feelings is **straightforward/difficult**.
9. Parents are very good at detecting their children's depression: **true   false**
10. If in error, parents are likely to **overestimate/underestimate** their children's depression.
11. Fears in children are a symptom of some emotional disorder: **true   false**
12. School refusal often indicates a child's fear of _____.
13. Which category of peer ratings is the most correlated with psychological disorders? _____
14. What type of norms are essential in assessing abnormal behavior in children? _____ norms
15. A learning disorder is defined as one or two standard deviations between _____ and _____.
16. There is a high degree of comorbidity between learning disorders and which two psychological disorders? _____ and _____
17. Learning disorders are easily treated: **true   false**
18. Encopresis and enuresis are usually **causes of/reactions to** psychological distress.
19. The bell and pad is a device that is effective in treating _____.
20. The current DSM-IV-TR is probably **overinclusive/underinclusive** in its listing of childhood psychological disorders.
21. Hyperactivity is the result of inattention: **true   false**
22. ADHD and oppositional defiant disorder are separate but _____ disorders.
23. More **boys/girls** are treated for psychological disorders. More **men/women** enter into therapy.
24. Girls are more likely to have _____ problems, and boys are more likely to have _____ problems.
25. Risk for _____ problems increase substantially when more than one family adversity risk factor is present.
26. What is the third leading cause of death among teenagers? _____
27. Picking up a crying infant makes it **easier/more difficult** to manage.
28. Children with serious conduct problems often have parents who use what type of parenting? _____
29. Negative attention is sometimes _____ to children.
30. Crime rates are about the same in the United States and in Europe: **true   false**
31. Research has shown that critical and demanding parenting is the **cause/result** of hyperactive child behavior.
32. A certain temperamental style has been linked to _____ disorders in adulthood.
33. Genetic factors appear to be strongly linked to ADHD: **true   false**
34. Children with externalizing disorders may be less _____ reactive than other children.

35. Research has shown that sugar increases hyperactive behavior:

    true   **false**

36. Children with externalizing disorder have problems with _____ control.

37. Aggressive children demonstrate immaturity in moral development:

    true   **false**

38. Children with mothers who are depressed are more likely to develop _____.

39. Children usually grow out of internalizing disorders: **true   false**

40. Antidepressants are effective in treating children with depression: **true   false**

41. Psychostimulants are effective in treating children with ADHD: **true   false**

42. Psychostimulants have a paradoxical effect on children with ADHD, which demonstrates the biological underpinnings of the disorder: **true   false**

43. Psychostimulants are taken for a couple of weeks and their effects last for several months at a time: **true   false**

44. Psychostimulants given at high doses provide maximum _____ but interfere with _____.

45. Medication is more helpful in the treatment of ADHD than behavioral family therapy:

    true   false

46. When juveniles are diverted from the juvenile justice system, they show higher rates of recidivism:

    true   false

47. Psychostimulant use among preschoolers has significantly increased:

    true   false

CROSSWORD

Answers are found at the end of this chapter. Complete the following crossword puzzle to reinforce your understanding of this chapter's key terms and concepts.

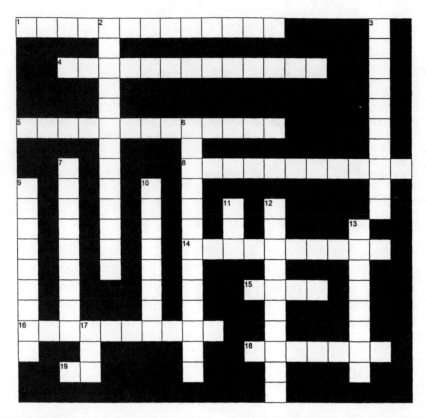

ACROSS

1. process of shaping children's behavior to conform to expectations of society
4. disorders which create difficulties for a child's external world
5. involves squirming, fidgeting, and restless behavior
8. child's inborn characteristics such as emotionality and activity level
14. close bond between infant and caregiver
15. characterized by hyperactivity, attention deficit, and impulsivity
16. inappropriately controlled defecation
18. a psychostimulant often used with children with ADHD
19. defined primarily by a persistent and repetitive pattern of serious rule violations

DOWN

2. parenting that is both loving and firm
3. ability to "bounce back" from adversity
6. disorders which primarily affect a child's internal world
7. depression characterized by lack of social responsiveness among infants
9. disorder marked by repeated motor and verbal tics
10. cluster of problems
11. treatment based on learning theory principles
12. repeat offending
13. inappropriately controlled urination
17. defined by a pattern of negative, hostile, and defiant behavior

MULTIPLE CHOICE

Answers are found at the end of this chapter. The multiple choice questions listed will test your understanding of the material presented in the chapter. Read through each question and circle the letter representing the best answer.

1. In his study on family adversity, Michael Rutter found that all of the following were predictors of behavior problems among children except
    a. low income
    b. overcrowding in the home
    c. conflict between parents
    d. paternal depression

2. In all but which of the following are major problems in evaluating children's internalizing symptoms?
    a. there are insufficient self-report measures to assess internalizing symptoms in children
    b. it is much more difficult for adults to assess children's inner experiences than it is to observe children's behavior
    c. children often are not reliable or valid informants about their internal life
    d. children's capacity to recognize emotions in themselves emerges slowly over the course of development and therefore they may not be aware of their own emotional turmoil

3. Reactive attachment disorder is most likely caused by which of the following?
    a. it appears to have genetic origins
    b. an unstable home environment in which caregivers are frequently changing
    c. extremely neglectful parenting
    d. its etiology is unknown

4. In all but which of the following are major subtypes of externalizing disorders?
    a. attention-deficit/hyperactivity disorder
    b. conduct disorder
    c. depression
    d. oppositional defiant disorder

5. Which of the following is the most helpful for scientists to have for predicting adult antisocial behavior?
    a. information obtained during birth and infancy
    b. information obtained during childhood
    c. information obtained during adolescence
    d. information obtained during adulthood

6. According to a panel of experts assembled by the National Academy of Sciences, at least _____ of the sixty-three million children living in the United States suffer from a mental disorder.
    a. five
    b. twelve
    c. seventeen
    d. twenty three

7. Which of the following is a sample that accurately depicts a larger group of people?
    a. representative sample
    b. random sample
    c. convenience sample
    d. heterogeneous sample

8. _____ implies that an externalizing problem has environmental origins, while _____ implies problems with some sort of biological cause.
    a. Attention-deficit/hyperactivity disorder; oppositional defiant disorder
    b. Oppositional defiant disorder; attention-deficit/hyperactivity disorder
    c. Conduct disorder; oppositional defiant disorder
    d. Oppositional defiant disorder; conduct disorder

9. Separation anxiety disorder is typically associated with all of the following except
    a. fears of getting lost or being kidnapped
    b. refusal to be alone
    c. persistent and excessive worry for the safety of an attachment figure
    d. refusal to interact with others when the attachment figure is not present

10. The attachment figure for an infant with an anxious attachment responds to the infant in which of the following ways?
    a. appropriately attends to the infant's needs
    b. inadequately or inconsistently attends to the infant's needs
    c. immediately attends to the infant's needs
    d. is completely unresponsive to the infant's needs

11. The FBI reports that about _____ percent of arrests for major crimes including murder, forcible rape, and robbery are of juveniles under the age of 18.
    a. 10
    b. 20
    c. 30
    d. 40

12. Which of the following is a well-known treatment device that awakens children with enuresis by setting off an alarm as they begin to wet the bed?
    a. bell and pad
    b. light and alarm
    c. sensitive signal seat
    d. responsive wetting device

13. Which of the following is characterized by self-stimulation or self-injurious behavior?
    a. conduct disorder
    b. developmental coordination disorder
    c. Tourette's disorder
    d. stereotypic movement disorder

14. ADHD is characterized by all but which of the following symptoms?
    a. impulsivity
    b. hyperactivity
    c. aggression
    d. inattention

15. Treatment with children often begins with which of the following?
    a. an attempt to get the adults (i.e., parents, teachers) to agree as to what the problem really is
    b. identifying a disorder and then building hypotheses to either prove or disprove it
    c. helping the child to identify his or her problems
    d. an attempt to treat the family, independent of the child, in order to facilitate change in the child's environment

16. Which of the following gender differences is not true in respect to internalizing and externalizing problems?
    a. more adult men enter into therapy than do adult women
    b. boys are treated more for psychological problems than are girls
    c. by early adult life, more females report psychological problems than males
    d. boys have far more externalizing disorders than girls

17. According to the "peer sociometric method" of assessing children's relationships, which of the following groups is characterized by a high frequency of "liked least" ratings and a low frequency of "liked most" ratings?
    a. average
    b. neglected
    c. rejected
    d. controversial

18. In all but which of the following are internalizing symptoms?
    a. somatic complaints
    b. fears
    c. aggressive behavior
    d. sadness

19. In all but which of the following factors influence how adults evaluate children's rule violations?
    a. frequency of the child's behavior
    b. duration of the child's behavior
    c. intensity of the child's behavior
    d. all of the above

20. Brandon is a three-year-old who frequently throws a tantrum when in the grocery store if he does not get what he wants. Because this is such an embarrassing situation for his mother, she will give Brandon whatever he desires in order to get his cooperation. In this case, Brandon is being _____ while his mother is being _____.
    a. positively reinforced; negatively reinforced
    b. negatively reinforced; positively reinforced
    c. classically conditioned; punished
    d. positively reinforced; punished

21. Infants typically develop a fear of _____ around the age of seven to eight months.
    a. strangers
    b. the dark
    c. monsters
    d. unfamiliar environments

22. Which of the following is the process of shaping children's behavior and attitudes to conform to the expectations of parents, teachers, and society?
    a. modeling
    b. socialization
    c. conditioning
    d. vicarious learning

SHORT ANSWER

Answer the following short answer questions. Compare your work to the material presented in the text.

1. Discuss the challenges of identifying internalizing problems in children. How do different sources of information (e.g., parents, teachers) vary on their estimation of internalizing problems?

2. Discuss the role of context in the etiology and maintenance of children's psychological problems. Provide one example.

3. Compare attention-deficit/hyperactivity disorder, oppositional defiant disorder, and conduct disorder. Describe the overlap between these disorders.

3. Why must a sample be representative of a general population? Provide one example.

ANSWER KEY

MATCHING I

1. u	14. q
2. p	15. x
3. y	16. j
4. v	17. g
5. i	18. f
6. t	19. k
7. z	20. o
8. h	21. r
9. n	22. b
10. w	23. l
11. a	24. s
12. m	25. c
13. d	26. e

MATCHING II

- a. 4
- b. 5
- c. 14
- d. 18
- e. 10
- f. 23
- g. 16
- h. 22
- i. 20
- j. 9
- k. 8
- l. 26
- m. 12
- n. 2
- o. 1
- p. 13
- q. 19
- r. 11
- s. 3
- t. 15
- u. 24
- v. 21
- w. 6
- x. 25
- y. 17
- z. 7

MATCHING III

1. b
2. a
3. e
4. f
5. d
6. c

MULTIPLE CHOICE

1. d
2. a
3. c
4. c
5. b
6. b
7. a
8. b
9. d
10. b
11. c
12. a
13. d
14. c
15. a
16. a
17. c
18. c
19. d
20. a
21. a
22. b

CONCEPT REVIEW

1. conduct disorder
2. 29 percent
3. childhood
4. normative
5. thinking
6. in the classroom
7. unintentional
8. difficult
9. false
10. underestimate
11. false
12. leaving a parent
13. rejected
14. developmental
15. aptitude; achievement
16. ADHD; oppositional defiant disorder
17. false
18. causes of
19. enuresis
20. overinclusive
21. false
22. overlapping
23. boys; women
24. internalizing; externalizing
25. externalizing
26. suicide
27. easier
28. neglectful
29. reinforcing
30. false
31. result
32. anxiety
33. true
34. emotionality
35. false
36. self
37. true
38. depression
39. false
40. false
41. true
42. false
43. false
44. behavioral control; learning
45. true
46. false
47. true

CROSSWORD

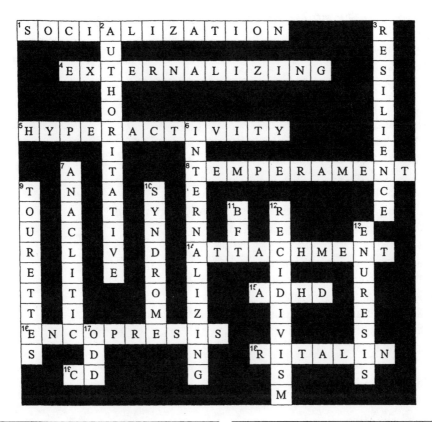

ACROSS

1. process of shaping children's behavior to conform to expectations of society
4. disorders which create difficulties for a child's external world
5. involves squirming, fidgeting, and restless behavior
8. child's inborn characteristics such as emotionality and activity level
14. close bond between infant and caregiver
15. characterized by hyperactivity, attention deficit, and impulsivity
16. inappropriately controlled defecation
18. a psychostimulant often used with children with ADHD
19. defined primarily by a persistent and repetitive pattern of serious rule violations

DOWN

2. parenting that is both loving and firm
3. ability to "bounce back" from adversity
6. disorders which primarily affect a child's internal world
7. depression characterized by lack of social responsiveness among infants
9. disorder marked by repeated motor and verbal tics
10. cluster of problems
11. treatment based on learning theory principles
12. repeat offending
13. inappropriately controlled urination
17. defined by a pattern of negative, hostile, and defiant behavior

CHAPTER SEVENTEEN

ADJUSTMENT DISORDERS AND LIFE-CYCLE TRANSITIONS

CHAPTER OUTLINE

Overview
    Typical Experiences
    Classification of Life-Cycle Transitions
The Transition to Adulthood
    Typical Experiences of the Adult Transition
    Classification of Identity Conflicts
    Epidemiology of Identity Conflicts
    Etiological Considerations and Research on the Adult Transition
    Treatment During the Transition to Adult Life
Family Transitions
    Typical Experiences of Family Transitions
    Classification of Troubled Family Relationships
    Epidemiology of Family Transitions
    Etiological Considerations and Research on Family Transitions
    Treatment During Family Transitions
Aging and the Transition to Later Life
    Ageism
    Typical Experiences of Aging
    Classification of Aging
    Epidemiology of Aging
    Etiological Considerations and Research on the Aging Transition
    Treatment of Psychological Problems in Later Life
Summary

OBJECTIVES

1. Define life-cycle transition.
2. Discuss the role of life-cycle transitions in the development of psychopathology.
3. Describe Erikson's psychosocial moratorium and identity crisis.
4. Define Marcia's four identity statuses.
5. Describe several common gender differences which occur in the transition to adulthood.
6. Identify ways in which power struggles, intimacy struggles, affiliation, interdependence, and scapegoating impact family structure.
7. Describe Gottman's four communication problems.
8. Describe several premarital and marital therapy treatment programs.
9. Compare Bowlby's and Kubler-Ross's model of grieving.
10. Identify typical psychological and physiological processes in young-old, old-old, and oldest-old adults.
11. Describe several gender differences in later life regarding relationships.

MATCHING I

Answers are found at the end of this chapter. Match these terms and concepts with the definitions that follow:

a.	Adjustment disorders	k.	Identity crisis
b.	Life-span development	l.	Intimacy versus self-absorption
c.	Life-cycle transitions	m.	Generativity versus stagnation
d.	Transition to adult life	n.	Integrity and despair
e.	Family transitions	o.	Family life cycle
f.	Transition to later life	p.	Early adult transition
g.	Interpersonal diagnoses	q.	Midlife transition
h.	Crisis of the healthy personality	r.	Late adult transition
i.	Identity	s.	Social clocks
j.	Identity versus role confusion		

1. ____ the challenge in establishing intimate relationships, balanced between closeness and independence
2. ____ clinically significant symptoms in response to stress that are not severe enough to warrant classification as another mental disorder
3. ____ career and family accomplishments with purpose or direction as opposed to lacking purpose or direction
4. ____ struggles in the process of moving from one social or psychological stage of adult development into a new one
5. ____ a series of normal conflicts related to change as the comfortable and predictable conflicts with the fearsome but exciting unknown
6. ____ becoming less driven by internal and external demands and developing more compassion for ourselves and others
7. ____ classification of psychological problems that reside within the context of human relationships rather than within an individual
8. ____ age-related goals for ourselves
9. ____ a period of basic uncertainty about self
10. ____ the challenge of adolescence and young adulthood, this stage involves integrating various role identities into a global sense of self
11. ____ continuities and changes in behavior from infancy through the last years of life
12. ____ looking back on one's life with either a sense of acceptance and pride or anger and despair
13. ____ global sense of self
14. ____ the changing roles and relationships of later life
15. ____ the developmental course of family relationships throughout life
16. ____ in the middle years of life; includes birth of first child and divorce
17. ____ in the late teens and early twenties; struggling with identity, career, and relationship issues
18. ____ moving away from family and assuming adult roles
19. ____ major changes in life roles like retirement, grief over death of loved ones, and aging and facing mortality

MATCHING II

Answers are found at the end of this chapter. Match these terms and concepts with the definitions that follow:

1. Moratorium
2. Identity diffusion
3. Identity foreclosure
4. Identity moratorium
5. Identity achievement
6. Alienated identity achievement
7. Empty nest
8. Power struggles
9. Intimacy struggles
10. Boundaries
11. Reciprocity
12. Demand and withdrawal pattern
13. Gene-environment correlation
14. Rational suicide
15. Scapegoat
16. Heritability
17. Heritability ratio
18. Criticism
19. Contempt
20. Defensiveness
21. Stonewalling
22. Androgynous couples
23. Behavioral marital therapy
24. Assisted suicide

a. _____ an elderly adult choosing to end his/her life
b. _____ couples in which both husbands and wives have high levels of masculinity and femininity
c. _____ the adjustment that occurs when adult children leave the family home
d. _____ a new identity status common in the 1960s, where one's definition of self is alienated from many values held by the larger society
e. _____ attacking someone's personality rather than his or her actions
f. _____ emphasizes the couple's moment-to-moment interaction, focusing on exchange of positive and negative behaviors, style of communication, and strategies for problem-solving
g. _____ where the wife becomes increasingly demanding and the husband withdraws further and further as time passes
h. _____ a statistic used for summarizing the genetic contributions to behavioral characteristics
i. _____ the category of being in the middle of an identity crisis and actively searching for adult roles
j. _____ a form of self-justification, such as denying responsibility or blaming the other person
k. _____ social exchange of cooperation and conflict
l. _____ a pattern of isolation and withdrawal
m. _____ attempts to change dominance relations
n. _____ a time of uncertainty about self and goals
o. _____ a family member who is held to blame for all of a family's troubles
p. _____ attempts to alter the degree of closeness in a relationship
q. _____ the category of having questioned childhood identity but not actively searching for new adult roles
r. _____ a nonrandom association between inborn characteristics and environmental experience
s. _____ the category of having questioned one's identity and having successfully decided on long-term goals
t. _____ an insult motivated by anger and intended to hurt the other person
u. _____ the rules of a relationship
v. _____ the relative contribution of genes to behavioral characteristics
w. _____ the category of having never questioned oneself or one's goals but instead proceeding along the predetermined course of one's childhood commitments
x. _____ a medical professional helping a disabled person end their life

MATCHING III

Answers are found at the end of this chapter. Match these terms and concepts with the definitions that follow:

- a. Ageism
- b. Menopause
- c. Estrogen
- d. Hormone replacement therapy
- e. Reminiscence
- f. Integrative reminiscence
- g. Instrumental reminiscence
- h. Transitive reminiscence
- i. Escapist reminiscence
- j. Obsessive reminiscence
- k. Narrative reminiscence
- l. Grief
- m. Bereavement
- n. Gerontology
- o. Young-old adults
- p. Old-old adults
- q. Oldest-old adults
- r. Behavioral gerontology

1. ____ the cessation of menstruation
2. ____ descriptive rather than interpretive
3. ____ misconceptions and prejudices about aging
4. ____ the recounting of personal memories of the distant past
5. ____ the multidisciplinary study of aging
6. ____ a female sex hormone that fluctuates during menopause
7. ____ the emotional and social process of coping with a separation or loss
8. ____ adults ages 85 and older
9. ____ an attempt to achieve a sense of self-worth, coherence, and reconciliation with the past
10. ____ preoccupation with failure; full of guilt, bitterness, and despair
11. ____ adults roughly between the ages of 65 and 75; those in good health and active in their communities
12. ____ a sub discipline of health psychology and behavioral medicine which focuses on the study and treatment of behavioral components of health and illness among older adults
13. ____ a specific form of grieving in response to the death of a loved one
14. ____ the administration of artificial estrogen
15. ____ full of glorification of the past and deprecation of the present
16. ____ includes both direct moral instruction and storytelling with clear moral implications; serves the function of passing on cultural heritage and personal legacy
17. ____ adults roughly between the ages of 75 and 85; those who suffer from major physical, psychological, or social problems and require some routine assistance in living
18. ____ the review of goal-directed activities and attainments reflecting a sense of control and success in overcoming life's obstacles

MATCHING IV
Answers are found at the end of this chapter. Match these names with the descriptions of their contributions to the study of abnormal psychology.

a. Erik Erikson   c. Karen Horney   e. John Gottman
b. Daniel Levinson   d. Elisabeth Kubler-Ross

1. ____ theorized that people have competing needs to move toward, to move away from, and to move against others
2. ____ widened the emphasis of adult development to social as well as psychological tasks
3. ____ developed a stage theory of grieving in bereavement
4. ____ developed a stage theory of psychosocial development from birth to death
5. ____ focused on communication patterns in marital interaction

CONCEPT REVIEW
Answers are found at the end of this chapter. After you have read and reviewed the material, test your comprehension by filling in the blanks or circling the correct answer.

1. The DSM-IV-TR has a comprehensive, detailed section on adjustment disorders and other conditions besides mental disorders that may be the focus of psychotherapy: **true**   **false**

2. Erikson focused more on the _____ side of "psychosocial" development, while Levinson focused more on the _____ aspects.

3. Research has shown that **adolescents/adults** experience more intense emotions.

4. The development of identity has been **focused on/neglected by** researchers.

5. The "forgotten half" refers to youth who do not _____.

6. Research suggests that the most successful young adults have parents who strike a balance between continuing to provide support and _____ and allowing their children increasing _____.

7. For women in traditional roles, identity often develops out of _____.

8. Marital satisfaction **increases/decreases** following the birth of the first child.

9. Family members with happy relationships _____ negative comments and _____ positive ones.

10. Research shows that men, but not women, experience high emotional arousal as _____.

11. About _____ of all existing marriages will end in divorce.

12. **Whites/blacks** are more likely to remarry following divorce.

13. Androgynous couples had marriages that were **higher/lower** in satisfaction than nonandrogynous couples.

14. Research indicates that the Premarital Relationship Enhancement Program **is/is not** effective in increasing marital satisfaction over time.

15. Behavioral marital therapy has been shown to be more effective than other therapy approaches: **true   false**
16. Couples therapy can be effective in alleviating a person's depression: **true   false**
17. **Men/women** have a shorter life expectancy.
18. Older people are less satisfied with their lives: **true   false**
19. Personality has been found to be consistent from middle age to old age: **true   false**
20. Physical activity and physical health are some of the best predictors of psychological well-being among older adults: **true   false**
21. Hormone replacement therapy increases the risk for cancer: **true   false**
22. Visual acuity actually increases with age: **true   false**
23. Older adults report fewer positive relationships and a declined sense of mastery over their environment than young and middle age adults: **true   false**
24. Researchers have found support for the stages of bereavement proposed by Kubler-Ross: **true   false**
25. Less intense bereavement predicts better long-term adjustment: **true   false**
26. The prevalence of mental disorders increases with age: **true   false**
27. The risk of completed suicide is higher among the elderly: **true   false**
28. Men apparently benefit more from _____ while women benefit more from _____.

CROSSWORD

Answers are found at the end of this chapter. Complete the following crossword puzzle to reinforce your understanding of this chapter's key terms and concepts.

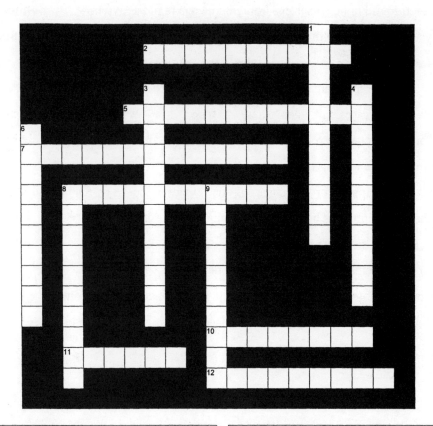

ACROSS

2. rules that mark psychological territory of individual or relationship
5. recounting of personal memories
7. a form of self-justification
8. specific form of grieving in response to death of a loved one
10. crisis characterized by basic uncertainty about self
11. encompasses a number of misconceptions about aging
12. cessation of menstruation

DOWN

1. multidisciplinary study of aging
3. relative contribution of genes to a characteristic
4. social exchange
6. disorders defined by development of clinically significant symptoms in response to stress
8. approach to marital therapy which emphasizes exchange of positive and negative behaviors
9. time of uncertainty about oneself and one's goals

MULTIPLE CHOICE

Answers are found at the end of this chapter. The multiple choice questions listed will test your understanding of the material presented in the chapter. Read through each question and circle the letter representing the best answer.

1. The decline in the divorce rate is mostly the result of
    a. more people completing marital therapy
    b. the changing age of the U.S. population
    c. divorce being less acceptable
    d. people most prone to divorce not marrying in the first place

2. Which of the following groups has the highest suicide rate?
    a. teenagers
    b. young adults
    c. middle-aged adults
    d. adults over the age of 65

3. Which of the following includes various struggles in the process of moving from one social or psychological "stage" of adult development into a new stage?
    a. life cycle transitions
    b. transition to adult life
    c. developmental tasks of adult life
    d. family transitions

4. Approximately _____ of couples seen in behavioral marital therapy do not improve significantly.
    a. 30 percent
    b. 40 percent
    c. 50 percent
    d. 60 percent

5. According to Erikson, which of the following stages is the major challenge of adolescence and young adulthood?
    a. integrity versus despair
    b. generativity versus stagnation
    c. intimacy versus self-absorption
    d. identity versus role confusion

6. On the average, marital happiness declines following_____.
    a. the death of a family member
    b. the birth of the first child
    c. the emptying of the family nest
    d. the fifth year of marriage

7. Which of the following refers to youth who do not attend college and who often assume marginal roles in U.S. society?
    a. "Transient Youth"
    b. "Generation X"
    c. "Alienated Youth"
    d. "Forgotten Half"

8. When reviewing the various models of adult development, which of the following must be taken into consideration?
    a. that history, culture, and personal values influence views about which kinds of "tasks" are normal during adult development
    b. that transitions or "crises" may not be as predictable as the models imply
    c. some people may not pass through a particular stage of development
    d. all of the above

9. Research indicates that depression is more closely linked to _____ for women, while it is more closely liked to _____ for men.
    a. marital conflict; divorce
    b. divorce; marital conflict
    c. poor support system; financial difficulties
    d. financial difficulties; poor support system

10. The ratio of men to women _____ at older ages.
    a. increases
    b. decreases
    c. is approximately equal
    d. stays relatively the same across the age span

11. Erik Erikson highlighted _____ as a common theme that occurs throughout life cycle transitions.
    a. uncertainty
    b. conflict
    c. remorse
    d. acceptance

12. Estimates indicate that about _____ of all of today's marriages will end in divorce.
    a. 30 percent
    b. 50 percent
    c. 40 percent
    d. 60 percent

13. Epidemiological evidence indicates that the prevalence of mental disorders is _____ among adults 65 years of age and older as compared to younger adults.
    a. lower
    b. higher
    c. about the same
    d. it is unknown due to the difficulty in studying this population

14. Which of the following identifies people who are in the middle of an identity crisis and who are actively searching for adult roles?
    a. alienated identity achievement
    b. identity moratorium
    c. identify diffusion
    d. identity foreclosure

15. All of the following are emphasized by behavioral marital therapy except
    a. the couple's moment-to-moment interactions
    b. strategies for solving problems
    c. extensive clinical interview of relationship patterns in the couple's families
    d. the couple's style of communication

16. Family life cycle theorists classify adult development according to which of the following?
    a. the tasks and transitions of family life
    b. the adult's memories of their childhood and adolescence
    c. the tasks and transitions of psychological challenges of adulthood
    d. all of the above

17. Psychological research suggests that the most successful young adults have which kind of parents?
    a. parents who are strict and authoritarian
    b. parents who are supportive and could be characterized as their children's "best friend"
    c. parents who strongly encourage individuation and provide opportunities for their children to take on numerous responsibilities at an early age
    d. parents who strike a balance between continuing to provide support and supervision of their children while allowing them increasing independence

18. Which of the following individuals theorized that people have competing needs to move toward, to move away from, and to move against others?
    a. Erikson
    b. Levinson
    c. Horney
    d. Kubler-Ross

19. _____ struggles are attempts to change dominance relations, whereas _____ struggles are attempts to alter the degree of closeness in a relationship.
    a. Intimacy; power
    b. Power; intimacy
    c. Conflict; relational
    d. Relational; conflict

20. A study of adults over the age of 70 found that both men and women listed which of the following as the most common contribution to a negative quality of life in their later years?
    a. poor health
    b. death of a spouse
    c. financial difficulties
    d. interpersonal problems

21. All of the following are true of the "V codes" in the DSM-IV-TR except
    a. they do not include an extensive summary of life difficulties
    b. they are similar to other diagnoses in the DSM in that they are diagnosed as mental disorders
    c. they include issues such as bereavement, identity problems, and phase of life problems.
    d. all of the above are true of "V codes"

22. Lisa and Mike have been married for four years. Recently, they have been arguing more than usual. Whenever they get into an argument, Lisa engages in a pattern of isolation and withdrawal, ignoring Mike's complaints and virtually ending all communication with him. According to Gottman, Lisa is engaged in which of the following?
    a. stonewalling
    b. contempt
    c. defensiveness
    d. criticism

23. In all but which all of the following are true of hormone replacement therapy?
    a. it alleviates some of the psychological strains associated with adverse physical symptoms of menopause
    b. reduces the subsequent risk for heart and bone disease
    c. increases the risk for cancer
    d. decreases symptoms of depression, which are often associated with menopause

24. Alternative lifestyles not withstanding, evidence indicates that _____ of the adults in the United States get married during their adult lives.
    a. 40 percent
    b. 60 percent
    c. 75 five percent
    d. 90 percent

25. One criticism of Erikson's theories is
    a. the stages are inappropriate for certain developmental levels
    b. the theories are too broad and general and are not applicable to a large proportion of the population
    c. they are not very accurate in outlining developmental stages
    d. the theories focus on men to the exclusion of women

26. According to psychologists Wong and Watt, which of the following is associated with less successful adjustment in later life?
    a. obsessive reminiscence
    b. transitive reminiscence
    c. instrumental reminiscence
    d. integrative reminiscence

27. Family therapists and family researchers often blame difficulties in negotiating family transitions on which of the following?
    a. low motivation
    b. problems with communication
    c. difficulty identifying problem areas
    d. all of the above

28. Which of the following is not a stage of adult development in Erikson's model?
    a. intimacy versus self-absorption
    b. integrity versus despair
    c. assurance versus apprehension
    d. generativity versus stagnation

29. Research on identity achievement indicates that _____ may have rejecting and distant families, while _____ may have overprotective families.
    a. identity diffusers; identity foreclosers
    b. identity foreclosers; identity diffusers
    c. identity achievers; alienated identity achievers
    d. alienated identity achievers; identity achievers

30. All but which of the following are stages included in the Family Developmental Tasks through the Family Life Cycle?
    a. childbearing
    b. launching center
    c. aging family members
    d. death and dying

UNDERSTANDING RESEARCH

Answers are found at the end of this chapter.

The Heritability of Divorce: The text presents a detailed description of a study in the Research Close-Up. Finding the answers to these questions will provide an understanding of this study and why it is important.

1. Behavior geneticists have increasingly emphasized that people make their own _____. Some people are risk _____ who constantly seek thrills, while others are risk-_____ who seek stable, predictable environments. Family transitions may be partially determined by a person's _____, which may be influenced by _____ factors. In this sense, _____ may be genetic. The sample in this study included more than _____ MZ and DZ twin pairs. MZ twins with divorced co-twins were more than _____ times as likely to be divorced as MZ twins with never-divorced _____. For DZ twins, the risk was less than _____ times higher if the co-twin was divorced than if the co-twin was never divorced. The heritability of divorce was calculated at _____.

2. Clearly, there is no divorce _____. Since divorce does not occur at random, children from divorced and married families differ in more ways than _____. Over the past hundred years, divorce rates have gone from _____ to _____. Environmental _____ can eliminate or increase divorce. Therefore, the issue is genes _____ environment. As well as personality traits, physical _____ or age at _____ may be factors. People may find divorce more _____ if their identical versus fraternal twin has been divorced.

SHORT ANSWER
Answer the following short answer questions. Compare your work to the material presented in the text.

1. Discuss the stages of Erikson's model of adult development. What do you consider to be the strengths of this model? What are some of its weaknesses?

2. Outline the psychological, social, and biological factors that may contribute to difficulties in family transitions. Which factors do you think are most important when identifying the etiology of family transition difficulties?

3. Review the categories of reminiscence identified by Wong and Watt. Which categories appear to be related to successful aging? Which appear to be associated with less successful adjustment in later life? Which category do you think will best describe your reminiscence later in life? Why?

4. Discuss categories of identity conflicts. Do you identify with any of these? Explain.

ANSWER KEY

MATCHING I

1. l
2. a
3. m
4. c
5. h
6. q
7. g
8. s
9. k
10. j
11. b
12. n
13. i
14. r
15. o
16. e
17. d
18. p
19. f

MATCHING II

a. 14
b. 22
c. 7
d. 6
e. 18
f. 23
g. 12
h. 17
i. 4
j. 20
k. 11
l. 21
m. 8
n. 1
o. 15
p. 9
q. 2
r. 13
s. 5
t. 19
u. 10
v. 16
w. 3
x. 24

MATCHING III

1. b
2. k
3. a
4. e
5. n
6. c
7. l
8. q
9. f
10. j
11. o
12. r
13. m
14. d
15. i
16. h
17. p
18. g

MATCHING IV

1. c
2. b
3. d
4. a
5. e

MULTIPLE CHOICE

1. d	6. b	11. b	16. a	21. b	26. a
2. d	7. d	12. b	17. d	22. a	27. b
3. a	8. d	13. a	18. c	23. d	28. c
4. c	9. a	14. b	19. b	24. d	29. a
5. d	10. b	15. c	20. a	25. d	30. d

CONCEPT REVIEW

1. false
2. psychological; social
3. adolescents
4. neglected by
5. attend college
6. supervision; independence
7. relationships
8. decreases
9. ignore; reciprocate
10. negative
11. 40%
12. whites
13. higher
14. is
15. false
16. true
17. men
18. false
19. true
20. true
21. true
22. false
23. false
24. false
25. true
26. false
27. true
28. marriage; happy relationships

UNDERSTANDING RESEARCH

1. environments; takers; adverse; personality; genetic; divorce; 1,500; six; probands; two; .525

2. gene; their parents' marital status; zero; 50 percent; thresholds; and; attractiveness; marriage; socially acceptable

257

CROSSWORD

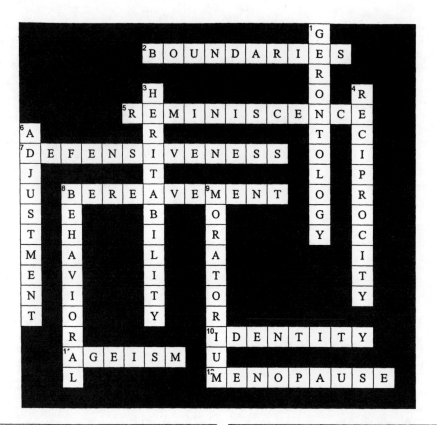

ACROSS	DOWN
2. rules that mark psychological territory of individual or relationship	1. multidisciplinary study of aging
5. recounting of personal memories	3. relative contribution of genes to a characteristic
7. a form of self-justification	4. social exchange
8. specific form of grieving in response to death of a loved one	6. disorders defined by development of clinically significant symptoms in response to stress
10. crisis characterized by basic uncertainty about self	8. approach to marital therapy which emphasizes exchange of positive and negative behaviors
11. encompasses a number of misconceptions about aging	9. time of uncertainty about oneself and one's goals
12. cessation of menstruation	

CHAPTER EIGHTEEN

MENTAL HEALTH AND THE LAW

CHAPTER OUTLINE

Overview
    Expert Witnesses
    Free Will versus Determinism
    Rights and Responsibilities
Mental Illness and Criminal Responsibility
    The Insanity Defense
    Competence to Stand Trial
    Sentencing and Mental Health
Mental Health and Civil Law
    A Brief History of U.S. Mental Hospitals
    Libertarianism versus Paternalism in Treating Mental Patients
    Civil Commitment
    The Rights of Mental Patients
    Deinstitutionalization
Mental Health and Family Law
    Children, Parents, and the State
    Child Custody Disputes
    Child Abuse
Professional Responsibilities and the Law
    Professional Negligence and Malpractice
    Confidentiality
Summary

OBJECTIVES

1. Discuss the issues of free will and determinism as they relate to the insanity defense.
2. Distinguish between the M'Naghten test, the irresistible impulse test, the product test, and the American Law Institute legislation for determining insanity.
3. Discuss the "guilty but mentally ill" verdict and explain the consequences of this verdict.
4. Distinguish between the verdict of NGRI with that of a "guilty" verdict
5. Discuss the issue of competence and its role in the legal system.
6. Contrast the libertarian position with the paternalist position regarding involuntary psychiatric commitment.
7. Discuss issues of reliability as they relate to predictions of dangerousness and suicide risk.
8. Describe the issues involved in a patient's right to treatment, a least restrictive alternative environment, and right to refuse treatment.
9. Discuss problems associated with deinstitutionalization.
10. Describe the role of mental health practitioners in child custody disputes.
11. Discuss the most common types of malpractice cases filed against mental health practitioners.
12. List situations in which psychologists are legally bound to break confidentiality.

MATCHING I

Answers are found at the end of this chapter. Match these terms and concepts with the definitions that follow:

a. Free will
b. Criminal responsibility
c. Determinism
d. Insanity
e. Insanity defense
f. M'Naghten test
g. Not guilty by reason of insanity
h. Irresistible impulse test
i. Deterrence
j. Product test
k. Guilty but mentally ill (GBMI)
l. Burden of proof
m. Standard of proof
n. Expert witnesses
o. Battered woman syndrome
p. Temporary insanity
q. Competence
r. Miranda warning
s. Moral treatment
t. Deinstitutionalization movement
u. Libertarian
v. Paternalist
w. Preventive detention
x. Civil movement
y. Parens patrial
z. Police power

1. ____ a defendant's ability to understand the legal proceedings that are taking place against him or her and to participate in his or her own defense
2. ____ a legal term referring to a defendant's state of mind while committing a crime
3. ____ the state as parent
4. ____ specialists allowed to testify about specific matters of opinion within their area of expertise
5. ____ a person being held accountable when he or she breaks the law
6. ____ the attempt to care for the mentally ill in their communities
7. ____ the idea that people have the capacity to make choices and act freely on them
8. ____ the view that emphasizes the state's duty to protect its citizens
9. ____ confinement before a crime is committed
10. ____ the psychological effects of being chronically abused by a husband or lover
11. ____ the involuntary hospitalization of the mentally ill
12. ____ the principle for determining insanity of whether the person is prevented from knowing the wrongfulness of his or her actions by a mental disease or defect
13. ____ the stress of an event temporarily causes a person to be legally insane
14. ____ the idea that an accused person is not criminally responsible if the unlawful act was the product of a mental disease or defect
15. ____ a movement founded on a basic respect for human dignity
16. ____ the police must inform a suspect during arrest of his or her rights to remain silent and to have an attorney present during police questioning
17. ____ the idea that human behavior is determined by biological, psychological, and social forces
18. ____ the idea that people will avoid committing crimes because they fear being punished for them
19. ____ the degree of certainty required
20. ____ the principle that people could be found insane if they were unable to control their actions because of a mental disease
21. ____ the view that emphasizes protecting the rights of the individual
22. ____ whether the prosecution or the defense has the obligation to prove guilt
23. ____ an attempt to prove that a person with a mental illness did not meet the legal criteria for sanity at the time of committing a crime
24. ____ the finding by a court that a person is not criminally responsible for his or her actions because of a mental disease or defect
25. ____ the state's duty to protect the public safety, health, and welfare
26. ____ the finding by a court that a person committed a crime, was mentally ill at the time it was committed, but was not legally insane at that time

MATCHING II

Answers are found at the end of this chapter. Match these terms and concepts with the definitions that follow:

1. Emergency commitment procedures
2. Formal commitment procedures
3. Base rates
4. Sensitivity
5. Specificity
6. Informed consent
7. Substituted judgment
8. Revolving door phenomenon
9. Child custody
10. Physical custody
11. Legal custody
12. Sole custody
13. Joint custody
14. Mediator
15. Child's best interests standard
16. Divorce mediation
17. Child abuse
18. Physical child abuse
19. Child sexual abuse
20. Child neglect
21. Psychological abuse
22. Foster care
23. Professional responsibilities
24. Negligence
25. Malpractice
26. Confidentiality

a. ____ where the children will live at what times
b. ____ a court order that allows an individual to be involuntarily committed to a mental hospital for a long period of time, such as six months
c. ____ population frequencies
d. ____ repeated denigration in the absence of physical harm
e. ____ a legal decision that involves determining where children will reside and how parents will share legal rights and responsibilities for child rearing
f. ____ the ethical obligation not to reveal private communications
g. ____ a neutral third party who facilitates the parents' discussions
h. ____ more patients are admitted to psychiatric hospitals more frequently but for shorter periods of time
i. ____ parents meet with a neutral third party who helps them to identify, negotiate, and resolve their disputes during a divorce
j. ____ a temporary placement of the child outside of his or her home
k. ____ appointing an independent guardian to provide informed consent when a person is not competent to provide it for himself or herself
l. ____ when professional negligence results in harm to patients
m. ____ the standard that governs custody disputes
n. ____ allow an acutely disturbed individual to be temporarily confined in a mental hospital for a few days
o. ____ how the parents will make separate or joint decisions about their children's lives
p. ____ true positives over the sum of true positives and false negatives
q. ____ involves placing children at risk for serious physical or psychological harm by failing to provide basic and expected care
r. ____ a situation in which only one parent retains custody of the children
s. ____ involves sexual contact between an adult and child
t. ____ a situation in which both parents retain custody
u. ____ a legal decision that a parent or other responsible adult has inflicted damage or offered inadequate care to a child
v. ____ when a professional fails to perform in a manner that is consistent with the level of skill exercised by other professionals in the field
w. ____ true negatives divided by the sum of the true negatives and false positives
x. ____ involves the intentional use of physically painful and harmful actions

y. ____ a professional's obligations to meet the ethical standards of the profession and to uphold the laws of the states in which he or she practices

z. ____ the requirement that a clinician tell a patient about a procedure and its risks, the patient understands the information and freely consents to the treatment, and the patient is competent to give consent

MATCHING III

Answers are found at the end of this chapter. Match these names with the descriptions of their contributions to the study of abnormal psychology.

a. Thomas Szasz
b. John Monahan
c. Lenore Walker
d. Henry Kempe

1. ____ researched the relation between violence and mental illness, and predicting dangerousness
2. ____ wrote about the "battered child syndrome"
3. ____ asserted that the concept of mental illness is a myth, and argued that abnormal behavior must be defined relative to some social or moral standard
4. ____ coined the term "the battered woman syndrome"

CONCEPT REVIEW

Answers are found at the end of this chapter. After you have read and reviewed the material, test your comprehension by filling in the blanks or circling the correct answer.

1. Mental health professionals typically assume which view?

    free will   **determinism**

2. Criminal law assumes which view?

    free will   **determinism**

3. The views of Szasz are widely accepted in the psychiatric community:

    true   **false**

4. The irresistible impulse test and the product test **narrowed/broadened** the grounds for determining insanity.

5. The problem of circular reasoning was introduced when mental health professionals decided to include _____ disorder as one of the mental diseases that could be the basis of an insanity defense.

6. In federal courts today, the burden of proof of a defendant's insanity lies with the **prosecution/defense.**

7. There remain some states in which a husband cannot be charged with raping his wife no matter what the circumstances: **true**   **false**

8. Substance abuse lowers a psychiatric inpatient's risk of committing violence:

    true   **false**

9. About _____ percent of all criminal cases involve the insanity defense.

10. Most defendants who are found Not Guilty by Reason of Insanity spend substantially less time in a mental hospital than they would have spent in prison: **true   false**
11. The goal of commitment following an NGRI verdict is _____.
12. Competence refers to the defendant's _____ mental state and insanity refers to the defendant's state of mind at the time of _____.
13. The poor conditions of mental institutions were brought to light shortly after World War II by _____.
14. American law provides for the confinement of someone who is about to commit a crime:

    true   false
15. What percent of the mentally disturbed have no history of violence? _____
16. Clinicians can usually predict violence quite accurately: **true   false**
17. Hospital where minors are admitted constitute an independent fact finder, but they have a clear _____ interest in committing the minor.
18. Between 1980 and 1984 the number of juveniles admitted to private psychiatric hospitals increased by _____ percent.
19. *Wyatt v. Stickney* established that hospitalized mental patients have a right to _____.
20. *Lake v. Cameron* established the patient's right to be treated in the _____.
21. The development of resources to treat people in their communities grew rapidly with the deinstitutionalization movement: **true   false**
22. Many community mental health centers do not offer services to the seriously mentally ill:

    true   false
23. Many patients that would have been institutionalized before are now in jail or are homeless:

    true   false
24. Mental health law is mostly based on the state's _____ and family law is mostly based on the state's _____.
25. Several large-scale studies have shown that divorce itself has little negative effect on children's mental health: **true   false**
26. Research evidence suggest that conflict between parents is strongly related to maladjustment among children following divorce: **true   false**
27. Mental health professionals are not permitted to break confidentiality, even to report child abuse:

    true   false
28. One common ground for successful malpractice suits against mental health professionals is the existence of a _____ relationship.
29. The Tarasoff case established a mental health professional's duty to _____ a potential victim of their client.

CROSSWORD

Answers are found at the end of this chapter. Complete the following crossword puzzle to reinforce your understanding of this chapter's key terms and concepts:

ACROSS	DOWN
2. ethical obligation not to reveal private communications	1. parent feigns, exaggerates, or induces illness in a child
5. offers juries option of finding defendant both guilty and mentally ill	2. involuntary hospitalization of the mentally ill
6. population frequencies	3. claiming one is not guilty because of a mental defect
7. involves defendant's ability to understand legal proceedings that are taking place	4. exception to criminal responsibility
9. process whereby third party helps participants identify, negotiate, and resolve disputes	8. insane because one cannot tell right from wrong
11. view that behavior is determined by biological, psychological, and social forces	10. capacity to make choices and freely act on them
13. duty to warn	12. warning issued during arrest

MULTIPLE CHOICE

Answers are found at the end of this chapter. The multiple choice questions listed will test your understanding of the material presented in the chapter. Read through each question and circle the letter representing the best answer.

1. Which of the following cases ruled that a state could not confine a non-dangerous individual who is capable of surviving safely on his or her own or with the help of willing and responsible family members or friends?
    a. Washington v. Harper
    b. Parham v. J.R.
    c. O'Connor v. Donaldson
    d. Lake v. Cameron

2. _____ commitment procedures allow an acutely disturbed individual to be temporarily confined in a mental hospital, typically for no more than a few days, while _____ commitment procedures can lead to involuntary hospitalization that is ordered by the court and typically lasts for much longer.
    a. Formal; emergency
    b. Emergency; formal
    c. Medical; crisis
    d. Crisis; medical

3. In all but which of the following are true of the "guilty but mentally ill" (GBMI) verdict?
    a. it holds defendants criminally responsible for their crimes
    b. it helps ensure that the defendant receives treatment for the mental disorder
    c. it was designed as a compromise to the "not guilty by reason of insanity" (NGRI) verdict
    d. a defendant found to be GBMI cannot be sentenced in the same manner as any criminal

4. In all but which of the following have been goals of deinstitutionalization?
    a. to prevent inappropriate mental hospital admissions through arranging community alternatives to treatment
    b. to release to the community all institutionalized patients who have been given adequate preparation for such a change
    c. to decrease the influx of patients by not allowing them continued access to mental hospitals and thus encouraging independence
    d. to establish and maintain community support systems for non-institutionalized people receiving mental health services in the community

5. Which of the following individuals argues that mental disorders are subjective "problems in living" rather than objective diseases, and thus believes that the concept of mental illness is a myth?
    a. Thomas Szasz
    b. E. Fuller Torrey
    c. Bertram Brown
    d. Henry Kempe

6. The majority of custody decisions are made by
    a. parents themselves
    b. attorneys who negotiate for the parents outside of court
    c. a judge and decided in court
    d. mental health professionals who evaluate the case

7. In all but which of the following are true of the parens patriae?
    a. it is used to justify the state's supervision of minors and incapacitated adults
    b. it is based on the state's duty to protect the public safety, health, and welfare
    c. commitment under these rationales was virtually unknown to the United States until the early 1950s
    d. it refers to the concept of the "state as parent"

8. Following a civil commitment to a mental hospital, mental patients' rights include all of the following except
    a. right to treatment
    b. right to design their own treatment plan
    c. right to refuse treatment
    d. right to treatment in the least restrictive alternative environment

9. Evidence suggests that the insanity defense is used in approximately _____ of all criminal cases in the United States.
    a. 1 percent
    b. 4 percent
    c. 7 percent
    d. 10 percent

10. In all but which of the following stages are part of Lenore Walker's stages of the "cycle of violence?"
    a. battering incident
    b. tension-building phase
    c. loving contrition
    d. verbal reprimands

11. On the average, defendants who are found "not guilty by reason of insanity" (NGRI) spend _____ time confined in an institution as they would have if they had been given a prison sentence instead.
    a. significantly less
    b. twice as much
    c. approximately the same
    d. roughly three times as much

12. Which of the following terms is defined as the ethical obligation not to reveal private communication and is basic to psychotherapy?
    a. confidentiality
    b. private communications
    c. classified information
    d. privileged communications

13. Mental disorders and the actions that result from them are typically viewed as
    a. choices
    b. conditions that are outside of voluntary control
    c. responsibilities that the mentally disordered individual must assume
    d. a and c

14. The acquittal of John Hinckley prompted all of the following except
    a. the new verdict "guilty but mentally ill" (GBMI)
    b. a revised definition of the insanity defense
    c. shifting the burden of proof from the prosecution to the defense in federal courts
    d. the creation of a much stricter standard of proof for the defense in the majority of states

15. In all but which of the following are issues of special relevance regarding involuntary hospitalization of the severely mentally impaired?
    a. criminal record
    b. civil commitment
    c. patients' rights
    d. deinstitutionalization

16. Research indicates that approximately _____ of the mentally disturbed are not violent.
    a. 30 percent
    b. 50 percent
    c. 70 percent
    d. 90 percent

17. In all but which of the following are grounds that tend to dominate commitment laws?
    a. being dangerous to others
    b. inability to care for self
    c. being dangerous to self
    d. inability to care for others

18. Over _____ of all reports of child abuse are found to be unsubstantiated after an investigation.
    a. one-eighth
    b. one-quarter
    c. one-half
    d. two-thirds

19. In all but which of the following were key figures in instituting moral treatment reform efforts for the mentally ill?
    a. Benjamin Rush
    b. Lenore Walker
    c. Phillipe Pinel
    d. Dorothea Dix

20. Empirical research on children's adjustment after divorce indicates that
    a. a substantial portion of the difficulties found among children after divorce actually begins long before the marital separation occurs
    b. the psychological functioning of children from divorced families does not differ from that of children from non-divorced families
    c. the difficulties children experience are directly related to marital conflict and divorce
    d. children from divorced families tend to have more internalizing problems than children from non-divorced families

21. Which of the following is known as the "product test" which indicated that "an accused is not criminally responsible if his unlawful act was the product of mental disease or defect?"
    a. Parsons v. State
    b. O'Connor v. Donaldson
    c. Durham v. United States
    d. Parham v. J.R.

22. One more common malpractice claim against mental health professionals is
    a. the misuse of psychotherapeutic techniques
    b. the inappropriate use of electroconvulsive therapy (ECT)
    c. the failure to disclose therapeutic interpretations to clients
    d. inappropriate hospitalization

23. Confidentiality between a therapist and a client can be broken under which of the following circumstances?
    a. the client is threatening to harm another person
    b. the client has disclosed sexual or physical abuse of a child
    c. the client is threatening to harm himself or herself
    d. all of the above

24. Which of the following is not true of the legal definition of competence?
    a. it refers to the defendant's ability to understand criminal proceedings
    b. it refers to the defendant's current mental status
    c. it refers to the defendant's willingness to participate in criminal proceedings
    d. the "reasonable degree" of understanding needed to establish competence is generally acknowledged to be fairly low

25. In the case of *Wyatt* v. *Stickney*, the federal district court ruled that at a minimum, public mental institutions must provide all of the following except
    a. a humane psychological and physical environment
    b. a sufficient number of qualified staff to administer adequate treatment
    c. individualized treatment plans
    d. "reasonable" rates for inpatient services

26. Which of the following details a suspect's rights to remain silent and to have an attorney present during police questioning?
    a. Miranda warning
    b. informed consent
    c. confidentiality
    d. parens patrial

27. Evidence suggests that in child custody cases, mediation
    a. does not necessarily reduce the number of custody hearings in court
    b. is more effective than the role that mental health professionals play in custody cases, and thus mental health professionals should limit their involvement in the legal system
    c. does not help parents reach decisions more quickly than if they were to go through custody hearings in court
    d. is viewed by parents as more favorable than litigation, especially fathers

28. Which of the following cases established the patient's right to be treated in the least restrictive alternative environment?
    a. Lake v. Cameron
    b. Osheroff v. Chestnut Lodge
    c. O'Connor v. Donaldson
    d. none of the above

29. Which of the following is true regarding the idea that mental disability should limit criminal responsibility?
    a. it is a relatively new concept among mental health professionals
    b. it dates back to ancient Greek and Hebrew traditions and was evident in early English law
    c. it has emerged in our legal system within the past 50 years
    d. it surfaced following World War II when large numbers of veterans experienced post-traumatic stress symptoms and committed violent acts

30. In his research on the prediction of dangerousness, John Monahan has found which of the following to be several times higher among prison inmates as among the general population?
    a. major depression
    b. bipolar disorder
    c. schizophrenia
    d. all of the above

SHORT ANSWER
Answer the following short answer questions. Compare your work to the material presented in the text.

1. Brian is a thirty five year old white male who was recently arrested for sexually abusing a seven-year-old girl. Although this is Brian's first offense, he has a history of addictive behavior. Explain how you think a criminal lawyer would conceptualize Brian's behavior and how a mental health professional would conceptualize his behavior. Discuss the similarities and differences of the two perspectives.

2. Discuss Szasz's position on free will, determinism, mental illness, and the insanity defense. Do you agree or disagree with Szasz? Why?

3. What are the underlying principles of libertarianism and paternalism? Which view do you agree with? Defend your position.

4. Discuss the implications of *Tarasoff* v. *Regents of the University of California*. If you would have been Poddar's therapist, would you have handled the situation differently? Why?

5. What are base rates? Discuss their utility in research.

ANSWER KEY

MATCHING I

1. q
2. d
3. y
4. n
5. b
6. t
7. a
8. v
9. w
10. o
11. x
12. f
13. p
14. j
15. s
16. r
17. c
18. i
19. m
20. h
21. u
22. l
23. e
24. g
25. z
26. k

MATCHING II

a. 10
b. 2
c. 3
d. 21
e. 9
f. 26
g. 14
h. 8
i. 16
j. 22
k. 7
l. 25
m. 15
n. 1
o. 11
p. 4
q. 20
r. 12
s. 19
t. 13
u. 17
v. 24
w. 5
x. 18
y. 23
z. 6

MATCHING III

1. b
2. d
3. a
4. c

MULTIPLE CHOICE

1. c
2. b
3. d
4. c
5. a
6. b
7. c
8. b
9. a
10. d
11. c
12. a
13. b
14. d
15. a
16. d
17. d
18. c
19. b
20. a
21. c
22. b
23. d
24. c
25. d
26. a
27. d
28. a
29. b
30. d

CONCEPT REVIEW

1. determinism
2. free will
3. false
4. broadened
5. antisocial personality
6. defense
7. true
8. false
9. 1
10. false
11. treatment
12. current; the crime
13. conscientious objectors
14. false
15. 90 percent
16. false
17. financial
18. 450
19. treatment
20. least restrictive environment
21. false
22. true
23. true
24. police power; parens patriae
25. true
26. true
27. false
28. sexual
29. warn

CROSSWORD

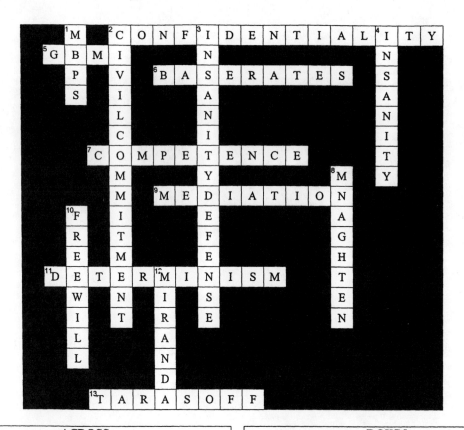

ACROSS

2. ethical obligation not to reveal private communications
5. offers juries option of finding defendant both guilty and mentally ill
6. population frequencies
7. involves defendant's ability to understand legal proceedings that are taking place
9. process whereby third party helps participants identify, negotiate, and resolve disputes
11. view that behavior is determined by biological, psychological, and social forces
13. duty to warn

DOWN

1. parent feigns, exaggerates, or induces illness in a child
2. involuntary hospitalization of the mentally ill
3. claiming one is not guilty because of a mental defect
4. exception to criminal responsibility
8. insane because one cannot tell right from wrong
10. capacity to make choices and freely act on them
12. warning issued during arrest